# A SERIAL KILLER IN NAZI BERLIN

The Chilling True Story of the S-Bahn Murderer

## SCOTT ANDREW SELBY

BERKLEY BOOKS, NEW YORK

THE BERKLEY PUBLISHING GROUP
Published by the Penguin Group
Penguin Group (USA) LLC
375 Hudson Street, New York, New York 10014

USA • Canada • UK • Ireland • Australia • New Zealand • India • South Africa • China

penguin.com

A Penguin Random House Company

Berkley trade paperback ISBN: 978-0-425-26415-7

Library of Congress Cataloging-in-Publication Data

Selby, Scott Andrew.
A serial killer in Nazi Berlin : the chilling true story of the S-Bahn murderer / Scott Andrew Selby.
p. cm.
Includes bibliographical references and index.
ISBN 978-0-425-26414-0
1. Ogorzow, Paul.   2. Berliner S-Bahn (Germany)   3. Serial murders—Germany—
Berlin—Case studies.   4. Serial murder investigation—Germany—Berlin—Case studies.
5. Berlin (Germany)—History—1918–1945.   I. Title.
HV6535.G33B477 2013
364.152'32092—dc23
2013032412

PUBLISHING HISTORY
Berkley hardcover edition / January 2014
Berkley trade paperback edition / December 2014

PRINTED IN THE UNITED STATES OF AMERICA

10  9  8  7  6  5  4  3  2  1

*Dedicated to all the victims of the S-Bahn Murderer*

In the coming war we shall fight not only on land, on sea, and in the air. There will be a fourth theatre of operations—the Inner Front. That front will decide on the continued existence or the irrevocable death of the German nation.

HEINRICH HIMMLER, SEPTEMBER 1937[1]

# CONTENTS

# CONTENTS

# CONTENTS

# Murders and Attempted Murders

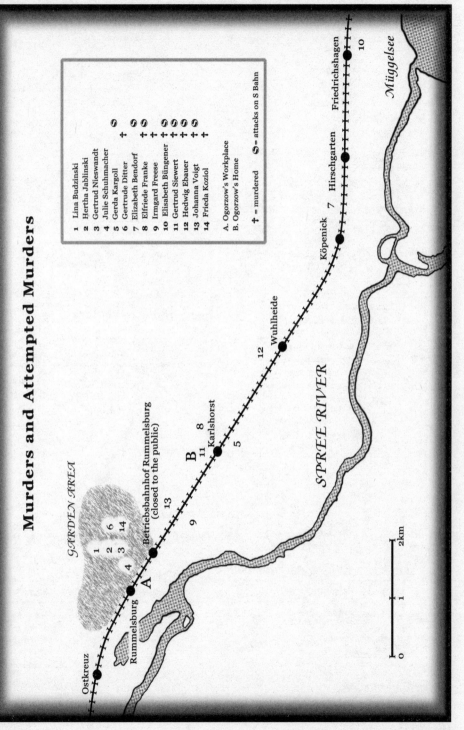

1 Lina Budzinski
2 Hertha Jablinski
3 Gertrud Nieswandt
4 Julie Schuhmacher
5 Gerda Kargoll
6 Gertrude Ditter
7 Elizabeth Bendorf
8 Elfriede Franke
9 Irmgard Freese
10 Elisabeth Büngener
11 Gertrud Siewert
12 Hedwig Ebauer
13 Johanna Voigt
14 Frieda Koziol

A. Ogorzow's Workplace
B. Ogorzow's Home

† = murdered    Ⓢ = attacks on S Bahn

GARDEN AREA

Betriebsbahnhof Rummelsburg
(closed to the public)

Ostkreuz

Rummelsburg

Karlshorst

Wuhlheide

Köpenick

Hirschgarten

Friedrichshagen

SPREE RIVER

Müggelsee

0    1    2km

Janet Dreyer

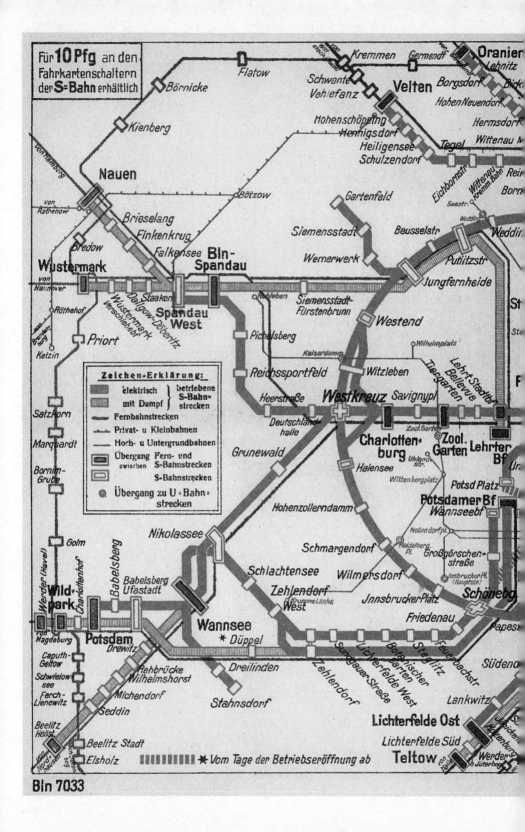

# LIST OF S-BAHN STATIONS ON KEY ROUTE

Ostkreuz

Rummelsburg

[Betriebsbahnhof Rummelsburg—
not open to the public during this time]

Karlshorst

Wuhlheide

Köpenick

Hirschgarten

Friedrichshagen

Rahnsdorf

Wilhelmshagen

Erkner

Fangschleuse

Hangelsberg

Fürstenwalde

# CHRONOLOGY OF BACKGROUND EVENTS— AUGUST 1939 TO JULY 1941

## 1939:

**AUGUST 23** Germany and the Soviet Union sign a nonaggression pact

**SEPTEMBER 1** Germany invades Poland (widely considered the start of World War II)

**SEPTEMBER 3** The UK, Australia, New Zealand, India, and France declare war on Germany; a German U-boat sinks an unarmed British passenger ship, starting the Battle of the Atlantic

**SEPTEMBER 5** The United States declares neutrality regarding this conflict

**SEPTEMBER 17** The Soviet Union attacks Poland

**OCTOBER 6** Germany and the Soviet Union now occupy a divided Poland

## 1940:

**APRIL 9** Germany invades Denmark and Norway; Denmark surrenders

**MAY 10** Germany begins the invasion of Belgium, France, the Netherlands, and Luxembourg; Luxembourg is occupied

**MAY 14** The Netherlands surrenders to Germany

**MAY 28** Belgium surrenders to Germany

**JUNE 9** Norway surrenders to Germany

**JUNE 22** France signs an armistice with Germany

**AUGUST 24** Germany accidentally bombs a church in London

**AUGUST 25** The UK bombs Berlin

**SEPTEMBER 7** The Blitz begins—Germany bombs London and other British cities on purpose

**SEPTEMBER 27** Japan, Italy, and Germany sign the Tripartite Pact—establishing the Axis Powers

## 1941:

**FEB 20** German and British land forces fight in Libya

**APRIL 6** Invasion of Yugoslavia by Bulgaria, Germany, Hungary, and Italy

**APRIL 17** Yugoslavia surrenders to Germany

**APRIL 27** Greece surrenders to Germany

**JUNE 22** Germany breaks its pact with the Soviet Union and invades it

**JULY 31** Hermann Göring orders Reinhard Heydrich to plan the Final Solution of the Jewish question (i.e., the Holocaust)

# DRAMATIS PERSONAE

## KEY VICTIMS

**ELIZABETH BENDORF** Attacked November 1940 on the S-Bahn

**LINA BUDZINSKI** Attacked August 1939 in the garden area

**ELISABETH BÜNGENER** Attacked December 1940 on the S-Bahn

**GERTRUDE "GERDA" DITTER** Attacked October 1940 in the garden area

**HEDWIG EBAUER** Attacked January 1941 on the S-Bahn

**ELFRIEDE FRANKE** Attacked December 1940 on the S-Bahn

**IRMGARD FREESE** Attacked December 1940 outside the Karlshorst station

**HERTHA JABLINSKI** Attacked December 1939 in the garden area

**GERDA KARGOLL** Attacked September 1940 on the S-Bahn

**FRIEDA KOZIOL** Attacked July 1941 in the garden area

**GERTRUD NIESWANDT** Attacked July 1940 in the garden area

**JULIE SCHUHMACHER** Attacked August 1940 in the garden area

**GERTRUD SIEWERT** Attacked December 1940 on the S-Bahn

**JOHANNA VOIGT** Attacked February 1941 on the S-Bahn

# DRAMATIS PERSONAE

## KILLER

PAUL OGORZOW S-Bahn employee

## LAW ENFORCEMENT AND GOVERNMENTAL PERSONNEL

JOSEPH GOEBBELS Minister of propaganda, gauleiter of Berlin,
  *Reichsleiter*
GEORG HEUSER Kripo detective
REINHARD HEYDRICH Director of the RHSA
HEINRICH HIMMLER Chief of the RHSA and the SS
WILHELM LÜDTKE Kripo police commissioner
ARTHUR NEBE Head of the Kripo (RHSA *Amt 5*)
DR. WALDEMAR WEIMANN Forensic pathologist and psychiatrist

# AUTHOR'S NOTE ON SOURCES

I've tried to minimize the use of endnotes in this book to make it a more enjoyable read. If information is not cited, it is either commonly known, such as dates of key events during World War II, or it comes from the *Kriminalpolizei* file on the criminal investigation into the S-Bahn murders. The original documents from this investigation are at the Landesarchiv Berlin, A.Pr. Br. Rep. 030-03 Tit. 198B Nr. 1782–1789.

The woman looked to be alone. That was Paul Ogorzow's first mistake. He was so eager to attack her that he went with this initial impression instead of taking the time to make sure there was no one around that could save her.

She was walking along a pathway through the gardens of suburban eastern Berlin in an area known as Berlin-Friedrichsfelde. Although she was near the station from where she could catch a train that would whisk her into the heart of Berlin, this residential area felt like the countryside. She'd walked this path between residents' allotments many times, through the lush gardens with their cherry trees, chestnut trees, apple trees, carrots, onions, potatoes, hedges, and assorted bushes and grasses.

Twenty-seven-year-old Paul Ogorzow hunted for victims in this area. He stalked and attacked women who were walking by themselves at night. And night had acquired new meaning in wartime Berlin—a government-imposed blackout meant the only meaningful illumination here at this hour came from the night sky.

He looked rather average—on the short side of medium height, white, with short black hair parted on the left. He mostly was clean-shaven, although he sometimes had a wisp of a mustache. His eyes were a bit beady, his lips thin, his hair thinning, and his ears stuck out, but his only truly noticeable feature was his nose. The left nostril looked normal, but the right nostril was oversized, the result of a broken nose he'd suffered in his youth that had not been properly set.

He sometimes wore his uniform during his attacks, in which cases that was generally all his victims noticed. His railway uniform, though, looked somewhat like many other uniforms worn during the Third Reich. In the dark, and with the suddenness of his attacks, it could be hard to observe the details that would reveal exactly what kind of uniform he was wearing.

This was not Ogorzow's first time looking for a woman to assault. By now, he'd emerged from the darkness to attack around thirty different women here. So far, the confusion of the war had helped him avoid much police attention, but he'd also been careful to attack his victims only when he felt confident that he could safely overpower them.

Taking advantage of the darkness on this evening, he rushed his victim. She only saw him coming at the last moment, when she reacted by screaming as loud as she could. Ogorzow wrapped his large hands around her neck and started squeezing, hoping to silence her and render her unconscious. She fought him though, tooth and nail, enough to be able to continue to breathe, and even to scream.

What she knew—and he did not—was that help was only a short distance away. Her husband and brother-in-law were nearby, and she hoped they would hear her screams and come to her aid.

They were horrified to hear her yelling for help and rushed to the scene. Ogorzow was a man of some strength, as he'd worked in manual and farm labor for most of his life, but he was not a big man. Also, he had expended a lot of energy trying to subdue his victim by the time the two men came upon him.

The husband and brother-in-law violently grabbed Ogorzow and yanked him off his victim. They began to pummel him. Once they were done beating him, they yelled at him that if he were still alive, then they would turn him over to the police.

Ogorzow had just experienced a sudden reversal of fortune—one moment, he felt as powerful as God, able to control whether his victim lived or died, his hands squeezing around her throat, and the next, he was being beaten by two men. He worried that they might kill him or, if he survived, alert the authorities so they could arrest him.

In the darkness, Ogorzow was able to break away from his attackers and hide among the numerous bushes and trees in this area. He knew this place well, having spent time here at night, looking for victims to attack. These two men searched for him, but they eventually gave up and took their loved one away for medical attention. By the time the three of them reported this incident to the police, Ogorzow was safe at his nearby home.

Afterward, Ogorzow thought back on his mistakes. Besides having attacked a woman who was not alone, he had left behind three witnesses. He'd counted on the speed of his attack, combined with the darkness on the garden path, to result in his victim not being able to properly describe him to the police. But a prolonged struggle had occurred, and he worried that the woman he'd attacked and her two saviors might be able to identify him.

He reflected on his narrow escape and how he could lower his risk of getting caught. Giving up his attacks was not even a consideration. He derived too much pleasure from assaulting women. Instead, he focused on what he could do to become a better criminal.

After this close call, Ogorzow realized that he needed to make sure that his victims could not scream out for help. So he would immediately choke them with his hands, threaten them with a knife, or hit them over the head with a blunt instrument. He was not sure yet what would work best, but he knew this was a problem he would have to solve if he was to avoid getting beaten up again—or, worse yet, caught by the police.

And he set his sights on a new hunting ground—one that ran right straight through the heart of Berlin, with an almost limitless supply of victims. Soon, he would expand his repertoire and become one of Berlin's—and maybe Germany's—most notorious serial killers.

## CHAPTER ONE

# The Garden Area

Up until after the incident in which he went from hunter to hunted, Paul Ogorzow only attacked women in the garden area near his home. The area where he lived was suburban, but between his home and a nearby commuter train station, there was a large area of garden allotments.

The Germans traditionally have these in cities so that people without space to garden at home have someplace to go to have a small garden of their own. A person can own or rent a small plot of land inside what they call a "colony" and grow ornamental flowers and plants, or, especially during wartime, fruits and vegetables. These spaces tend to have small structures on them where people store their gardening equipment and anything else they need to have an enjoyable day in this facsimile of the countryside. Many colonies allow people to live there during the summer.

In this particular colony, there were small houses that people lived in year-round. This area was actually made up of two allotment garden colonies joined together—Gutland I and Gutland II—but as a practical matter, this was one area of continuous garden plots.

Paul Ogorzow saw people gardening when he walked or rode his bicycle to the nearby train station. He had no need for a garden house since his apartment building had a small garden that he lovingly tended.

A book on the cultural topography of Berlin explained how these allotment gardens, combined into colonies, worked: "Characteristic of the great German cities is the attempt to counterbalance their high residential densities by the creation of gardens for individual use on the city fringes. . . . Unlike the British allotments, mere portioned fields where the wind blasts unchecked through the sodden Brussels sprouts and tools are kept in shanties made of old packing cases, the Berlin garden colonies are extremely orderly and well-organized affairs, made attractive by their mature fruit trees. Behind formidable fences and locked gates, the profusion of flowers, the patches of lawn, and the garden furniture make their primarily recreational function apparent, while the 'summer-houses' can approach the solidity and dimensions of cottages, in which the family can spend the night. . . . In the period of acute housing shortage caused by wartime bombing, many 'summer-houses' came to be permanently occupied, producing a kind of untidy suburbia."[1]

Past these allotments, there were suburbs. Around eight thousand people lived in them, including many employees of the railroad company, like Ogorzow. Some of the people who lived in these houses walked home from the train at night through the garden area. They walked in darkness, as the streetlights here were turned off as part of the city's wartime blackout. Many of these inhabitants were women whose husbands were away in the German military.

Historian Dr. Laurenz Demps, an expert on Berlin during the Nazi era, described this area as follows: "The area of garden plots is directly next to the [train] tracks. We can imagine the allotments of that time, as we know it today. They were usually small garden-plot houses. In 1938, 25,000 families lived in such small garden-plot houses in Berlin. They were very simple; very primitive. The street lighting, path lighting, was simply not there. There was a lot of green. It was very dark and not very busy—especially in the evening."[2]

This was an area that was already poorly lit even before the blackout was implemented. But with the blackout, even the few electric lamps that lit some of the paths through these garden plots were turned off for the duration of the war. It would be hard to intentionally create a better environment for a serial killer and rapist to prowl. Seen from the perspective of the women who lived in the area, it was a scary place to have to walk through to get to and from the train station.

This is where Ogorzow's attacks on women developed. He started by shining his flashlight on women to startle them. The conditions of the blackout involved serious regulations about what kinds of lights could and could not be used outdoors. So these women would usually be walking without their own flashlights on.

As a reporter living in wartime Berlin explained, "Most people carry small flashlights, but their use is strictly circumscribed. You are supposed to use them only near the ground to avoid tripping over curbstones, and then only for an instant. Should you flash it around to learn your whereabouts or find the street number you are seeking, you will probably be shouted at."[3] So Ogorzow was allowed to carry a flashlight, but he was violating the rules of the blackout by using it to frighten people.

The only form of light that was permitted to be on at all times outdoors was an eerie green glowing round pin on people's jackets. It was coated in a phosphorous paint that absorbed energy during the day from the sunlight and emitted a faint glow in the dark. This was not enough light to be able to see where one was going—all it accomplished was enabling other people to avoid walking into you. Or in Ogorzow's case, it allowed him to see people coming from a distance and to tell if they were alone.

Ogorzow started by hiding out in the garden area during the night and waiting until he saw a woman approaching. He might see her by the glow of her phosphorous pin or the occasional lighting of a flashlight for a split second to check the path. Or he could hear someone coming and tell from a silhouette in the moonlight that it was a woman coming his way. A sudden shining from his flashlight or from the light on his bicycle would startle and disorient her.

While walking in the darkness, this woman's eyes would have adapted to the low levels of light by dilating her pupils to allow more light into her eyes. There's more to seeing in the dark though than just having dilated pupils. There are also light-impacted pigments called photopigments that would have built up in her eyes while she was in the dark. Light breaks these down, but in the dark, they continue to build up and result in sensitivity to light.

A textbook on psychology described what happens when someone who has been in the dark a long while is suddenly exposed to light: "You would experience a bright flash of light and perhaps even pain as the large number of available photopigments makes your eyes very sensitive to the light. It would take about 1 minute for your eyes to adjust to the light."[4]

For the woman suddenly, and unexpectedly, hit with a bright light, this meant that she had trouble seeing and might even feel some pain from the light. If this light came from some sort of non-threatening source, like a street lamp malfunctioning and accidentally turning on despite the blackout, it would have been frightening enough. Or if someone walking the other direction was using a flashlight despite the rules and accidentally hit her with its beam. But here, there was no accident—instead the light seemed to come out of nowhere. Even worse, after the first few times, a man yelling crude sexual innuendos and threats accompanied this flash of light.

A typical reaction to this fright was to run yelling in a search for help. However, it could be hard to explain just how terrifying this experience was. It was the sort of thing the police could easily dismiss as a prank, albeit a particularly malicious one.

To the women it happened to, though, this felt like something out of a horror film. A late night or early morning walk through a garden area with meandering paths, suddenly interrupted by a man who'd been lying in wait for just such a moment. A bright flash, some yelled words, and the ominous feeling that things could suddenly take a turn for the worse if this man decided to launch an actual physical attack.

For Paul Ogorzow, the thrill he'd felt when scaring women just by blinding them with a flashlight quickly faded. Next, he started yelling abusive, vulgar things at them as well. When this no longer gave him a rush, he upped the stakes by actually grabbing or punching women. Like a drug addict who needs to use more and more to get the same high, Ogorzow felt compelled to take things further with his victims. Eventually, he escalated to sexually assaulting women and then, finally, to killing them.

Like most serial killers, he did not start out by murdering his victims. Rather, it was a slow process of escalating violence. Famed FBI profiler John Douglas wrote about how this works, explaining that a developing predator "sets about to practice more of the acts that leave him feeling powerful and satisfied, sorting out the factors or actions that get in the way of the experience. He discovers expanded areas and situations where he can practice his domination and control of others. And he learns from his own experience, perfecting his technique to avoid detection or punishment. He learns how to become a success at what he does. The more success and satisfaction he has, the tighter that feedback loop becomes."[5]

John Douglas went on to give an example of this process: "The young man whose particular thing is voyeurism may move on to fetish burglary of things belonging to women he spies on. Once he becomes comfortable with breaking and entering and knows how to get away with it, he may then escalate to rape. Depending on the circumstances, if, for example, he realizes he could be identified by his victim if he doesn't take preventive action, rape can end in murder. And if he then finds that killing gives him an even greater arousal and an increased sense of power and satisfaction, he's entered a new dimension of control and the murders very well might continue."[6]

Paul Ogorzow engaged in just this kind of increasingly violent behavior. Before he started attacking women on the commuter train system, Ogorzow escalated to attempted murder in the garden colony near his home.

Around one in the morning on August 13, 1939, Ogorzow prowled in this garden area looking for a female victim. World War II had not yet started, but it was clear that war was coming. Three months before, the German government had issued regulations that called for the immediate implementation of measures required for a blackout. While the actual blackout would not start for another two weeks, public spaces, such as the garden area, already had their lighting shut off. The idea was that with a very short amount of notice, the population would be ready to cut off light from escaping into the night.

Ogorzow hunted in the dark, hoping to find a woman walking to or from the nearby train station. At this hour, it would most likely be a factory worker coming home from a long shift producing weapons or other industrial materials needed for the German war effort. That would be a plus for him as it increased the odds that the victim would be too tired to put up much of a fight. And her focus might be on just getting home and going to bed, instead of paying full attention to her surroundings.

He spotted a woman in her early forties, Lina Budzinski, and followed her as she walked down the dark paths to her home. She could hear his footsteps. Frightened, she ran to her property, entered the garden plot in front of her small house, and started to close the gate behind her. While closing the gate, she heard the heavy breathing of Ogorzow struggling to catch up with her. When she was just a few feet from safety, Ogorzow hit her from behind, knocking her to the ground. She was unable to scream for help, as the blow to her head dazed her.

Ogorzow did not say anything to her during this attack. They were still outside, in the small garden in front of her home. Although Miss Budzinski was too out of it to yell, she was still conscious. She had suffered a concussion. This injury resulted in her temporary inability to speak or otherwise fully control her body. There were a whole host of other symptoms that accompanied this, including having difficulty thinking clearly, but for now, the most pressing matter by far was whether she would be able to do something that would enable her to survive this attack.

She could see and hear everything that was happening to her and tried desperately to get her body to work. She wanted more than anything to run away, or at least scream out for help from her neighbors.

The silence made her attacker seem all the more ominous. With the hit on her head, and the darkness of the no longer lit garden area, it felt hard to understand how this man had emerged out of nowhere to attack her.

While she was still in a daze, she felt the sharp pain of a knife entering her back and being pulled out. And then her attacker stabbed her again, hard. The pain was excruciating. Ogorzow removed his knife, raised his weapon up in the air and plunged it down fast for a third stabbing. If Miss Budzinski did not manage to overcome her head injury and do something, she would soon die at Paul Ogorzow's knife-wielding hand.

For a fourth, and final, time, he used his knife to penetrate her back. There was blood running out of her body in five different places now—the four knife wounds and the hit to her head.

Somehow, she managed to overcome her head injury and flee from her attacker. Perhaps all the adrenaline running through her system helped. She made it into her house and slammed the door behind her, this time successfully keeping Ogorzow out.

Ogorzow quickly fled the scene. Miraculously, Miss Budzinski survived this attack. At the hospital, the surgeons patched her up well enough for the police to talk to her. As her attacker never said a word, she could not tell them anything about what he sounded like or what he might have been thinking during this brutal attack.

The police questioned her extensively about the assault. The elimination of lighting on the public paths of the garden area, though, meant that Miss Budzinski had seen very little of her attacker. All she could tell the police was his approximate size.

While the police in Nazi Germany struck fear into the hearts of the many people who had good reason to be afraid of the regime, as a nonpolitical Aryan woman, Miss Budzinski would have had no such concerns. These policemen were not here to investigate her, but to try to learn what they could to help catch the man who had done this to her. And so she cooperated with them fully.

The police still considered her a potentially useful witness and hoped to use her eventually to identify her attacker. If they ever caught a suspect, they wanted to at least see if she could identify him as her attacker.

Despite the trauma, after the attack Lina Budzinski stayed in Berlin, where she later married and took the last name of Mohr.

## CHAPTER TWO

# The Detective

Murder and attempted murder were investigated by the Criminal Police (*Kriminalpolizei*, or Kripo), which generally handled nonpolitical serious crimes. Police Commissioner Wilhelm Karl Lüdtke was in charge of the Serious Crimes Unit of the Kripo in Berlin, which dealt primarily with homicides.

A single attack on a woman was not a high-profile enough case to require Lüdtke's direct participation in the investigation. It was only later, as the victims increased in number and women were killed, that he took charge.

Lüdtke was lucky to have a job with the police at all, let alone a high-ranking position in Berlin. In 1939, he was not a party member, even though many of those with ambitions to get ahead in the

German bureaucracy had joined after the Nazis took power in 1933. And the true believers had joined before then.

Back when there were other parties to vote for, he had been a member of the German Democratic Party. It was a social liberal party that believed, among other things, in protecting the rights of ethnic minorities such as German Jews. Lüdtke, though, had more problems than just not being a Nazi and having been a supporter of a now-disbanded liberal party; he'd openly worked against the Nazis prior to 1933.

He was born on June 22, 1886, in the small town of Alt Fanger in what was then Pomerania, Germany, and now is northwestern Poland. His father, Karl Johan Lüdtke, was a farmer and his mother, Johanna Lüdtke (maiden name Pansch), was a housewife. He graduated from high school in Pomerania at eighteen and then joined the German army. He served in the army from 1904 to 1909, which was before World War I. When his military service ended, he became a uniformed policeman in Frankfurt, Germany.

In August 1914, he was promoted to the Criminal Police (Kripo). World War I had begun just the month before, so there was room in the ranks to move up as other policemen left to join the war.

If he had stayed in this relatively nonpolitical position, Lüdtke would have likely never had a run-in with the Nazis, but in 1929, he was promoted to run the political police in Frankfurt and Harburg-Wilhelmsburg. He'd worked his way up the ranks and was now a criminal commissioner.

He held this job from 1929 to the start of 1933, a time period filled with bloody and murderous street battles between the different political forces vying for control of Germany. The Communists and Nazis were the two main groups that Lüdtke was supposed to keep from killing each other. With this job, he made powerful enemies when he interfered with Nazi party rallies, among other actions.

On January 30, 1933, as a result of his work running the political police department, he lost his job with the Kripo. The regional leader of the Nazi Party in Eastern Hanover, Otto Telschow, had Lüdtke removed from office. As the Nazis consolidated power in early 1933, Lüdtke was tried in front of a disciplinary court for interferences with the public activities of the Nazi Party, such as demonstrations and rallies. Although it had been his job at the time to do precisely that, the Nazis were not interested in the fact that he had just been following orders.[1]

Despite this black mark on his Kripo record, Lüdtke managed to use the connections he'd built up over the years in the police to get a new job and keep his rank. He left behind the region of Eastern Hanover and started work in Berlin on May 1, 1933. He now tried to stay out of political matters and concentrated on solving the crimes belonging to the department he ran, the Serious Crimes Unit of the Berlin Kripo.

# CHAPTER THREE

## The Footrace

In 1939, Ogorzow was still developing his method of attack. With Miss Budzinski, he had hit her first on the head to incapacitate her and then proceeded to stab her repeatedly. During other attacks, he had used his hands to choke the women he attacked so that they physically were incapable of yelling for help. In his early days, he had mostly used his fists to beat up women, which did nothing to stop their screams.

Paul Ogorzow was worried about possible repercussions from his attack on Lina Budzinski. She was still alive, and he was not sure if she had been able to see him well enough in the dark to identify him. He had not been wearing a mask or otherwise covering his face, so if she had gotten a good look at him, he could be in serious trouble. He waited though and nothing happened. No one came looking for him and no posters went up with a drawing of his likeness.

Despite the risk it entailed, he eventually returned to the garden area to harass and attack women. He was afraid, though, that he might get caught, and so he reverted to engaging in lower-level offenses again for a while, such as yelling at women and scaring them with his flashlight.

Once he became comfortable with this level of activity, he returned to a more serious level of crime. Four months after he had almost killed Lina Budzinski, he was ready to violently attack, and maybe even kill, the next woman he came upon who was alone in the darkness.

By now, World War II was well under way. On August 23, 1939, Germany and the Soviet Union signed a nonaggression pact. A week later, on September 1, Germany attacked Poland. That same night, the blackout officially began in Germany.

In September, a number of countries, including France and the United Kingdom, declared war on Germany. The United States declared that it would be officially neutral. On September 17, the Soviet Union invaded Poland as well. In early October, the Soviets and the Germans occupied all of Poland. They divided the country between themselves.

At 1:15 in the morning of December 14, 1939, Ogorzow spotted a woman walking alone in the garden area. Her name was Hertha Jablinski. While her first name sounds strange in English it was not that unusual in Germany at the time—Hertha was one of the names of the ancient German fertility goddess Nerthus.

Miss Jablinski was nineteen years old and was walking home from her war related work. She was tired and ready to call it a day.

She'd taken the train and now was walking alone in the dark through the garden colony. There were trees and small plots filled with fruits, herbs, and vegetables. Before the war, there had been more flowers and decorative plants, but with rationing, it made sense to grow things that didn't look as pretty but could be eaten.

The garden colony was empty at this time of night. The main commuter train line in Berlin, the S-Bahn, stopped here. While hundreds of thousands of people rode this rapid transit train every day, generally just a few people, if any, got off the S-Bahn here at this time, and they quickly dissipated, each going his or her own way on the myriad paths that branched away from the train station.

While walking in the garden area, Miss Jablinski could hear the footsteps of someone walking behind her. She looked back over her shoulder and saw nothing. It was too dark and this person was too far behind her on the path.

There had already been rumors of attacks in this area, so when she heard the footsteps quicken, as if the person was trying to catch up to her, she started to panic.

As the adrenaline pumped through her body, her fight-or-flight response kicked in. She could try hiding in the dark, but if the person following her had a flashlight, he might find her. Fighting seemed a poor option as she did not have a weapon. So she ran as fast as she could.

Ogorzow broke out into a run as well. They were now engaged in a high-stakes footrace, the end of which was Jablinski's home. If she made it there in time to get inside, she would be safe. If he caught up to her first, he would attack.

She lived nearby, so she did not risk stopping by a random garden house in the hope that someone would be home and would come out to help her at this ungodly hour if she banged on the door. The blackout meant that even if someone was at home and awake with the lights on, she wouldn't be able to see that from the path. The person's blackout curtains would prevent any light from spilling out and revealing that someone was home.

Behind her, Ogorzow broke out into a run as well. He was stronger and faster and managed to gain ground on her quickly.

Ogorzow won this high-stakes footrace. When he caught up to Miss Jablinski, he didn't yell at her or hit her over the head. Without saying a word, he stabbed her in the neck. Then again, and again, and again. Eerily, just as in his attack on Miss Budzinski, he was silent during the entire event.

Although she was shocked at first, she gathered her wits about her and screamed as loud as she could. In response, Paul Ogorzow stopped his attack. He paused a moment and then ran away. As much as he desperately wanted to continue stabbing Hertha Jablinski, he was deeply afraid of being caught.

Now, on her own, Miss Jablinski managed to get help and stop the bleeding. She was lucky that he had not cut an artery or she almost certainly would have bled to death on this garden path. At the hospital, surgeons stitched up her wounds, but they would leave scars behind once they healed.

## CHAPTER FOUR

# Do Not Cry Yet

Once again, Paul Ogorzow was worried about getting caught. Although it was dark, his most recent victim, Hertha Jablinski, had gotten a decent look at him. She wasn't able to tell the police much about his facial features, but he didn't know that at the time.

Only when the days turned into weeks and the weeks into months did Ogorzow feel secure that the police had not learned enough from Jablinski to be able to find him. It was difficult for him to control his urges to assault women during this time, but he was able to do so.

Even though he was not attempting to kill women then, he continued to prowl in the garden area at night. Sometimes he went out just to find women to yell at and scare with his flashlight. He would go out on foot or ride his bicycle. He also continued to physically attack women during this time, but not with a level of violence that the police considered to be attempted murder.

The police were aware that a man was harassing and attacking women in the garden allotments, but as there had been no murders and few clues, it was not a high-priority case.

Eight months after his attack on Hertha Jablinski, Ogorzow finally felt secure enough to try again for a full-fledged assault on a woman who was making her way through the garden allotment area during the blackout conditions.

At half past one on the morning of July 27, 1940, Mrs. Gertrud Nieswandt was walking through the garden area. She was twenty-five years old and was going to her parents' house. As she made her way in the darkness, Mrs. Nieswandt heard someone walking behind her. She quickened her pace but did not break into a run. Perhaps she was not aware that a man was using the darkness and isolation of this area to attack women. There had been nothing in the news about these attacks; the only information that spread was rumors among the people who lived here. Mrs. Nieswandt, though, lived elsewhere.

Behind her, Ogorzow was slowly gaining ground. He had learned from his attack on Hertha Jablinski that if he broke into a loud run, it would spook his intended victim. So he picked up his pace, in a carefully calculated move to try to catch up to her before she reached her destination, whatever that might be, without scaring her into yelling out that a man was chasing her.

Although it was late, and they encountered no one else on this path, Mrs. Nieswandt could not be certain that the footsteps behind her meant that someone was stalking her. There were other people who worked late hours and needed to walk home from the train station.

By the time Ogorzow caught up to her, she had almost reached safety. They were now standing together in front of the porch of her parents' house.

At this point, it was clear to her that something was very wrong. She did not know this man who was standing near her. If she had known that a man had been seriously hurting women in this area, she would have likely yelled out the moment she realized that he was near her. Instead it was a confusing moment, in which she may have thought this man was merely going to try to ask her out. With so many men away in the military, it was not uncommon for those men still in Berlin to try to take advantage of the fact that there were many lonely women in the city.

Given that at this moment Ogorzow could tell that this woman was not panicking, he tried to keep things calm by saying something relatively innocuous.

He asked her, "Are you going in here?"[1]

She answered him almost automatically with an "Of course."

Mrs. Nieswandt had no interest in having a conversation with a man she didn't know in front of her parents' house in the middle of the night. She wanted him to go away, but she did not feel threatened enough by what he'd said and done so far to actually scream out for help.

She thought a simple threat would be enough to get rid of this man, and so she said, "Leave, or else I will yell."

Ogorzow was worried about his victims screaming for help. In the past, when they screamed, he ran away. Not only did this mean he had to stop his criminal actions mid-attack, but as he ran away, he also felt fear that he would be caught. He needed to strike now, fast, before this woman actually did scream out and call attention to them.

Paul Ogorzow replied, "Do not cry yet." At the same time as he was saying this, he hit Mrs. Nieswandt, hard. As a result, she fell to the ground. Once she was down, he bent over and used his pocketknife to stab her in the neck. His knife landed less than half an inch away from her carotid artery. If he had hit that artery, she would have quickly bled out and died. There was still blood flowing from her neck, but nothing like there would have been if his strike had landed in a slightly different place.

He intended for this first stab to incapacitate his victim and prevent her from screaming for help. He raised his arm up with his now bloody knife in it. This time, his intention was not to stop her from crying out, but to fulfill his own desire to hurt her in a sexualized way. He plunged his knife into her about two inches from her genital region.

As he pulled his knife out, he realized that Mrs. Nieswandt was screaming. Despite his stabbing her neck, he'd done nothing to prevent her from yelling, other than the shock of being knocked to the ground and under attack.

Ogorzow was worried that family members or friends would come out of the house that Mrs. Nieswandt had been heading into before he attacked her or neighbors would stream out of their houses and capture him. He ran as fast as he could to get away before that happened.

Mrs. Nieswandt survived this attack and reported it to the police. They added the details of what happened to her to the growing list of offenses committed by an unknown man in this area.

## CHAPTER FIVE

# A Blow to the Head

On the evening of August 21, 1940, about three weeks after his attack on Gertrud Nieswandt, Paul Ogorzow lay in wait for a new victim to come along. This time he would combine his flashlight harassment with a physical attack.

On this night, the forty-year-old Mrs. Julie Schuhmacher was returning home after a long day at her war-related work. At 10:50 P.M., she was walking in the garden area near the Rummelsburg S-Bahn station when a flashlight suddenly blinded her. Her eyes had grown accustomed to the darkness, and it hurt to have a burst of light in them. She was blinded. The fact that the light came out of nowhere made it worse, as it felt like a malicious act and not something that had happened by accident.

She cried out for the unknown person who did this to stop. There was no verbal response from her harasser, Paul Ogorzow. Instead, he took advantage of her temporary blindness and confusion to emerge from hiding and attack her. He'd learned from his prior attacks that he needed to quickly render her unable to fight back, yell out, or get away.

He hit her on the head with a heavy blunt object. It was a lead cable that he'd found at work and carried around in his jacket sleeve to use as a weapon. Unlike an attack with a knife or his fists, a hit to the head with this object was enough to knock his intended victim out. Mrs. Schuhmacher fell to the ground unconscious.

And now that she was knocked out, Ogorzow raped her.

He had escalated from physical assaults to sexual assault. With each serious attack in the garden area, he became more comfortable with using violence against women.

Hitting his victim over the head with a blunt lead object had worked as well as he'd hoped. It had knocked Mrs. Schuhmacher out with a single blow. He kept the lead cable with him when he left the scene of the crime. He planned to use it again.

Mrs. Schuhmacher awoke afterward, with her attacker long gone. Given the light that was flashed in her eyes and the hit to her head, along with the fact that she was unconscious during the actual sexual assault, she was not able to provide the police with much in the way of useful information.

A forensic exam in the hospital found semen in her genital region, and she informed the police that she had not recently had consensual sex, so the police were now aware that they had a rapist in the garden area.

Of the four major attacks in this garden area that preceded Ogorzow's first attack on the commuter train system, this was the only one that involved an actual sexual assault. The preceding three attacks did not have this component, the police later theorized, because the victims had been able to scream out for help or escape before he had the opportunity to do more harm to them. Or perhaps the reason was that he needed the experience of hurting women badly with weapons and his fists before he was ready to commit rape.

These four attacks (Lina Budzinski, Hertha Jablinski, Gertrud Nieswandt, and Julie Schuhmacher) stood out for the amount of violence involved in them. The police classified these crimes as attempted murders.

The police eventually documented more than two dozen other, less violent attacks by Ogorzow that took place around this same time in the garden area between the S-Bahn stop and his home. There could have been even more than that, as some victims did not go to the police, and Ogorzow himself lost track of his criminal activities there.

## CHAPTER SIX

# A Family and Party Man

After his attacks, Paul Ogorzow went home to his family. Unlike the stereotype of a serial killer, Ogorzow wasn't a loner.

He lived with his wife Gertrude, their son, and their daughter in an apartment at Dorotheastrasse 24, which was a ten-minute walk from the Karlshorst S-Bahn station. They'd been married for three years and appeared to neighbors to have a normal family life. Ogorzow's wife was two and a half years older than him, having been born on March 16, 1910, with the maiden name of Ziegelmann.

Most of his attacks took place while he was supposed to have been at work, so his family thought nothing of his having been gone during that time. If he were late coming home, having just attacked a woman, he would lie by saying that he had been working overtime.

When questioned later on, his neighbors recalled seeing him

spending time playing with his young children and tending to his fruit and vegetable garden. He especially appeared to love the cherry trees that grew there.

The broken nose that Ogorzow had suffered in his youth, which had been improperly set, caused him to suffer from chronic nasal infections. These infections in turn caused him bad headaches at times. He'd also contracted gonorrhea on three occasions and had problems with the treatments for this sexually transmitted disease. The only visible element of these health problems was that his nose looked disfigured.

His wife later told police that Ogorzow was constantly jealous, suspecting (without any basis in reality) that she was cheating on him, and beating her on the pretext of her supposed adultery. He would sneak home early to try to catch her in the act of cheating on him. But he never did.

She remained faithful to him during their entire marriage. It turned out that her lack of commitment was all in his mind. This can be seen as a case of projection, as Ogorzow himself cheated on his wife numerous times, not even counting the violent sex crimes that he committed.

Despite this, the married couple had what they both considered a healthy sex life, with intercourse two to three times each week.[1] Paul Ogorzow also had a woman on the side. He'd often sneak away from work to visit her. She was a married woman whose husband was away in the German military. But just as with his attacks on women, his wife had no idea about this part of his life.

Paul Ogorzow would turn twenty-eight about a month after his attack on Mrs. Schuhmacher. He'd been born on September 29, 1912, in the village of Muntowo in what was then East Prussia, a province of the German Empire. This area is now part of northeastern Poland.

He was born Paul Saga, with no father listed on his birth certificate, and had a difficult upbringing as the illegitimate child of Marie Saga, a servant on a farm. There is not enough information about his childhood to know if he engaged in any of the behavior that criminal profilers would later associate with developing serial killers.

A book on teen killers described these behaviors as "the 'homicidal triad'—also known as the 'homicidal triangle' or the 'psychopathological triad'—a combination of three childhood behaviors that many murderers, especially serial killers, exhibit in their early years. These include enuresis (bed-wetting), pyromania (setting fires), and animal torture. . . . J. M. MacDonald first described the homicidal triad in his article 'The Threat to Kill,' published in the *American Journal of Psychiatry*, and it is sometimes referred to as 'the MacDonald Triad.'"[2]

Whether Paul Ogorzow wet his bed beyond the age that most children stop (around five), or set fires or tortured animals, there's not available documentation on this period of his life, and those who knew him at that age have passed away. This cluster of behaviors, which has become entrenched in American popular culture as indicative of a young serial killer, is controversial, and some believe it to be without merit in determining future activity. The German Police did not look into whether any of these three factors were present in Ogorzow's childhood as this was long before this theory was first proposed.

At around age twelve, a man named Johann Ogorzow adopted him. Paul Ogorzow grew up as a manual laborer—first, he was a farmworker, and later he worked at a steel mill, before moving to Berlin and starting work at the railroad company.

It helped his advancement at the railroad company that many of the men with whom he would normally be competing for jobs had left to join the military. So far, he had not been drafted, even in time of war; his job for the railroad was a skilled one that still needed to be done. Also, as a loyal member of the National Socialist German Workers' Party, aka the Nazi Party, he was in an advantageous position when it came to promotions. He'd joined the Nazi Party on April 1, 1932, a year before it gained power over Germany. This meant that he had a relatively low party number, and it gave him a bit of status in the Reich, as those who joined before 1933 were considered to be among the party's true believers. After the Nazis gained power in 1933, many joined the party in order to help their careers, while beforehand it could have been disadvantageous to be aligned with it.

There was no uniform for party members to wear; instead the party issued them a round membership pin. On it a black swastika, with a thin silver border, was set in the middle of a white background. A thick band of red circled the enamel pin, with the words *"National-Sozialistische D.A.P."* in all-white capital letters wrapped around the swastika.

Ogorzow was more than just a party member though. He was also in the party's paramilitary organization—the *Sturmabteilung*, also known as the SA, the Storm Troopers, or the Brownshirts. The term "Brownshirts" came from the color of their uniform.

Even among their fellow Nazis, members of the SA were often thought of as a ragtag collection of brutes and thugs. They were used primarily as goons to do the party's street fighting in the early days of Hitler's rise to power. Brownshirts terrorized opposing political groups, like the Communists, as well as persecuted minorities such as Jews and Gypsies. After Hitler established his control over Germany, he turned against the leadership of the SA and had hundreds of them killed in 1934 in a purge now called "the Night of the Long Knives."

Having only been in the SA for two years at that point, Ogorzow held far too low a rank to be purged. In order to help publicly justify this purge, the Third Reich publicized the fact that the head of the SA as well as many of the other purged members were closeted homosexuals. Of course, Hitler had been well aware of this fact before the purge occurred. The Night of Long Knives had been a matter of internal politics and a perceived threat to Hitler's hold on power, and so the Nazis had murdered some of their own leaders.

Ogorzow fit into the SA, with its working-class culture. It was during his early days in the organization that he saw the most action. Along with other SA men, he fought in pitched street battles against Communists, socialists, and trade unionists. They also beat up those the Nazis considered undesirable, such as Jews, gypsies, and, ironically, homosexuals. Among other tasks, they were used as muscle to prevent customers from entering Jewish-owned businesses.

This violence served as training for Ogorzow in his latter attacks on women. He found that he enjoyed the rush of power he felt in pushing people around and beating them up. And by engaging in such violence, he became more comfortable with it.

In November 1938, the men of the SA took part in a brutal, all-out attack on Jewish citizens of the Reich. The excuse for this attack was an incident that had taken place in Paris on November 7, 1938. Polish-born Jews in Germany were being deported to

Poland. But Poland, not yet a conquered country, refused to let them in. It was a nightmare for the thousands of people stuck between these two countries. One such family was Riva and Sendel Grynszpan's.

Their teenaged son Herschel lived in Paris, and when he heard about the perilous situation his parents were in, he went to the German embassy in France and asked to be brought to an official. He was seen by the most junior official on duty, a man named Ernst vom Rath. Herschel Grynszpan shot Ernst vom Rath, repeatedly. Ironically, vom Rath had expressed anti-Nazi views, including concern over the mistreatment of Jewish people. Ernst vom Rath died two days later on November 9.

The Nazis used this murder as an excuse to engage in organized violence against Jews, while pretending that it was a spontaneous outburst from the population. Reinhard Heydrich, the head of the Gestapo (*Geheime Staatspolizei*, which means Secret State Police), issued detailed, secret instructions to the SA and the Security Police (*Sicherheitspolizei*) on this matter.

In what has come to be called *Kristallnacht*, also known as the Night of Broken Glass, the SA and other Nazi groups attacked Jews and locations linked to Jews, such as synagogues, businesses, and residences. This took place across Germany and Austria, and was organized such that non-Jewish property was to be protected. So, for example, in Berlin, a synagogue in a Jewish area would be burned, while one next door to an Aryan-owned business would be smashed up instead.

Many young, healthy Jewish men were rounded up and detained, then shipped off to concentration camps. Others were simply beaten to death.

Having been an active part of the SA, Ogorzow became increasingly comfortable with violence. He'd risen to the rank of SA *Oberscharführer* (senior squad leader). It was the second noncommissioned officer rank in the SA, just above his prior rank of *Scharführer* (squad leader).

His activities with the SA desensitized him to beating people. Such violence, of course, was supposed to be directed against perceived enemies of the Nazi Party, not German housewives.

The garden allotments that had been Ogorzow's hunting grounds, an area he lived near and knew intimately, no longer felt safe to him. While the extensive green areas that filled this place provided him with plenty of cover, and the blackout meant that the area had no lighting in it, he was now afraid.

He'd attacked a woman who he had mistakenly thought was alone, and her brother-in-law and husband had beaten him badly. Even in his prior attacks, a woman screaming out for help had often foiled his plans, and so he thought about a new place where he could attack women and not face this danger.

He passed through the garden area on his way to and from one of the S-Bahn stations near his home. It may have been during one these trips that he realized that the trains themselves could serve as a new, safer, hunting ground for him. He knew them just as intimately as he did the garden area near his home, and by carefully waiting to attack until the only ones in a compartment were him and his intended victim, he could greatly minimize the risk of interruption or anyone hearing his victims' screams. And the trains themselves were darkened—not the complete darkness of the garden area, but still enough to make them an attractive place for a violent criminal like him.

## CHAPTER SEVEN

# The Blackout

The S-Bahn train compartments were dark (a little light was allowed though, so they were merely poorly lit, not pitch-black), as was the city of Berlin, because the Nazi regime had mandated a blackout in order to make it harder for British bombers to hit their targets.

The first British bombs landed in Berlin on August 25, 1940. Little actual damage had been done during that attack (the British only managed to destroy a garden house), but the city was on edge now that the war had finally come to its doorstep.

The famed historian William Shirer was in Berlin that night, and he wrote that despite the "material damage [being] negligible . . . the effect on German morale was tremendous. For this was the first time that bombs had ever fallen on Berlin. 'The Berliners are stunned [I wrote in my diary the next day, August 26]. They did not think it could ever happen. When this war began, Goering assured them it couldn't. . . . They believed him. Their disillusionment today therefore is all the greater. You have to see their faces to measure it.'"[1]

The head of the German air force, Reichsmarschall Hermann Göring, famously announced about a year before, in September 1939, "No enemy bomber can reach the Ruhr. If one reaches the Ruhr, my name is not Göring. You may call me Meier."[2] By this he meant that he was so confident that the British would never bomb Germany, that if the impossible happened, and Germany was bombed, he would trade in his high-status identity as Göring for the common, everyman status of Meier. It was like a prince saying he would become a blue-collar worker if a certain event came to pass.

Despite Allied bombs raining down on the Ruhr region, and past it, on Berlin itself, Göring did not change his name. However, cynical Berliners, when they thought it safe to do so, would refer to him as Hermann Meier. And air raid sirens became informally known among the embittered as "Meier's trumpets."[3]

The night before Great Britain bombed Berlin, the Germans had accidentally bombed a church and civilian housing on the outskirts of London. Their mission had been to hit an oil terminal. Hitler did not want London bombed.

The prime minister of the United Kingdom, Winston Churchill, was furious about this attack and ordered the immediate bombing of Berlin. While their first raid killed no one, the next attack on Berlin killed eight. About two weeks after the first bombs fell in Berlin, Germany began the Blitz (the German word for lightning), a 267-day-long campaign of German bombing of British cities.

Aerial bombardment of cities meant that places like London or Berlin were blacked out during the night so as to make it harder for planes to find targets. Nowadays, planes usually find targets using a global positioning system (GPS), but in World War II that was still thirty years in the future. Nor did those going on bombing runs have the advantage of night-vision goggles. Air-to-ground radar would come into use as the war progressed, but it still was not nearly as useful as being able to see a target. Other means of navigating to targets included astronavigation (used by the British) and radio navigation (used by the Germans).

As a practical matter, pilots needed to actually see targets with their own eyes to know where to bomb. Other ways of bombing tended to result in bombs landing far from their intended targets.

Daylight bombing runs were much more accurate than attacks by night, but with the German air force still a power to be reckoned with and antiaircraft fire coming from batteries on the ground, it was very dangerous for the Allies to fly bombing sorties while the sun shined. Bombers were much slower than fighter planes and were especially vulnerable during the day. At night, painted black, flying high in the sky, such bombers were harder to intercept.

On the other end of the spectrum, during times of storms or heavy cloud cover, while they were safe from enemy fire, it would be hard for bombers to find targets to hit. They would not know if they were above the center of Berlin's government district or a farm twenty miles away. The key then for planes to find targets to hit was for them to look for the telltale sign of modern civilization—lights at night.

The populations of these cities faced the dangers of a bomb hitting their homes, their places of work, their various modes of transportation, or wherever they happened to be walking. And as William Shirer wrote, the British air force "came over in greater force on the night of August 28–29 [1940] and, as I noted in my diary, 'for the first time killed Germans in the capital of the Reich.'"[4]

While the United States would not enter World War II until December 7, 1941, President Franklin Roosevelt had spoken out early on against the aerial bombardment of cities. On September 1, 1939, he proclaimed, "The ruthless bombing from the air of civilians in unfortified centers of population during the course of the hostilities which have raged in various quarters of the earth during the past few years, which has resulted in the maiming and in the death of thousands of defenseless men, women, and children, has sickened the hearts of every civilized man and woman, and has profoundly shocked the conscience of humanity. If resort is had to this form of inhuman barbarism during the period of the tragic conflagration with which the world is now confronted, hundreds of thousands of innocent human beings who have no responsibility for, and who are not even remotely participating in, the hostilities which have now broken out, will lose their lives."[5]

President Roosevelt went on to appeal to all sides to stop bombing civilian populations, but the problem remained that as long as one side was willing to do it, the other belligerents felt compelled to do so as well.

Hitler promptly released a statement to the press: "The opinion expressed in President Roosevelt's message that it is the law of humanity to refrain under all conditions of military activity from bombing non-military objectives is fully in accordance with my viewpoint and in accordance with what I have always represented. Therefore I agree unconditionally to the proposal that governments participating in current hostilities give a public declaration to this effect. For my part, I already announced publicly in my Reichstag speech on Friday that the German air forces have received orders to restrict their action to military objectives."[6]

Hitler's statement was contingent on the British not bombing civilians, and in the end, both sides continued to bomb cities.

These attacks were not even accurate in terms of being able to hit military targets within a city environment. For example, in September 1941, the British would analyze their past bombing attacks on Germany and find that only 20 percent of their planes bombed within five miles of their targets.

During the war, Berliners were free to wander around at night and go to normal activities like the theater, a restaurant, or a bar. The insides of such places were usually full of smoke, as the blackout meant that doors and windows could not be left open, and the air inside would soon grow stale and smoky. Restaurants in particular were often packed, as one did not need ration cards to get food there, just money. And this meant that if one had the money, there was food to be had without any hassle.

If an air raid siren went off, signaling that British bombers had been spotted, then everyone had to get off the streets and into the nearest air raid shelter. A reporter explained in August 1940 that in Berlin, "the streets were quickly cleared when the alarm sounded. Buses, street cars, subway trains were halted according to regulations."[7]

Any German citizens caught on the street during the air raid had to pay a fifty-mark fine, which was then equivalent to twenty U.S. dollars. As the reporter was an American, he was allowed to continue on with a warning and the sense that if he wanted to risk his own life to get to work during an air raid, that was on him. Only once the all-clear signal was sounded could civilians go out again.

The main regulations for implementing the blackout in Germany were issued by the Nazi government on May 23, 1939.[8] The blackout had not yet begun, as it was not needed until Germany was actually at war, but Hitler planned to attack Poland later that year and so needed the regulations in place beforehand. It would take time for the Reich to be ready to implement the blackout.

The Blackout Regulation, the informal name for the Eighth Regulation Implementing the Air Protection Act, spelled out how the blackout would work. This regulation was divided into two main parts. The first part dealt with general regulations that impacted private spaces, while the second part covered special regulations, which dealt primarily with public space issues such as how transportation and signage would work.

Section One explained that these regulations covered implementation of the blackout throughout the Reich.

Section Two proscribed that "responsibility for implementation of the blackout" fell on those who owned a property or at least exercised actual control over it. This was combined with the next section, which set forth that as a general rule the costs of implementing the blackout requirements fell on those responsible for implementing them. The only exceptions being if the person had a contract that said otherwise or if specific legislation addressed this issue for them. These two provisions combined meant that it would be up to a home or business owner to do what was needed to prevent light from spilling out into the night. And any associated expenses, such as purchasing heavy-duty blackout curtains for windows, would be that person's responsibility.

Section Four, "Preparation of Blackout Measures," required that people ready themselves to implement the blackout immediately, so that the government could announce at any time that they wanted it to begin right away. The real date for when the blackout would begin would be the invasion of Poland, but that date was a closely guarded secret, and so instead of including an actual date for when people would need to start implementing the blackout, the Blackout Regulation mandated that the populace ready themselves now. The announcement of when the blackout would actually begin would come later on.

Section Five, "Commencement and Duration of the Blackout," explained that the police would announce the start and end of the blackout. Once it began, the default timing for it would be from dusk to dawn every day.

Section Six covered the very narrow circumstances under which relief from the mandatory blackout would be granted. This primarily applied to essential factories that needed light to operate and could set up a connection to the air raid warning system so they could go dark if bombers were actually coming.

Section Seven covered monitoring of the implementation of the Blackout Regulation. Those making sure that the people followed these rules were given the police powers needed to enforce them and to punish those who did not abide by them.

The second part, special regulations, contained twenty-one sections that covered everything needed to convert a modern industrial city, powered by electricity and filled with cars, buses, trams, and trains, into something that did not leak light into the night. There were a host of issues, big and small, that needed to be covered to enable this massive transformation and to try to accomplish it while still allowing the city to be productive at night and to minimize the loss of life that would result from the removal of proper outdoor lighting.

This section included rules on such subjects as the nature and implementation of blackout measures; the dimming of light sources; preventing the exit of light from buildings and vehicles; traffic lights; road sign lighting; the lighting of land vehicles such as cars and bicycles; road safety; and more.

Train platforms became dark as a result of Section Sixteen (traffic lights), Clause One: "The lighting of streets, roads, squares, railway and port facilities, waterways, and properties of all kinds, to the extent not otherwise provided below, are to be shut down."[9]

Road safety was a major issue, and Section Twenty-Eight prescribed that weatherproof white paint, highly visible in the dark, be applied to the curbs of major traffic points such as crosswalks, bus stops, and intersections. This paint was also to be applied about a meter up on any dangers near the road, such as fences, trees, bends, houses, and more. Otherwise, cars might veer off the road and crash into these obstacles.

The third part consisted of a single section, numbered twenty-nine, which covered the authorization needed to amend the second part of the regulation. It granted this power to the reich minister of aviation and commander of the air force, Hermann Göring, although any changes to rules about traffic lighting needed to be approved by the minister of the interior and the minister of transport.

The Reich held elaborate practice runs for the blackout before starting World War II. In July 1939, Berlin prepared for Germany's upcoming attack on Poland by blacking out the whole city. The population of this city of four million people all played some role in this exercise, from the civilians who responded to the air raid sirens by quickly entering the closest air raid shelters to the first responders who attended to those who acted as if they were injured or dying.

Planes flew overhead and dropped fake bombs while the city's defenders tried to shoot them up with fake antiaircraft fire. As the Associated Press reported, "The raiders theoretically shattered hundreds of buildings, tore up streets, overturned street cars, and caused casualties among civilians. . . . Buildings poured forth specially manufactured smoke while red flares added to the simulation of buildings set afire by bombs. Detonations like exploding bombs could be heard."[10]

On September 1, 1939, Germany attacked Poland, and the blackout began. Strangely, that same night, the air alarm went off, even though no Polish bombers had come to attack and a practice air raid had not been announced. In December, a foreign correspondent wrote, "When evening falls, Berlin becomes literally a 'city of dreadful night.' This blackout must be lived to be understood. It is almost total. Trams and buses still run, but virtually dark. The few automobiles that circulate have their headlights hooded save for a small slit, which emits only a faint ray. You pick your way warily through inky-black streets, sensing rather than seeing the passers-by."[11]

German propaganda posters emphasized this element of threat and the need for diligently following the rules and regulations related to the blackout. One particularly memorable poster featured a malevolent skeleton riding on top of a plane painted with a Royal Air Force roundel while hurling down a black ball on a German city. At the bottom left of the poster, we see how the bomber found a target—a person stands in an open doorway leaking light out into the street. The same building has windows that are lit up as they lack blackout curtains. Scrawled across the poster are the words "The Enemy Sees Your Light! Blackout!"[12]

Another German blackout propaganda poster also featured a

skeleton in the sky. In this one a plane flew on a clear starry night. The skeleton is some kind of supernatural force, death incarnate, that spits out a bomb onto a building with a lit window and no blackout curtain. The text reads, "Light. Your Death!"[13]

The Nazis did not simply provide propaganda and rules—they of course also enforced the blackout using the tools of their totalitarian state. In addition to the usual authorities, such as police, there were those specifically responsible for checking that the blackout conditions were being respected, such as local air raid wardens.

Herbert Vogt, who lived in Berlin during this period, later wrote about how Germany enforced the blackout conditions: "In shops, offices, and private homes, the windows had to be covered with black curtains so that not a ray of light showed from the outside. Many people constructed rigid contraptions to bolt on to the window frame, which considerably simplified the nightly ritual of 'putting up the blackout.' Those who were careless or late risked the humiliating experience of [an air raid] warden's stentorian voice roaring for the whole street to hear the word that quickly became a catch phrase: 'Put that light out.' In case there was no response, any pedestrian was allowed to throw a stone in the window, or many times a policeman would pull out his pistol and shoot the light out. Repeat offenders had to pay a fine or, in some cases, were arrested."[14]

Local air raid wardens would walk around at night, and if they spotted any light emerging from a building, they would post a warning to notify the resident to fix this problem and to embarrass him as part of this process. One such posting said in big, bold letters, "This house is badly darkened!"[15] It went on to explain that this endangered not only those living here, but also their neighbors. Once the problem was fixed, the notice could be removed.

Not everyone used blackout curtains. Many people in Berlin covered their windows with paper so that no light could escape at night, even though that meant they didn't get any light coming through their windows during the day either. For them, this was easier and cheaper than installing special curtains that had to be drawn every evening.

Within days of the start of the blackout, the Nazis passed a law dictating strict punishments for those who took advantage of the darkened conditions to commit crimes. On September 5, 1939, the Third Reich issued a "Decree Against Public Enemies," the name of which literally translated would have been "Regulation Against Folk Pests" (*Volksschädlingsverordnung*).

The United States Holocaust Memorial Museum's *Holocaust Encyclopedia* explains, "Under the terms of the law, a crime against person or property, or against the community or public security, could carry a death sentence if the accused was charged with exploiting the special conditions of war—such as blackouts or a lack of police supervision—to carry it out. . . . It is worth noting that *Volksschädlinge*, the key term in the law's title, is translated as 'folk pests' or 'vermin.' As such, the law equates those exploiting the special conditions of war to carry out crimes with the type of agricultural pests that are destructive and generally outside the sphere of moral responsibility. Just as a gardener attacks the bugs and vermin that threaten his plants, so too, the Nazis believed, the national community had to eliminate those who compromised the health and well-being of the body politic."[16]

On October 24, 1939, a reporter for *Life* magazine wrote in a letter, "The courts are clamping down on petty crimes committed in the dark and some of the sentences are rather astounding when one considers that the penalty for murdering one's wife may be two years in the pen. A law establishing the death penalty for persons convicted of taking advantage of the blackouts to snatch pocketbooks or commit hold-ups has been passed. A Hanover court has just sentenced three boys 17, 18 and 21 years of age, for whacking a woman shop clerk on the head and robbing her of 150 marks she was taking to the bank. All three are to have their heads chopped off because the law makes no distinction for youth. Had they robbed her by daylight, the sentence would have been a few months in prison."[17]

A serial killer and rapist taking advantage of blackout conditions would certainly fit within this notion of a pest that threatens the well-being of the German community. Such a pest would need to be identified and captured by the Criminal Police so as to protect the home front and the citizens of Berlin. The resulting sentence would be death, as Ogorzow had to be aware, given the publicity surrounding this law.

Berliners eventually grew used to living in blackout conditions and thought nothing of riding the trains in the low light allowed on them, although they remained murky at best. Only every other light-bulb was plugged in, and the output of those that were on was reduced by half. In sum, this meant that inside the train there was one-quarter of the light that had existed before the blackout.

And this had never been much light anyway. The trains did not have the fluorescent tubes that people are accustomed to these days; instead there were incandescent globes along two rails on the roof of the carriage, with a pair of bulbs every six feet or so. During the blackout one light in each pair was lit, with the opposing light being turned off. This alternated throughout the train, resulting in a zigzag pattern of small pools of light. One could still see inside the train, but not well.

The windows were shut and covered over for the duration of the war. This meant that even during the day if people smoked in the train or just if there was a sweaty mass of people using it, the smell could build up to something terrible.

Passengers could still open and close the doors, though, as that was necessary to board or exit the train. There were doors on both sides of the train, as some stations would have a platform on one side, while others would have one on the opposite side. Confusion over getting on and off the train in the blackout conditions resulted in serious accidents on a regular basis. While there was some light in the train, the boarding platforms of the train stations were themselves dark.

The outsides of the trains were not painted black. Instead, they remained the colors that the S-Bahn had been using since 1924, a very distinctive combination of ruby red and yellow ocher. The bottoms and tops of the sides of the trains were painted ruby red and the middle area, around the windows, was yellow ocher. The same basic color scheme is used on the Berlin S-Bahn today.[18] During the blackout, the outside of the train often had phosphorus paint on it as well so that people could see a faint glow in the dark as it arrived.

## CHAPTER EIGHT

# The First S-Bahn Attack

In the little more than a year since Germany began World War II by invading Poland, the Third Reich had enjoyed tremendous military success. The Soviet Union was still its ally, and the only significant foe it faced in Europe was the United Kingdom.

Germany had invaded Norway and Denmark on April 9, 1940. Denmark surrendered that day. Norway surrendered on June 9. On May 9, Germany began its invasion of Belgium, France, the Netherlands, and Luxembourg. France had built a massive collection of defenses, known as the Maginot Line, along its border with Germany. Instead of trying to fight his way through this collection of concrete bunkers, tank obstacles, retractable turrets, garrisoned troops, and other defensive measures, Hitler ordered his troops to attack from the north by conquering the countries that lay above France.

Belgium, the Netherlands, and Luxembourg all quickly fell to the Germans. France signed an armistice on June 22, 1940, that among other provisions gave Germany direct control over the north and west of the country, while a collaborationist French government known as the Vichy Regime controlled most of southern France. There were other divisions of France as part of this agreement, including territory controlled by Italy, but these were the two major chunks of what had been the French Third Republic. The United States had not yet entered the conflict.

Although the world was engulfed in a massive war, Ogorzow remained in the heart of Nazi Berlin, where he worked a civilian job.

After the incident in the garden area in which a woman's husband and brother-in-law beat him, Ogorzow had learned a few lessons the hard way. One was to make certain that his victim was alone before attacking her, so nobody could hear her screams and come to her rescue. The second thing was to kill his victims—a dead woman could not cry out for help or talk to the police.

Paul Ogorzow wore his railroad uniform as he rode the S-Bahn train in Berlin on the night of September 20, 1940, on the hunt for a woman to attack. Until now, Ogorzow had not used the S-Bahn itself as a way to find and attack women, but he'd recently come to realize that in a train compartment he could make certain that there was no one present besides him and his victim.

Although tonight would mark the first time that Ogorzow attacked a woman on the S-Bahn, he was very familiar with this environment. He'd ridden the S-Bahn to and from work on a regular basis for a long time. He'd been working on the railroads of Berlin for six years now. He'd started in 1934 with a temporary job as a manual laborer for the German National Railroad Company

(*Reichsbahn*) in Berlin. For this job, he worked construction, laying railroad track as part of a large work crew. It was hard, backbreaking work, but in the economic chaos of 1934, he was lucky to have a job.

This temporary job turned into a permanent one with the *Reichsbahn*. He then worked his way up from manual labor, such as turnpike maintenance, to his current job with the S-Bahn. The *Reichsbahn* operated the S-Bahn, so he was still working for the same company.

There was something creepy about the S-Bahn at night under the Nazis. The S-Bahn logo at the time featured a gravestone shape of alpine green with a large stylized white "S" above the word "Bahn." Today, the symbol is similarly colored but a circle; the shape of the old logo was ghoulish given the deaths that were to occur on this train system.

The S-Bahn stations had large Nazi flags and bunting displayed in them. The flag consisted of a red background with a white circle in the middle containing a black swastika.

As most stations were outdoors, passengers had to wait in darkness for the trains to arrive at night. Even when trains arrived and people opened their compartment doors, only a little light flooded out because of the restrictions of the blackout.

Although some of its parts were much older, the modern S-Bahn was formed in 1924, through the combination of various, mostly over-ground, commuter railways in and around Berlin. The system was electrified, with a third-rail power source, during the 1920s; some of the older trains had been run on steam, made from burning coal.

The term "S-Bahn" may stand for "city fast train" (*Stadtschnell-*

*bahn*), but that is not certain. An expert on the Berlin S-Bahn, Thomas Krickstadt, described the confusion over what S-Bahn actually stands for. "There is no evidence what exactly 'S-Bahn' means, but the term *'Stadtschnellbahn'* is the most probable explanation. To understand the story behind the name, you have to go back a bit. Until 1928–1929 the group of state-operated railway lines in Berlin had the name *Stadt-, Ring- und Vorortbahnen*, German for 'City, Circle and Suburban Railways,' which was rather an unwieldy name for a trademark. Then, with the electrification of the state-operated railway system, the trains got faster and had a modern touch. On one station a self-made logo 'SS-Bahn' appeared, which obviously stood for *'Stadtschnellbahn.'* Soon after, a new symbol (a white 'S' in a green gravestone like shape) was invented as a trademark and the term 'S-Bahn' became popular (in opposition to the city-operated underground railway system called 'U-Bahn' with a white 'U' in a blue square as its symbol)."[1]

There are two other popular explanations for what the "S" in "S-Bahn" stands for—*Stadtbahn*, the German word for "city train," or *Schnellbahn*, German for "fast train." According to customer service at the company that currently operates the S-Bahn in Berlin, the full name is *Stadtschnellbahn*.[2]

The Nazis built a key part of this system for the 1936 Berlin Olympics. Their final addition to the S-Bahn was in October 1939, shortly after Germany invaded Poland.

A book on the history of Berlin explained, "The S-Bahn had its origins in the notion of a '*Ringbahn*,' originally derived from the military, who wanted to ensure that in the event of a mobilization the various Berlin terminal stations would be linked together by a line that would also serve the Tempelhof training grounds. The actual position of the ring line was a compromise between the desire to maximize utilization by being as close as possible to the core of the city and the desire to minimize land-acquisition costs by avoiding areas of existing urban development. . . . After electrification in 1924–9 the journey time for a full circuit of the S-Bahn ring was 63 minutes. . . . A final element was provided at the end of the 1930s by another link across the S-Bahn ring, this time running north-south in a tunnel beneath the heart of the city, intersecting the 'diameter' S-Bahn line at Friedrichstrasse station, which developed into a major multi-level interchange of both S-Bahn and U-Bahn lines. . . . In 1939 the U-Bahn was still a relatively small system supplementing the S-Bahn in the more densely settled inner part of the city."[3]

Berlin at that time had a cutting-edge public transportation system that connected the whole city. Residents did not need a car to get around, which was a huge plus during the gasoline rationing of World War II.

The S-Bahn was a key part of this system, along with the primarily underground subway system, the U-Bahn (*Untergrundbahn*). Although these were both rapid transit commuter train systems in the same city, the two systems were run by different entities—the National Railroad controlled the S-Bahn while the Berliner Verkehrsbetriebe, popularly called the BVG, ran the U-Bahn. As such, Ogorzow's work had nothing to do with the U-Bahn.

Other elements of Berlin's public transportation system at the time included a tramway and a bus network, including trolley buses. The company Ogorzow worked for, the National Railroad, was not involved in these alternative means of transportation.

Ogorzow worked as an auxiliary signalman of the Berlin-Rummelsburg S-Bahn station, located in the Lichtenberg borough of Berlin. Two experts on the S-Bahn explained what duties Paul Ogorzow's job entailed: "An 'auxiliary signalman' or (as we call it) auxiliary staff at a signal tower (word-for-word translation of *Hilfsstell-wärter*: 'Auxiliary guard of a signal tower') had to care about faults at points (German word is *Weiche*, other English words are 'switch' or 'flank'), signals or rails and to repair these faults. For example he had to free unheated points from ice or snow in winter. Other examples: Mechanical signal towers use metal wires to change signals and the auxiliary staff had to make sure that these wires are functioning. Signals were lighted by gas in those times. Gas came from gas cylinders that had to be replaced when empty. The gas lamps often needed maintenance, like replacing the wick. All these tasks were duties of the auxiliary staff."[4]

Ogorzow was not close with his coworkers, but he did not stick out either. His superiors viewed him as a good worker, and he did much of his work alone.

On the evening of September 20, 1940, when Paul Ogorzow was riding the S-Bahn looking for a woman to attack, Miss Gerda Kargoll was taking the train home.

However, while riding the S-Bahn, she fell asleep. She was tired from a long day, and had been drinking a bit, which combined with the motion of the train to put her to sleep. When she woke, she'd ridden past her station. She got off the train at the Rahnsdorf station and waited to take a train going back in the direction she'd just come from.

Kargoll was worried because her train ticket only covered her originally intended ride from work to her home. If stopped by a ticket inspector, she would have to pay a fine for riding farther than she had paid for.

There was a system in place in which a trip within the inner part of Berlin was one price, but the farther out one went, the more the ticket cost. By the time one reached the outer reaches of Berlin, it could be an expensive trip.

A single trip in the inner area (known as the *Ringbahn*) cost 30 pfenninge for second class. Pfenninge were the linguistic equivalent of cents, so 30 pfenninge meant 0.30 reichsmarks. To take this same trip in second class cost 20 pfenninge.[5] This is what Kargoll had paid for her trip.

While many of the women that Ogorzow attacked on the train had weekly or monthly passes that saved them money compared to buying single tickets each day, Miss Kargoll had a single ticket. Ogorzow himself had a free pass to use the train, as he worked for the *Reichsbahn*.

Miss Kargoll had already had her ticket checked once, when she entered her originating S-Bahn station. In order to walk inside the station, she handed her ticket to the person working in a small office that controlled entrance and exit from the train system. Here, a ticket inspector stamped her ticket with a one- to three-letter stamp that indicated the station where her trip originated.

If she had made it to the end of her trip, she would have displayed her stamped ticket to the ticket inspector there before being able to exit her destination station. He or she would have looked at the origination stamp to figure out if the cost of her ticket was enough to pay for this trip. If not, Kargoll would have had to pay additional monies before she would have been allowed to leave the station.[6]

This meant that Kargoll would be safe as soon as she arrived at her original destination station, but while she was traveling back there, if a ticket inspector stopped her, she would face a fine for riding with a ticket that did not cover her trip. The worker at the ticket office at her final destination, however, would have no idea that she had taken this long route there.

Given the two classes of available transport, second or third class, this system needed personnel to occasionally spot-check passengers in transit to make sure that their tickets matched the class they sat in. A pure honor system would not work for long, and it was not feasible to check every passenger on the train itself. This spot-check system was meant to make sure that people had not snuck onto the train without a ticket somehow, as well as that people did not pay third-class rates and then ride in second class. It was not meant to find people like Gerda Kargoll who rode too far on the train before retracing their trip to arrive at their desired station. But if someone stopped her, she could be subject to a fine nonetheless.

Ogorzow, who was wearing his railroad uniform, could tell that this woman was distressed about something. He walked up to her and cordially asked what was the matter.

Miss Kargoll explained her situation, as she took him to have some authority in such matters. In reality, as a signalman, tickets were not something that he had any business dealing with. Having him with her did make her feel safe, though, because if a ticket inspector did stop her, Ogorzow could partially back up her story, and his very presence as her traveling companion might deter an inspector from fining her, as a professional courtesy.

Ogorzow told Kargoll that she would be fine riding with him. He invited her to ride with him in the second-class compartment even though she had a third-class ticket. Since he had a *Reichsbahn* uniform, she felt that he had the authority to provide her with this free upgrade. And she did not question his helpfulness.

A typical Berlin S-Bahn train was divided into "quarter trains," or four two-car units. Strangely, the S-Bahn had no first-class cars, only second-class, which made up a quarter of each train, and the rest of the train was third class.

This system was in place because the S-Bahn was not a stand-alone entity, but was run by the National Railroad Company, so it employed their terminology for classes. As an S-Bahn enthusiast recently explained: "There used to be four classes with the *Reichs-bahn* but not all of their trains had all classes. I believe only the long-distance trains had first class. Fourth class was introduced in 1852 to make traveling for the poor more affordable. It was abolished in 1928."[7]

The second-class compartments on the Berlin S-Bahn had drastically fewer passengers than did the third-class compartments. It was for this reason that Ogorzow decided to attack women who rode in the second-class section.

Gerda Kargoll again fell asleep for a short while. When she woke, she asked Ogorzow what station they were approaching. He told her—it was Wuhlheide station. When the train stopped there, Ogorzow watched the doors closely, hoping that no one else boarded their compartment. Given the late hour and the fact that they were in second class, it was unlikely that anyone would join them.

No one did. The two of them were alone.

There was not much time between S-Bahn stations. Along this line, it could vary from three to five minutes. Once Ogorzow saw his opportunity, he needed to move fast in order to attack Kargoll before they reached the next station.

Just after 11:30 P.M., as soon as the train left Wuhlheide station, Ogorzow made his move. He quickly strode to where Kargoll was seated. She did not try to run or otherwise panic, as he was wearing a uniform and he had been sympathetic before when she had told him about having ridden the train too far. He'd even allowed her to ride in second class with him.

Without hesitating, he wrapped his large hands around her delicate neck. He started to manually strangle her using both his hands, hoping to knock her unconscious and then quickly rape her, before killing her. Ogorzow did not have any weapons with him, just his hands.

Kargoll fought him much harder than he'd expected. She was fighting not just to draw breath, but also to make her way from her seat to the sliding door on the side of the train that could be opened even between stations.

Somehow, drawing on adrenaline and the strength she had gained from working at a factory, Kargoll managed to make her way to the door before collapsing.

Strangulation is a terrible thing to experience. The New York Prosecutors Training Institute recently explained what this feels like: "Clinically a victim who is being strangled first experiences severe pain, followed by unconsciousness, and then brain death. The victim will lose consciousness by any one or more of the following: blocking of the carotid arteries (depriving the brain of oxygen), blocking of the jugular veins (preventing deoxygenated blood from exiting the brain), and/or closing off the airway, causing the victim to be unable to breathe. Only eleven pounds of pressure placed upon both carotid arteries for ten seconds is necessary to cause unconsciousness. If pressure is released immediately, consciousness will be regained within ten seconds. After 50 seconds of continuous oxygen deprivation the victim rarely recovers."[8]

While Kargoll was merely unconscious, Ogorzow mistakenly believed that he had killed her.

He opened up the door she had fought so hard to get to. He could do it one-handed; the doors were designed to be easy to open and close. The doors had two door panels, each with its own metal handle. All Ogorzow had to use was one of these handles, and both panels opened sideways, disappearing into the frame of the train carriage.

This attack had taken longer than he'd expected because his victim had fought against him. He wanted to get rid of what he thought was her dead body before he arrived at the next station.

With the wind rushing against him, he threw Kargoll's unconscious body off the moving train. He was surprised to discover as he did so that he felt an incredible high as he touched her body and saw it fly into the night.

After throwing Gerda Kargoll off the train, Ogorzow tossed her belongings, including her purse with all its money still in it, right after her. He could live with himself as a sexual predator and a killer of women, but for some reason, he did not steal.

It was just before the train reached the station at Karlshorst. He closed the door before the train arrived at the platform. Through the use of a compressed air system, any open doors would automatically close before leaving a train station, but because the train was still in motion, Ogorzow had to manually shut the door by pulling on one of its handles. At the time, most of the handles were made of brass, but as the war progressed, cheaper metals were substituted.

If anyone had been standing out on the darkened platform, they would not have noticed anything amiss as the train pulled into the station.

Despite the fact that Ogorzow had not molested Kargoll, he experienced a sexual thrill from this attack. The forensic pathologist who would come to work on this case, Dr. Waldemar Weimann, later wrote that the combination of attacking this woman, having her body in his arms, and throwing her off a moving train "all called in Paul Ogorzow sensations produced by unprecedented violence. He then became addicted to it, attracted again and again to repeat that horrible situation."[9]

Unusually, in addition to being a forensic pathologist, Dr. Weimann was also a psychiatrist. This explains why he was comfortable making such an assessment about Ogorzow's psychological state.

So while Ogorzow had decided to start killing his victims as a way to protect himself, he discovered that he enjoyed killing women. As he threw Kargoll's seemingly lifeless body from the speeding train, he looked out into the black night. Adrenaline pumped through his veins. This had been the most singularly thrilling experience of his entire life. Killing, he realized, felt even better to him than did committing sexual assault.

Ogorzow was very aware of the S-Bahn timetable and the fact that there were only a few minutes between stations on this line. Given that he could not start his attack until the train left a station (the blacked-out windows prevented anyone from seeing anything from the platform, but he had to make sure no one could hear his attack either) and that he needed to dispose of his victim before reaching the next station, he had a very short amount of time in which to attack a woman, drag her to the door, and then throw her off the train, followed by all her belongings. There was not enough time to do more than touch his victims. He could not sexually assault them. And yet he continued to attack women on this mode of transportation despite the tight timeline it imposed on him, because the attack combined with his dragging the victim's body and throwing her off the train, gave him a strong, sexual feeling of power and pleasure.

While Ogorzow had thought Gerda Kargoll was dead, she miraculously survived not only his strangling her, but also his throwing her from a train traveling around forty or fifty miles an hour.

She landed on a soft pile of sand by the side of the track. This was an amazing stroke of luck, as the vast majority of the ground alongside the train track was stony. Perhaps this sand had been put there once as a resource to help put out a fire, and it had since been forgotten about. The police were not certain why it was there, only that it had saved Miss Kargoll's life.

She woke up on her own, on the embankment by the train tracks, where she slowly put together what had happened to her. She could see that she was lying in sand, and she was in pain from her injuries. Even with this sand to land in, it was still rough to be beaten up and then thrown from a moving train. She screamed for help, and eventually someone heard her cries and came to her rescue. The police were called, and they investigated this strange situation of a woman claiming to have been thrown from the S-Bahn.

Although he had yet to actually murder anyone on the train, this marked the beginning of Ogorzow's activities as the S-Bahn Murderer. The term had not yet been coined, but this was only his first attack on the S-Bahn.

## CHAPTER NINE

# The Investigation Begins

The Berlin police were notified that a woman had been found by the train tracks on the morning of September 21, 1940. When they interviewed Gerda Kargoll, she remembered nothing between the start of being strangled and waking up by the side of the railroad tracks. The police wrote this off as most likely being a hoax or else a drunken accident, where she fell off a moving train in the dark and then made up a story to cover up her own role in her injury.

She had not been sexually assaulted, and she still had her belongings, so she had not been robbed. She had found her purse a short distance down the tracks, the distance the train had traveled in the time it took Ogorzow to throw it off.

Gerda Kargoll suffered from a concussion and multiple abrasions as a result of her fall. She was hospitalized for four and a half weeks.

After her discharge, she continued to suffer terrible headaches as a result of the injuries to her head.

Without a robbery or a sexual assault, the police found it hard to believe that someone would, without warning, strangle her and then throw her from the train. A simpler explanation was that she was either mistaken or lying. It didn't help matters that she had been drinking earlier that evening and had fallen asleep on the train two different times that night according to her own version of events.

The police had grown used to a higher number of accidents in Berlin than there had been prewar. This made them all the less likely to believe that someone had actually thrown Kargoll from the train, as opposed to it being an accident. The blackout produced accidents in the city on a regular basis, including many related to the train. During one month alone, December 1940, twenty-eight people died from blackout-related accidents on the train tracks in Berlin. Such accidents included people walking across the tracks and not seeing that a train was coming, as well as people falling off the platform in dark train stations. Automobile-related fatalities were also common, owing to the dimmed headlights on cars and the lack of street-lights.

Numerous criminals struck during the blackout, such as Paul Mathes, whom the Germans executed during the middle of Ogorzow's killing spree. The German Police had caught Mathes stealing a large amount of coal, and they considered this "particularly heinous because it was carried out during a blackout."[1] He was sentenced to death on January 17, 1941 for this nonviolent crime. He was executed by guillotine.

When Kargoll was found in September 1940, Nazi Germany was at the height of its power. France had fallen to the Nazis three months before, and the UK was in a precarious position. They were afraid Hitler would invade, and the main way left for the British to fight was by sending out planes to bomb German targets. Daylight bombing allowed for some degree of accuracy, but it was extremely dangerous for the pilots, who ran a high risk of being shot down. So raids were conducted at night, making it virtually impossible to hit a specific target.

The nights in Berlin were a time of darkness and potential danger. Bombs could fall from the sky with only a short bit of notice that an attack was under way. Shrieking alarms would signal that people should flee to basement shelters, public air raid shelters, or anywhere they could quickly find cover.

For those riding the S-Bahn, what happened during an air raid depended on whether their train was heading to the outer sections or if it was on an inner-city line. Experts on the S-Bahn described how this worked: "A suburban train had to stop on the next station and all passengers had to leave the train there. Then the train had to rush to the next location on open track (away from any station) and the train personnel (engineer and conductor) had to take shelter under the train. After the air raid, all trains slowly returned to normal traffic, where the tracks were fine. . . . For the inner-city lines, old train drivers told the following: As soon as air formations were discovered miles away from Berlin, public enterprises were informed. Fifteen minutes later the public was informed with the air raid signal. So the train personnel had fifteen minutes to halt trains and to lead the passengers to the nearest shelters. Examples of big shelters in the city were at S-Bahn station Anhalter Bahnhof on the Schöneberger Straße or at S-Bahn station Friedrichstraße on the Reinhardtstraße."[2]

In Berlin, the basements of many buildings became makeshift

air raid shelters for their residents. Despite the Nazis' long-term awareness of the devastating possibility of aerial bombardments on their cities, they did not adequately prepare for this situation. While high-level government officials like Adolf Hitler could take refuge in bomb shelters built deep underground and with enough reinforced concrete to protect them even if a bomb hit, normal Berliners had to use the basement of the house or apartment building they lived in.

While such basements offered some safety, if a bomb hit them directly, the residents huddled inside would be unlikely to have enough protection to survive. Despite this grim reality, the people of Berlin became used to the sound of the air raid siren at night and the race to some sort of shelter.

This process was especially stressful for women with children, who were responsible for quickly taking their offspring to relative safety. A journalist for *Life* magazine described the daunting routine Berlin women with children had to go through each night: "Every mother must prepare for a nightly air-raid alarm before going to bed. In addition to the ordinary clothing, warm underclothing, long stockings and a coat must be placed on each child's bed. For small children a heavy cap and blanket are also necessary. A suitcase must be constantly ready for a hurried descent into the air-raid cellar. First, the suitcase must contain all the important documents and identification papers, then provisions for the children such as cakes of zwieback, picture books for the larger children and toys for the smaller ones. Then a small towel must be provided for each and naturally diapers for the babies. Each evening before going to bed the mother must fill a thermos bottle with fennel tea and also prepare the bottle for the baby. After placing these in the suitcase, she closes it and places it with the gasmasks in a position where it can be easily grasped."[3]

This was a tremendous amount of work to go through on a nightly basis. And visits to the air raid shelter could easily last three or four or more hours on any given evening. This often meant an entire apartment building's worth of tenants, including small children and babies, crammed into the basement. All the while, it was possible that death would rain down from above. It was a nerve-wracking experience that often resulted in a loss of sleep.

Paul Ogorzow's family often had to go through this experience without him. Unlike many families in Berlin, he was not serving in the military, but he would still be gone many nights either working or, unbeknownst to his wife and kids, prowling for women to attack. So it would be up to his wife, Gertrude, to take their young son and daughter to the basement shelter of their four-story brick apartment building. When the neighbors asked where her husband Paul was, she would answer that he was at work, and if it was past his regular hours, she would tell them that he was working overtime, as that was the lie he told her.

While many Jews in Berlin were ordered by the government to help with building air raid shelters and turning basements into shelters, they were prohibited from using any shelters that had Aryans in them. So if there had been any Jews in the Ogorzows' building, they would not have been allowed to use the shelter with their neighbors but would have had to risk the bombing run without the imperfect, but better than nothing, protection of the basement.

After a bombing run by the British, the streets of Berlin were often strewn with new piles of rubble. The hospitals would fill up with the injured and the morgues with the dead. Once people started dying from bombs dropped in Berlin in August of 1940, the population grew scared that they might die in the night.

And so the people of Berlin were already not feeling safe in the dark, even before Paul Ogorzow actually killed anyone.

## CHAPTER TEN

# The First Murder

As October 3, 1940, turned into October 4, Paul Ogorzow headed out into the night. He was not hunting for victims on the train, though, or in the garden area. This time he already had a specific target in mind—a woman he'd met on the S-Bahn.

Three or four days beforehand, Ogorzow had been standing at the Rummelsburg S-Bahn station when he saw Mrs. Gertrude "Gerda" Ditter waiting for a train. He went up to her and asked if he could visit her sometime. She said yes and told him where she lived. It was an address in the garden colony area of Berlin-Friedrichsfelde, where Ogorzow had formerly prowled for women to attack.

Mrs. Ditter was twenty years old with two young children. Her husband, Arthur Ditter, was away in the military. With so many men away fighting, it had become easier for someone like Paul Ogorzow, who was still in Berlin, to find married women who were willing to have an affair.

Ogorzow visited Mrs. Ditter for the first time that night, and she let him into her home at Kolonie Gutland II, path 5a, number 33. Each house in the garden area had an address of Kolonie Gutland I or II, then a path number and letter, and finally a house number.

They started off talking. It began as a casual encounter, the sort of prelude before two people who barely know each other commence an affair. It was a small house and they were in the kitchen, while Mrs. Ditter's two small children were sleeping in the living room.

Ogorzow wanted to keep Mrs. Ditter comfortable with his presence until he was ready to attack, so he was careful not to say anything that might alarm her. The last thing he wanted was for her to figure out that something was wrong before he began his assault.

Just as with some of his train attacks, there was an abrupt shift in their interaction when Ogorzow decided that now was the time he would strike. The switch between normal behavior and killer was a fast one for him. It was a conscious decision, made when he felt that it was safe for him to attack. He had complete control over this moment, when he crossed the line from the acceptable to the criminal.

Without any warning, Ogorzow abruptly ended their conversation with a violent attack on Mrs. Ditter's person.

He began this attack by grabbing her with both of his hands wrapped around her slender neck. He squeezed so hard that he fractured her hyoid bone. "The hyoid bone forms part of the axial skeleton and two characteristics make it unusual (for a bone): it is a single U-shaped bone that does not have a partner, and it does not articulate with any other bone," a textbook on forensic biology explained. "It is found in the anterior region of the neck between the mandibles and the larynx and its function is to act as a sling to support the tongue and for some of the neck and pharynx muscles. Damage to the hyoid bone, especially one or both of the horns of the 'U,' is a characteristic sign of manual strangulation."[1]

In cases with only skeletal remains, a broken hyoid bone is a strong indicator that the person was strangled. It is hard to break it otherwise.

Despite this serious injury, Mrs. Ditter was still alive. Paul Ogorzow kept one hand on her neck, to hold her steady, while removing his other hand. He used his free hand to take a knife out of his pocket and then stabbed her in the neck. His knife cut severed her left carotid artery and she quickly bled out. As she died, she became Ogorzow's first murder victim.

Ogorzow then fled the scene. He walked out the front door. None of Mrs. Ditter's neighbors saw him leave her place. This was not surprising given the darkness of the blackout and the fact that most people were asleep at this time. He walked through the garden area until he reached the suburban neighborhood where he lived. Ogorzow reached his apartment on Dorotheastrasse 24, where his family was likely already fast asleep. His wife and small children had no idea that he had just crossed an invisible line by killing someone.

The timing of Mrs. Ditter's murder was quite strange as it coincided with a very turbulent period in her life. The authorities believed that she led what they considered to be an inefficient life, and they had planned to remove her two small children from her care and place them in an orphanage. They had previously warned her about this possibility.

This was the work of the National Socialist People's Welfare organization (*Nationalsozialistische Volkswohlfahrt*), known by the acronym of NSV. This was a social welfare organization created by the Nazi Party. Among its various responsibilities was child welfare.

The man responsible for carrying out this order, Konrad Braun, arrived at Mrs. Ditter's house around noon on October 4. No one answered his knocks, and he discovered that the door to the front garden area of her home was unlocked. He let himself in, and then found that the door to the house itself was also unlocked. He then entered Mrs. Ditter's home and walked around, looking for her.

With the conditions of the blackout, it was hard to see inside the house. Windows that had been blocked to prevent light from going out also stopped light from coming in.

In the kitchen, Braun lit a match to better see, and discovered Ditter's body. It was immediately apparent to him that Gertrude Ditter (maiden name Barth) was deceased. Her long black hair was tucked behind her neck, exposing the bruises on it. She had a scarf on, but it hung loose on her so it covered her collarbone, not her neck area. She was wearing a dark-colored loose dress or nightgown with thigh-high stockings held up by a garter belt. Mrs. Ditter was not wearing shoes.

Her body was propped up where she had died, with the clutter in the small kitchen working to keep her vertical. Her right foot was under a small table while her head was stuck between this table and a kitchen container. Her right hand lay on top of a bench.

The children themselves were fine. They were found in the living room of the tiny home. One was in his cot, while the other was in a stroller.

Braun then contacted the local police to report his grisly discovery. When the uniformed officers arrived, they briefly considered the possibility of suicide, given that Mrs. Ditter was found dead on the very day that the government was to take away her children and that they saw no signs of defensive wounds on her body.

Suicide fell under the jurisdiction of the Order Police (*Ordnungspolizei*, known as Orpo), who handled relatively lower-level police matters. These were mostly uniformed police, whose distinctive green uniforms resulted in their nickname—the Green Police. They included administrative police who often did not need to wear uniforms—they did the kind of work for which many other countries used civilian workers.

However, people do not normally commit suicide by manually strangling themselves and then stabbing themselves in the neck. So the police on the scene quickly decided it was likely a homicide.

With it being a homicide, the Orpo referred the case to the Berlin Kripo's homicide squad at about a quarter past three that afternoon. And so the Kripo promptly took over responsibility for this case from the Orpo, who had the case for only a few hours. If it had been a suicide or an accident, the Orpo would have handled this matter on its own. There was a clear hierarchy between these two groups, with the Kripo above the Orpo in status, power, and responsibility.

Criminal Commissioner Zach now headed the investigation. At this point, it was a routine murder case. Just as in contemporary America, detectives wore plain clothes, not uniforms. One of the main differences between their dress and that of contemporary detectives was that they generally wore hats outdoors, as that was the custom of the time.

As they did not have uniforms, these detectives needed a way to quickly reveal their authority to take over a crime scene such as Mrs. Ditter's house. For this purpose, they had warrant discs. An expert wrote that these "were die struck, exactly like a coin, and were of very high quality. The police agency identification number assigned to each officer was hand-punched into the space provided on the reverse side of the disc."[2] The side with the number said, "*Staatliche Kriminalpolizei*" for State Criminal Police and the front side had the German imperial eagle clutching a swastika encircled by a wreath.

The disc itself had a hole punched in it so it could be kept on a chain, secured to the detective's belt like a skateboarder's wallet. While the police had identification cards, they were not supposed to be used in circumstances such as these, when flashing one's warrant disc was the way to gain entry to a house. A warrant disc functioned in much the same way as a police shield or badge does today.

In investigating this case, the Kripo detectives observed, "Immediately nearby the deceased—namely, under her right hand on the ground—there was a kitchen-knife with the blade under a dirty cloth. Whether this knife was the one used in the murder is not yet clear. Fingerprints have not yet been found on the knife."[3]

They sent the knife to be tested for fingerprints and to determine whether it was the murder weapon. The Forensic Institute of the Security Police at the Office of the Reich Criminal Investigations Department examined this kitchen knife carefully, with all the latest scientific tests.

After a thorough investigation, they determined, "Human blood was not able to be detected on the kitchen knife. Additionally, no other meat or fat remnants were found on the knife. Beyond that, it can be explained with certainty that this knife cannot be considered as the murder weapon. This fact is especially evidenced by the detail that the fine layer of mold on the handle and blade was intact, which could not have been the case if this knife had been used in the last few days. Further, there was a dark crumb, about four millimeters long, stuck firmly to the point of the knife, which had nothing to do with blood, but was rather made up of plant-root, sand, and seeds. A little clump at the back handle end was also only made up of sandy soil and small bits of plants. Red areas on the back of the knife turned out to be rust; here, also small specimens of little feathers were found which are not from chicken or duck."[4]

The murder weapon was not found on the scene at all. It was a knife that Ogorzow had brought to the scene of the crime and taken with him when he left. So there was no weapon for the police to examine.

Dr. Dolgner, based nearby in Berlin-Friedrichsfelde, examined the body before it was moved. He declared Mrs. Ditter officially dead. His preliminary examination revealed the cause of death to be a stab wound on her left carotid artery.

The Kripo arranged for Mrs. Ditter's body to be delivered to Dr. Waldemar Weimann so that he could conduct an autopsy.

Dr. Weimann dictated a transcript of his findings. He observed signs of asphyxiation, including hemorrhaging marks in the eyes. He did a thorough check of Mrs. Ditter's fingers, hands, arms, and legs and found no signs of defensive wounds. This lack of defensive wounds, in an attack that involved a knife, suggested that the victim knew her killer. The totality of evidence suggested to Dr. Weimann that Mrs. Ditter invited her attacker into her home and he then strangled her with his hands before he attacked her with a knife. So that by the time the knife was part of the attack, she was not able to defend herself.

Given the lack of defensive wounds, the Kripo had someone they very much wanted to question. Then, as now, the first suspect when a woman was murdered was often her husband. He was in the German army, which had him stationed in Potsdam at the time of the murder. The distance between there and Berlin was only about thirty miles, but the husband was not free to come and go from his barracks.

The police worked very fast to locate him, however, and find out precisely where he had been during this crime. They arrived at Arthur Ditter's barracks just hours after his wife's body was discovered. The police were locking him into a timeline and a history of his relationship with his wife before her body was even cold.

The police interrogated him and then typed up a very detailed five-page statement with all the information that he had provided them about his now deceased wife, Gerda, and his whereabouts for all times between when she was last seen alive and when her body was discovered by Konrad Braun. Arthur Ditter signed this document, as did Kripo Detective Zach.

Mr. Ditter gave the police his work and educational history in addition to background on his relationship with his wife. They'd met as kids at school, and their mothers in turn had also been school friends. When Gertrude turned sixteen, their relationship became a romantic one. Gertrude's mother did not approve of this relationship, as she wanted her daughter to marry a government official and believed that Arthur's prospects in life were not great. A big part of this, according to Arthur's mother, was that Arthur was not a German citizen.

The complicated change in control of territory in Europe in the early twentieth century resulted in Arthur's father being considered a Czech citizen. This was a huge problem for Gertrude's mother.

Arthur's mother, confusingly named Gertrud Ditter, the same name as his deceased wife except without the "e" at the end of her first name, explained this citizenship issue to the Kripo detectives: "Because my husband was born an Austrian; his home town fell in 1919 to the former Czechoslovakia and, through this, my husband became a Czech citizen. Gerda's mother did not want her daughter to marry a Czech man. My husband and I wrote to the Führer that he was born German and, therewith, Arthur became a citizen."[5]

By the Führer, she meant Adolf Hitler. Presumably someone in his office handled this matter and it never rose to Hitler's personal attention. Many Germans wrote to Hitler personally, expecting that he could handle matters for them. In this case, it worked.

The young couple married in November 1938 and had two children, a daughter named Helga and a son named Wolfgang. When Ogorzow murdered Mrs. Ditter, Helga was around four months old and Wolfgang was a bit over a year and a half old.

Mr. and Mrs. Ditter had purchased their garden house in Kolonie Gutland II for one hundred and fifty reichsmarks. The associated fees for this place, what Germans call rent and Americans call maintenance fees, were sixteen reichsmarks a year. This was very little money—Mr. Ditter made much more than this in a single week.

As Mr. Ditter explained, it was his wife's decision to continue to live in this garden house: "I gave my wages almost exclusively to my wife so that she could keep herself busy. I kept almost nothing for myself because I neither drink nor smoke. Recently, when I was employed as a track shifter, I was giving my wife about forty-five reichsmarks a week. She was frugal and was able to make do with this amount of money. However, she almost always told others that she didn't have any money. That was a habit of hers. But she always had groceries in storage. I always got along well with my wife. There were never serious arguments. It only happened two times in our marriage that we bickered—because I blamed her for not being tidy enough or watching the children enough. My wife waved it off and said she couldn't manage the work—it was too much. I always wanted to move into a real apartment. My wife was against this, though. She wanted to save that rent money."[6]

If they had moved to a proper apartment, instead of the small colony house, perhaps Gertrude Ditter would not have suffered this terrible fate.

The German army had drafted Mr. Ditter into military service. He told the detectives that this meant he had no free time during which he could have visited his wife in Berlin: "During my military service, I haven't had a single vacation. I was only allowed to leave once by myself, and that was to go to the dentist. Later, other comrades drove me to the dentist. The last time I was there was at the end of September 1940. Otherwise, I haven't left the barracks except for performing military duties. Also, I was not in Berlin in the last few days. During my time as a soldier, I have only been in Berlin once, and that was to the parade for the Italian foreign minister Galeazzo Ciano. But that was still at the end of the last month. I didn't get to see any relatives at that time."[7]

Arthur Ditter informed the Kripo of all of his recent activities:

"Yesterday, I was working until about 5 P.M. I was shooting. After returning from shooting, I ate lunch and then received the command to report by the gunnery sergeant. The sergeant told me secretively that my wife had died and that I had vacation until Sunday evening at 10 P.M. The day before yesterday, on Thursday the third of October 1940, I had service in the barracks. We had shooting. At 5 P.M., we were finished with shooting—that means we had to clean the guns until 6 P.M. After this, I had to write a resume. The company leader made me do this. Then, I had to tidy my things, clean my uniform, boots, etc., and I went to bed at about 8:30 or 8:45 P.M. At 9:00 P.M. is curfew. Surely I did not leave the barracks on these days or in the evening. My comrades from barrack room 94a can attest to this."[8]

The police were able to verify the information that he gave them, and so Arthur Ditter was quickly cleared as a suspect.

Mr. Ditter did provide detectives with some additional information. He didn't know who would do this to his wife, but he mentioned a dispute with his neighbor, Hermann Herlitz of garden house number 32. This was over the pigeons that Mrs. Ditter kept at their property. She also had hens and rabbits, but the pigeons were the basis of this dispute. While Mr. Herlitz, like many of the people who lived in this colony area back then, also had animals, it was the noise of the pigeons that upset him.

Mr. Ditter alleged that Mr. Herlitz picked similar fights with a large number of neighbors over petty, neighborly disputes. There was nothing to indicate that Mr. Herlitz had used violence in any of these altercations though.

The police still investigated him and interviewed mutual neighbors of his and the Ditters', but that line of investigation went nowhere. They also talked to Mr. Herlitz's girlfriend of five years, Auguste Bohm, and she explained the dispute over the pigeons. This turned out to not be much of a dispute, as besides a few harsh words over it by Mr. Herlitz, nothing had happened. As for Auguste Bohm, she expressed her displeasure at Gertrude Ditter's pigeons by not greeting Mrs. Ditter when she saw her in the streets.

Auguste Bohm provided an alibi for Herlitz. Bohm said to the police, "When Herlitz came home as usual on this Thursday evening, shortly before 6 P.M., he first ate something and then got feed for our animals. He was not away for more than an hour. When he came back, it was still light outside. After this, he didn't leave our property. We went to bed really early, as is usual in recent times. It was probably about 8 P.M. Herlitz hardly left our bedroom during the night—I would have noticed. When he gets up in the night, I almost always hear it. The next morning, he went to work as usual. Even then he couldn't have gone to Ditter's garden house because he went in the direction of path 5a towards Triftweg."[9]

They talked to Mr. Herlitz on October 6 and did not find out anything incriminating. A neighborly dispute over pigeons seemed an unlikely motive for such a brutal attack.

However, the police uncovered evidence suggesting that there may have been issues of fidelity in the Ditter relationship. They found a letter in the couple's home written by a woman, a G. Weinberg from Fürstenwalde, that they were curious about. Arthur Ditter told them a bizarre and implausible story to explain this letter.

His explanation tied in to the job he'd held just before the army drafted him. In a very strange coincidence, he worked for the Reichsbahn at the train-switching yard at Rummelsburg. This location would be ground zero for the S-Bahn murders, and it was here that

Paul Ogorzow worked as an auxiliary signalman. Later on, the police did not generate any evidence that he and Ditter knew each other or that this was anything more than the sort of strange coincidence that sometimes pops up in the course of such an investigation. Of course, at the time the police were questioning Mr. Ditter, they had no idea who Paul Ogorzow was.

The story Mr. Ditter told about this letter was an odd one: "About fourteen days before my draft into the military, or maybe three weeks, I was working at the switching yard at Rummelsburg. A younger woman came out of a train compartment in the second class and asked if there were mailboxes nearby. My coworker 'Stark'. . . . told me: 'You can put the letter in the mailbox.' The previously mentioned woman gave me the letter and asked me to put it in the mailbox. I brought this letter with me, put it in my jacket pocket, and then didn't think about it again. Some days later, my wife found it in my things, ripped it open, and read it. Since doing that, we didn't dare to send it. I wanted to put it in another envelope and send it, but my wife told me not to. So, that's why the letter is in my apartment."[10]

This version of events could be true. If so, it suggests that Ditter's wife did not trust him in regards to other women. If it was a lie, then perhaps Mr. Ditter had cheated on his wife and did not want the Kripo to know of this. Even with an airtight alibi, in Nazi Germany, it was not a good idea to draw the attention of the authorities. If the police believed that he had been cheating on his spouse, they might decide to the pin the murder on him and claim that he'd hired someone to do it for him. He had no way of knowing that these particular detectives had no interest in finding a scapegoat. They wanted to capture the actual killer.

More damning, though, was a document the police found that Mr. Ditter had written to his wife. It was titled, "My Confession." When asked about it, Arthur Ditter said, "I wrote this note years ago. We were not even engaged with each other yet. It's not important at all. I just was trying to get her to become more attached to me. At that time, my wife went out once in a while to the movies with a certain Fritz Gann, who lives in our garden colony. . . . However, I don't think in the slightest that Fritz Gann had anything going on with my wife or that he has to do with the death of my wife."[11]

The police were curious about this strange note. After having first asked Mr. Ditter about it, and written down his explanation, they confronted him with the actual document. In response, Mr. Ditter told them, "I wrote this note because my wife asked me to after the first time we had sex. My wife dictated the text, but only the beginning, and I wrote the end by myself. The subtitle, 'If Gerda Barth swears to me that she will no longer lie to me and go out with other men, give out her address, or do any other nonsense'—is so that she wouldn't go to the movies with Gann anymore and then keep it a secret from me."[12]

Mr. Ditter's explanation did not fully clear this matter up. Both the backstory and the note itself were quite odd. However, the police accepted Mr. Ditter's account of how he came to write this unusual letter given that he had a solid alibi for the night of the murder. This note did suggest, however, that there were issues of fidelity in the Ditters' marriage and that perhaps Mrs. Ditter had cheated while her husband was away. Unknown to the police at this time, Mrs. Ditter had given out her address to a strange man (Paul Ogorzow) she met while waiting for the S-Bahn, and that was what had led to her death.

However, there was nothing at the scene or in the investigation thus far to tie this murder to the S-Bahn. While Mrs. Ditter had ridden the train, so did most everyone in Berlin. There was no way for the detectives to know that she had met her assailant there days before.

The police were aware of other crimes against women that had been committed in this area during the blackout. As Berlin historian Dr. Laurenz Demps later explained, this "brutal murder . . . was something new for them—even though there had been multiple rape attempts and instances of rape in this garden area."[13]

In addition to investigating suspects with connections to Mrs. Ditter, they also focused on the possibility that the man who killed her was the same one who had been harassing and attacking the women of this garden colony area.

On October 7, the Berlin Kripo announced a thousand-reichsmark reward for information that led to solving this crime. They posted reward posters with information about this crime as well as questions they hoped the public could help them with:

**Warning!!! Do Not Destroy!!! Relay Contents!!!**
**Woman murdered in "Gutland II" colony**
**1000 RM reward!**

On Friday, October 4th, 1940, Gerda Ditter, a 20-year-old married woman, was found murdered in her garden plot, Berlin-Friedrichsfelde, "Gutland II," Way 5a, Number 33, with a deep knife cut in the left side of her neck. The woman was additionally strangled. Nothing was stolen.

Mrs. Ditter was seen last on October 3, 1940, at about 5 P.M. near her apartment.

For a long time, in colony "Gutland," and in the surrounding area, solitary women have been immorally harassed and some have also been wounded with a knife—especially in the dark—by an unknown offender. It is to be assumed that this situation concerns the same offender.

It is the duty of every citizen to actively participate in identifying this demon!

Description of the suspect:

30 to 40 years old, 1.65–1.70 meters tall, bawdy facial expression.

Clothing: mostly blue visor caps, short jacket (leather?), sports-shirt with open collar, long dark pants, often has or is riding a bicycle.

The answers to the following questions are of urgent importance:

1. Who saw or talked to Mrs. Ditter on the night or in the day of the murder; either alone or maybe in the company of a man?
2. Who can describe her daily activities in more detail?
3. In which businesses did she often purchase things?
4. Did someone see Mrs. Ditter somewhere or at some time with the above-described man?
5. Who can say anything else about the suspect?

Every notification—even things which seem unimportant—is important and will be, by request, handled in a strictly confidential manner.

The Criminal Police Department of Berlin issued the above-mentioned reward for information from the public which leads to the identification and seizure of the offender. This reward is not meant for officials whose occupational obligation it is to track offenses or crimes. The disbursement of the reward will follow upon closure of the legal process. Every member of the police department is capable of taking in updates, especially the homicide division "Ditter," police headquarters of Berlin, Alexanderplatz, entrance Dircksenstraße, number 13/14, floor IV, room number 902, extensions 699 and 738.

Berlin, October 7, 1940.

Homicide Division "Ditter"[14]

This reward poster was put up in and around the garden area where Ogorzow preyed on women. While the poster did reveal that a murder had been committed in the area and that women had been harassed there, it played down the level of such attacks. It did not spell out that there had been actual rapes, instead using the euphemism "immorally harassed."

Also on October 7, the Kripo published a detailed announcement of this crime in the Reich Criminal Investigation Department newspaper (*Deutsches Kriminalpolizeiblatt*). This was a newspaper that was not intended for the general public; instead it was meant to be read by law enforcement personnel. This way they could share information on cases so that if any police officers knew something related to a given case, or saw a connection to another case, they could get in touch with the detectives involved.

This announcement included the material contained in the reward poster as well as additional information intended only for law enforcement. It was more blunt about the activities of the suspect in this area: "The criminal should be searched for in circles of sexual-offenders. Since 1938, a sexual-offender has been making trouble in the area. He attacks solitary women in the late hours of the evening or at night; mostly from behind. He chokes them and then abuses them sexually."[15]

The police looked at where Mrs. Ditter shopped, in the hopes it would lead them to a suspect, or at least give them additional insight into this victim. This was a time long before supermarkets were the norm, and the police knew that the local shops were a good source of gossip.

On October 10, they wrote, "The findings have shown that Mrs. Ditter almost only bought goods from the grocery store of Frenzel, Berlin-Friedrichsfelde, Triftweg 9, and the dairy man Hampe, Berlin-Friedrichsfelde, Volkradstraße 10. The findings in both businesses have shown that there is no evidence that Ditter associated with other men. In general, people speak well of her there."[16] So this was another dead end for the police.

On October 15, the Kripo sent out a local news release related to this crime. Just as with the original reward poster and the announcement in the police newspaper, no connection was made between this crime and the attacks on women on the S-Bahn. This was not because the police were covering up this connection. It was because they were unaware that any such connection existed. They did however view this murder as possibly related to the sexual assaults and harassments in the garden area. As for the arrests the news release mentioned, these referred to people who were temporarily detained by the police for questioning such as relatives and neighbors, before being cleared.

This release read as follows:

# THE FIRST MURDER

Berlin, October 15th, 1940
1,000 RM Reward. Lichtenberg woman—murder still unsolved
A couple [implying a man/woman in a relationship]
is being searched for as witnesses!

Despite intense investigation towards solving the murder of the 20-year-old married woman Gerda Ditter, who, as reported, was found murdered on the fourth, Friday, midday, in her garden colony home in Colony Gutland II in Berlin Lichtenberg-Friedrichsfelde, the [Kripo] have not been able to trace the criminal. Mrs. Ditter was killed by being strangled and stabbed in her neck. The crime most likely happened during the night.

With reference to the established reward of 1,000 RM, all sections of the population are being asked to actively participate in solving this crime.

During the course of the manhunt carried out by criminal investigators over the day and night, many suspected people were arrested; none of these, however, were found to have been involved in the crime.

The manhunt for the investigation of the suspected man who was, as reported, in Colony Gutland II and the surrounding area some time before the crime and who, at that time, harassed lone women in the night, is still in process, as he has not been able to be apprehended. Hints, which could lead to the determination of who he is or to his arrest, are, as before, being accepted by the [Kripo]. The suspect is 30–40 years old, 1.65–1.70 meters tall, was wearing mostly blue visor-caps or sports-caps, a short jacket, maybe leather—it's probably a heavy jacket—a sports-shirt with an open collar, and long, dark pants. He often had a bicycle with him.

Recently, it was found that, in the evening before the discovery of the murder, on Thursday the third of the month at about 11 P.M., not far from the garden house of Mrs. Ditter, on a cattle/sheep track at the corner of Way 5a, a couple was standing and talking to each other for a while. The testimony of these two still unknown people is very sought after by the [Kripo]. They are being requested to come forward immediately.

Pertinent information which could lead to finding the previously described suspect, or in any other way could lead to solving the crime, is being accepted by the homicide division "Ditter" (Police Headquarters, room 902, phone number 51 0023, extensions 699 and 738) under assurance of confidential handling.[17]

The police hoped that this news release would result in useful clues, or perhaps even the name of the killer himself. That did not happen, though, and the couple the police sought had nothing to do with this crime, which was committed by one man operating on his own. The police had claimed to be looking for them as possible witnesses, but there had been some hope that they had had something to do with the crime. They did not even have any use as witnesses.

The description that the Kripo had of Ogorzow was all the information they had about the man behind the attacks on the women in this area. There was no description of who had come to Mrs. Ditter's house that night to kill her. They were only speculating that it could be the same man who was responsible for the crime spree against women in this garden area.

By early November, the Kripo had identified roughly thirty suspects. After a thorough examination of these suspects, none were believed to be the killer.

They also chased a red herring in the form of a hearsay report of a scream on the night of the crime. This tip came in after the reward had been announced.

Mrs. Helene Schollain, a resident of Colony Gutland II, informed the police that she had heard rumors of a scream that night. This was all hearsay. She had not heard this alleged scream herself.

Mrs. Schollain told the Kripo a convoluted story of one person telling another about this supposed scream and so on: "On Monday, 10/7/1940, Mrs. Liebetraut, [residing at] Heinrichstraße 27, told Mrs. Schollain that she heard that, during the night when Ditter was murdered, a scream was heard from an unknown person. According to Mrs. Liebetraut, this came from a neighbor of Mrs. Ditter. There was even the assumption that it might be the neighbor Mrs. Bohm, who, out of fear of revenge of Mr. Herlitz, who lives with her, doesn't dare to say anything. Mrs. Liebetraut heard about the scream through her father, Mr. Gerbert, who apparently heard it from a coworker."[18]

This sounded like a rumor based on the well-known (within the neighborhood) dispute between Mr. Herlitz and Mrs. Ditter over Mrs. Ditter's pigeons. But the police could not be certain if there were something to this or not without investigating it.

The police talked to Mr. Herlitz's live-in girlfriend, Mrs. Auguste Bohm, on October 16 about this alleged scream, and she told them, "I did not hear any scream(s) on Thursday evening. If that were the case, I would say it without hesitation, without trying to protect someone."[19]

The police were not surprised that Mrs. Liebetraut was willing to snitch. Nazi Germany was full of people willing to inform on their neighbors to the authorities, and the announcement of a huge reward only contributed toward that tendency.

A police history set forth how the Nazi state used informants: "There were two general categories of informers in Nazi Germany. First, there were those who had a more formal relationship with the Gestapo and often had connections to the activity they were informing on. The state often paid this type of individual, the most important of whom were known as *Vertrauensleute*, or V-persons. . . . The numbers of those formally enlisted, however, pale in comparison to the second major category: volunteers who came forward to inform on or denounce an acquaintance or neighbor or even a spouse or child, to the Gestapo. These did so through letters, both anonymous and signed, tips and even visits to the local Gestapo office."[20]

So in addition to the people who came out in response to the prospect of a big reward, there were those in Nazi Germany who enjoyed denouncing others for free. It was a way to get revenge on a neighbor, neutralize a romantic rival, or simply feel important as a loyal citizen of the Third Reich.

Unfortunately for the police in this case, the tips they had received so far were worthless scraps of information like that provided by Mrs. Liebetraut. And these bad tips wasted police resources, as they needed to track down all of the people involved and interview them.

Meanwhile, a killer was still out there, hunting the women of Berlin.

## CHAPTER ELEVEN

# A Blunt Object

During the night of November 4, 1940, Paul Ogorzow again took to the S-Bahn to find a woman to attack. Under his jacket, he carried with him a concealed heavy piece of lead cable, the same one he'd used before to knock out Mrs. Julie Schuhmacher.

Ogorzow had come to discover, based on his past experiences, that a heavy blunt object better suited him than using his bare hands or a knife. He'd found that trying to choke a woman with his hands or threatening her with a knife might still allow his victim to resist his attack. Sometimes the women cried out; on other occasions, they tore at him and scratched him. One woman he harassed in the garden area had hurt him with her keys. The state of forensics at the time was such that even if any of these women did have bits of Ogorzow's skin under their nails it would not have done the police much good. No one turned in any strands of hair to the police. If Ogorzow had lost any in these struggles, the police never obtained it. All that it would have told them at the time was what color his hair was and if he dyed it.

Indeed, Ogorzow may have discovered the hard way that he was almost as likely to cut himself as his victim during a knife attack. It is very common for a criminal who wields a knife to injure himself while using it. A book on forensic biology discussed such "self inflicted wounds on the assailant" as follows: "Assaults are often chaotic events and the assailant may wield their weapon in a wild manner even if the victim is already dead. If the victim is vigorously defending themselves the scene is likely to be both noisy and violent. It is therefore not unusual for the assailant to wound himself, especially if he is using a sharp implement. In addition, the weapon may become covered in blood and therefore difficult to grip and if a knife without a guard is being used the hand holding it may slip down over the blade if it suddenly hits a hard object. Usually, the assailant acquires wounds in the form of cuts and stabs to the hands . . . although other parts of the body may be hurt."[1]

Ogorzow had learned with his experiences in the garden area that an unexpected blow to the head with a heavy instrument was a better approach than using his hands or a knife, as it quickly diminished the ability of his victims to fight back.

On this evening of November 4, 1940, thirty-year-old Elizabeth Bendorf had just finished her shift as a train ticket salesperson at the S-Bahn station Friedrichshagen and was waiting for a train to arrive in the station to take her home.

It was common in 1940 for German women like Bendorf to work outside the home. As a result, women often rode the S-Bahn alone at night when their shifts ended. With so many men away in the military, women had come to dominate the factories of Berlin, working to churn out the industrial products needed for the war effort. While the Nazis would have preferred to have women at home in a traditional role as mothers and homemakers, the war required that female labor be used to produce the armaments and other materials required to fight. And with men away, there were openings at non-war-related jobs as well, such as selling tickets for the S-Bahn.

Other powers fighting this war had similar issues with needing women to leave the realm of domestic work to do factory work that had previously been done by men. In the United States, the character of Rosie the Riveter was used to encourage women to leave the household sphere and do assembly line work at factories. One example of U.S. government propaganda aimed at getting women to work said, "Can you use an electric mixer? If so, you can learn to operate a drill."[2]

A German propaganda poster captures this sentiment with a foreground image of three women (a factory worker, a nurse, and a farmer), behind them a factory and a farm, and in the sky above them a drawing of a man wearing a combat helmet. The idea being that these women would free up men to fight. The text stated, "Starting with You!"[3]

Such propaganda was based on the idea that women would temporarily perform tasks in traditionally male-dominated fields and then return to their domestic work when the war was over and the men came home.

Ogorzow saw Elizabeth Bendorf waiting by herself for the train. He indicated with an inviting motion of his hands that she should use the second-class compartment, instead of the third-class one for which she was ticketed. Since he was wearing a railroad company uniform, and she was wearing hers, she thought this was a professional courtesy to let her upgrade to a better compartment. She was not worried that there was anything more nefarious involved. Second class was more comfortable and so would be a more relaxing ride for her after a long day at work.

The main difference between second and third class was the seating. Third class had hard wooden benches, worn down from decades of Berliners sitting on them. Most of the seats were in pairs facing each other with a narrow aisle between them. The seating looked like what many modern trains use in their dining car, minus the tables. On a crowded train, each bench could hold two people, who would then be stuck staring at the two people sitting inches away from them.

This made for much more cramped travel seating than most modern subway systems, which use seats facing the same direction or a long line of seating along the two outer walls of the compartment.

Second class featured the same basic seating arrangement as third class, but with upholstered seating. In addition to this added bit of comfort, second class offered a generally quieter and roomier compartment, as the vast majority of S-Bahn passengers rode third class.

In reality, Ogorzow did not care about this woman's comfort or extending her any kind of courtesy; he wanted her in the second-class compartment for his own reasons—it was likely to be empty, while the third-class compartment was more likely to have other passengers riding in it.

Their train arrived after eleven in the evening. They sat across from each other in the otherwise empty train compartment and made small talk. This was later characterized as a discussion about trivial things. This shows that Ogorzow was able to handle himself in social situations. He was not a misfit. He could converse easily with women, even to the extent of making a woman he did not know, who was traveling alone on a train at night, feel at ease. It helped, of course, that he wore a uniform, which gave him an aura of authority.

Ogorzow saw that they were alone. But he waited; he was not yet ready to attack. He wanted to make sure that he had the maximum amount of time to attack his victim and dispose of her body. Having made small talk, he'd already wasted much of the time between the station where they'd boarded the train and the upcoming one.

At the Hirschgarten station, Ogorzow waited by the train compartment's door, hoping that no one else would enter the second-class section. The train doors did not automatically open when the train reached a station; instead, any passengers that wanted on or off the train had to manually pull on a door handle. The only automatic function was the closing of doors before the train left the station. So Ogorzow was listening in the darkened compartment for the sound of anyone pulling a door open. During peacetime, the windows on the train, including the ones built into the doors themselves, would have let him see if anyone was about to board, but with the blackout they were covered.

The older S-Bahn series had four doors on each side, while the newer ones only had three. In the dark, it could be hard to tell which side of the train the platform was on. Ogorzow had to remember where it was at the Hirschgarten station and keep an eye out on the doors on that side of the compartment.

As the moments passed, it seemed less and less likely that anyone would board. Finally, the train started to leave the station, and he knew that it was now safe for him to attack. Without wasting time, he lowered the thick piece of lead cable he had hidden in his jacket so that it was now in his hand. He then raised his arm up and hit Elizabeth Bendorf hard in the head with this blunt metal instrument.

Despite this blow and the concussion it caused, Bendorf managed to retain consciousness. She fought back and screamed as loud as she could. Unfortunately for her, on this moving train, no one in the other compartments heard her. Ogorzow was in a panic now too. He was ultimately a coward, and he took no pleasure in his victims fighting back. He had anticipated that a hard hit to the head with this lead object would be enough to knock a woman out.

Bendorf defended herself against Ogorzow as best she could, but given that she was suffering the effects of a concussion and had no weapon with her, he managed to hit her on the head again. Each time he succeeded in hitting her, it caused her more pain and mental confusion. She could no longer process the flood of sensory information coming into her brain, let alone command her arms and legs to do anything.

He kept hitting her, hard, on the head until she finally slumped down onto the train's floor. Only then did he halt his attacks. Paul Ogorzow now believed that his victim was either knocked unconscious or that he'd killed her. However, she was neither, but merely temporarily stunned as a result of all the blows to her head.

Ogorzow turned his back on Bendorf and opened the compartment door. The train was still moving, and a cold wind rushed into the open second-class compartment. He felt close to re-creating that moment when he'd first thrown a woman from a moving train. The anticipation was building up and he began to feel a rush similar to the one he'd felt when he'd tossed Gerda Kargoll from the moving S-Bahn.

In the moments this took, Bendorf began to move again.

When Ogorzow turned around and walked toward her, he was shocked. He'd thought this attack was almost over, that the only thing left was to toss her out of the train, but here she was still alive and trying to get away. Any disappointment that he felt quickly faded, as it was readily apparent that she was not moving fast enough to pose any real threat to him. She'd already sustained a heavy beating and was barely functioning.

Ogorzow had no trouble using his piece of lead cable to hit her in the head once more. He thought that this single additional blow would be enough to knock her out or kill her.

Miraculously, even having been hit on the head one more time, Bendorf was still conscious. While aware of what was happening to her, she was now too dazed to move her body at all. Although she could do nothing to stop her assailant, she still was able to watch in horror as he dragged her to the open train door.

Ogorzow's proclivity for hitting women on the head meant that Bendorf was not his first victim to find herself in the nightmare situation of seeing the imminent threat he posed while being unable to do anything about it. Over a year before, Lina Budzinski had suffered the same kind of horrific experience when Ogorzow hit her in the head and left her conscious for a while but unable to control her body enough to move or scream while he attacked.

Ogorzow pulled Bendorf by the feet toward the door. Once she was in front of the open door, with the Berlin cityscape rapidly passing by outside, he attacked her again.

This time, he was no longer concerned with rendering her unable to fight back. That first part of his attack had a degree of rationality to it—he didn't want his victim to be able to resist him. But now that he'd accomplished that task, he was focused on attacking and hurting a woman for no rational reason at all.

He hit her repeatedly on her back with the lead cable and kicked her savagely.

After she endured these blows, he assumed that she was either dead or nearing death. He did not bend down to actually check whether she was still alive. He was quickly running out of time and was growing exhausted from all the energy he'd put into this attack.

While dragging her to the door, he briefly touched her in a sexual manner. She was not aware of this, as she was unconscious.

Now, it was time for the part that he seemed to enjoy the most— he threw her from the moving train before it arrived at the next station, Köpenick. The night outside was black, with the lights off throughout the city. This meant that he could not see where Bendorf's body fell.

After this attack, Ogorzow left his weapon behind on the train, hiding it in the compartment. Perhaps he didn't want to keep what he mistakenly believed was a murder weapon any longer. He had no sentimental attachment to this weapon. It would be easy enough to get another blunt piece of metal with which he could hit women. If he were worried about fingerprints, a careful rubbing of the handle of the lead cable against his uniform would be enough to wipe it clean and he would have needed to handle it with the sleeve of his uniform or another piece of cloth to avoid leaving behind any new prints as he hid it.

Having temporarily satiated his dark desires, Paul Ogorzow took the S-Bahn home. As he headed back to his wife and kids, he may have thought about how his latest victim screamed despite his best efforts to preemptively silence her. Perhaps this experience made him grateful that he'd attacked her on the moving S-Bahn train. If he'd been in the garden area and she'd managed to scream, based on his past actions, he would not have been able to complete his attack. Instead, he would have run away in case anyone had heard her.

Like Ogorzow's first victim on the S-Bahn, Gerda Kargoll, Bendorf too miraculously managed to survive her attack. She did however suffer a very serious concussion that required extensive hospitalization. It took her eight days in the hospital to recover enough for the police to be able to interrogate her. Although she was able to describe how she'd been attacked, she did not recall the kind of details that the police were hoping to obtain from her. In fact, they had little more to go on than what they had learned from the first S-Bahn victim. She did not realize that her attacker had briefly molested her during this attack, so the police were not aware of this as well. If they had known, it would have provided a possible motive for these attacks, some kind of sexual perversion.

Now that a second woman had been attacked, the police no longer had doubts about the first victim's story. It helped that, unlike Kargoll, Bendorf had not been drinking. Until now, Gerda Kargoll's case had been investigated as an accident. The Orpo handled accidents. Attempted murder, though, was a matter for the Kripo.

Not surprisingly, given the darkness, the abrupt nature of the attack, and the injuries suffered, neither woman could give the Kripo much to go on. The first victim (Kargoll) thought her attacker was around twenty-five, while the second (Bendorf) thought he was more in the range of forty. They both said that he was a white male wearing a dark uniform consistent with a railroad outfit. They placed his height at between five feet four inches and five feet five inches. As for his face, neither got a good look and they gave contradictory descriptions.

Bendorf's injuries showed that in addition to being thrown from a train, she had been hit hard in the head by a blunt object. This evidence bolstered her credibility.

Based on when and where she'd been attacked, the police were able to determine which train carriage she had been thrown from. Her having been in second class meant that only one of four compartments on that train could have been the scene of the crime.

They thoroughly searched it, and although they did not find bloody fingerprints, they did find a weapon. As this was second class, there were cushions on the seat, unlike the hard wooden benches of third class. Behind one of these seat cushions they found the bloody object that Bendorf had been hit with.

It was a two-inch-thick, twenty-inch-long piece of lead-encased telephone cable, with numbers on one side. Here was a workable clue, because unlike say a piece of iron rebar that could have come from any construction site, this was a very specific kind of cable that was only used in Berlin by the phone company. And the numbers on it were unique ones, stamped by machinery.

The police worked hard to research the origins of this mundane but now important object. They learned that about a year and a half ago, telephony cable had been laid alongside parts of the S-Bahn railroad track.

The police contacted the phone company, Deutschen Telephonwerken, and learned that numbers were stamped on the side of the cable to indicate how many meters from the start of the cable each piece was. With this knowledge, the police discovered that this particular piece had been sliced off somewhere by the Rummelsburg S-Bahn station. The police looked into the workers who laid this cable and systematically eliminated them as suspects based primarily on their alibis for the times of the attacks.

The Kripo detectives concluded that there were two likely ways the attacker could have obtained this cable. First, it could have been tossed aside by a worker while he was installing the telephone line, and the assailant later found it by the side of the track. This suggested that the assailant was someone familiar with the railroad, as the general public did not normally walk by these rails. However, it was not a sure thing, as someone could have hopped a fence into this area. Second, workers collected scrap pieces of cable and stored them in a warehouse that was open only to Reichsbahn employees. Every bit of scrap metal had value in the wartime economy. Consequently, all kinds of scrap was being collected and stored here. This possibility pointed toward a railroad employee as the culprit.

This early clue pointed the investigation in the right direction, but there were thousands of people who worked for the railroad, and the police were not even sure that the perpetrator would have needed to be a railway worker to obtain this weapon.

It would take tremendous amounts of manpower and other

resources to comb through all the people who worked for the railroad, and so far that was not justified. There had been only two attacks on the S-Bahn to date and both women survived. Only as Ogorzow's criminal attacks continued, and the body count added up, would the police expend the resources necessary to look at all the railroad workers in Berlin.

# CHAPTER TWELVE

# Death on the Train

It was now December and Ogorzow had yet to actually kill anyone on the S-Bahn.

He'd tried twice, and each time at first mistakenly thought he'd succeeded. But somehow these two women had survived both the brutal attacks and being thrown from a moving train.

Ogorzow had killed, though, just not on the train. He'd strangled and stabbed Mrs. Gertrude Ditter. Since this occurred in the privacy of her home with only her small children present, sleeping nearby, he was able to wait long enough to make sure that she was actually dead.

On the S-Bahn, he was operating on a very strict timetable, with little time to attack his victims and dispose of their bodies. He couldn't risk having someone he'd attacked still inside the compartment when it entered a train station. While not many people rode the second-class compartment late at night, there was always a chance that someone would board this part of the train at the next station.

As December 3, 1940, turned into December 4, Ogorzow rode the S-Bahn, looking for a new victim. It had been a month since he'd thrown Elizabeth Bendorf from the train. The thrill had not lasted that long, but he'd fought his desire to strike again so that he could see what the repercussions were to his last attack. He worried about getting caught, and so he took his time between attacks at this stage to make sure it was safe before he struck again.

Ogorzow carried with him a new blunt, heavy object to use as a weapon, an iron rod about fifteen inches long. It weighed a few pounds, and as with his old weapon, he'd found it during his work at the railroad company. It was the sort of thing that is still found at construction sites around the world. These days this sort of rod is usually made of steel, though, not cast iron. Kids often pick up such reinforcing bars, known as rebar, and play-fight with them. Ogorzow carried his concealed inside the left sleeve of his jacket uniform.

At the Karlshorst station, Ogorzow saw that there was already a female passenger sitting in the second-class train compartment. She was alone. He boarded the train, and it was just the two of them in this section as the train started to move.

With every assault Ogorzow committed on the S-Bahn, he became more confident in his actions. This translated into less and less hesitation before his attacks, as well as the increasing use of overwhelming force at the start of each attack. This evolution in Ogorzow's assaults was the result of a combination of overcoming any internal barriers to using violence, such as societal norms and fear of being caught, and learning from past mistakes to become a more efficient criminal. Whereas before he first made small talk or waited a station or two before taking action, now he struck right away, as soon as the train was under way.

Like with many things in life, the more he did these attacks, the more comfortable he became with them. As with his early days as a Brownshirt, when he first took part in pitched street battles against Communists and other rivals to the Nazis, he grew desensitized to using violence. After the Nazis had seized power, when Ogorzow and his fellow Storm Troopers beat up German Jews and destroyed their property as part of *Kristallnacht*, he shed any inhibitions he may have had against attacking innocent civilians who wanted no part of his violence.

Ogorzow didn't want to risk losing this opportunity, in the event that the female passenger left at the next station or someone else entered the train's second-class section. And he knew that his time was limited. Once he attacked, he felt that he needed to throw his victim from the train before it reached the next station.

The passenger was Elfriede Franke, a twenty-six-year-old nurse wearing her uniform. The attack was as vicious as it was sudden. Ogorzow pulled the iron rod out of his jacket sleeve and went over to Franke. Without saying anything, he hit her hard over the head with it.

He'd learned from his last attack. When he'd hit Elizabeth Bendorf a month ago, he had not used enough force to achieve his goal of incapacitating her. Instead, she had managed to fight back against him, despite multiple blows to her head. This time he made sure that he did not make the same mistake.

The blow came down so hard on Elfriede Franke that it shattered her skull and damaged her brain. She fell down onto the train's floor. She was dead.

Even with the speed and effectiveness of his attack, there still was not much time for Ogorzow to enjoy this moment. He never had much time with his victims on the train, as the interval between stations was so short. He would have liked to have more time, but this was a drawback he accepted as the cost of using the S-Bahn for his attacks.

He set down his weapon and walked over to the compartment door to open it. Unlike with his last attack, this time when he turned around and returned to his victim there were no surprises.

He had dragged his last victim by her feet to the open door. There's no reason to believe that he did things any differently this time. Staring out into the darkness of blacked out Berlin with the cold winter wind rushing over him, he felt excited.

He experienced a kind of cocaine-like high—a feeling of being all-powerful—as he threw Elfriede Franke's body into the night. Although this moment felt amazing to him, he needed to return to the real world, starting with the mundane task of pulling the handle to close the door when he was done.

As wonderful as he felt, there still was an element of frustration. He was not able to commit a rape on the train, as there was never enough time. Even here, where he had acted right away and killed his victim with a single blow, he still was not able to sexually assault her corpse. Over the course of his many attacks, when it came to sexually assaulting a woman, he did not seem to care one way or the other if she was alive, dying, or recently deceased.

He never left a victim on the train to be there when it arrived at the next station. The first time the reason for this was his fear of

Police photograph of Paul Ogorzow.
*Author's Collection*

German blackout poster: "The Enemy Sees Your Light! Blackout!"
*Author's Collection*

German blackout poster: "Light Means Your Death!"
*Author's Collection*

Re-creation of blackout conditions in second class of old S-Bahn train.
*Robin Gottschlag, courtesy of "Historische S-Bahn e.V.," Berlin, 2012*

Waiting platform for Berlin S-Bahn, Karlshorst station.
*Roland Anton Laub (photolaub.com), 2012*

S-Bahn train pulling into the Rummelsburg station.
*Roland Anton Laub (photolaub.com), 2012*

Present-day view of the side of the Karlshorst S-Bahn station.
*Roland Anton Laub (photolaub.com), 2012*

Apartment building where Ogorzow lived, still standing today.
*Roland Anton Laub (photolaub.com), 2012*

Entrance to the apartment building Ogorzow lived in.
*Roland Anton Laub (photolaub.com), 2012*

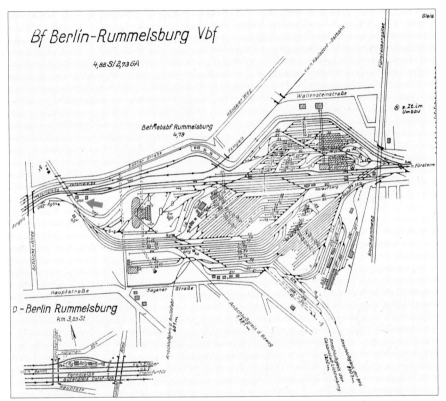

Map of Rummelsburg S-Bahn station showing signal tower Vnk (1962).
*Author's Collection*

Front of signal tower Vnk, where Ogorzow worked.
*Sven Keßler, 2004*

Rear of signal tower Vnk.
*Sven Keßler, 2005*

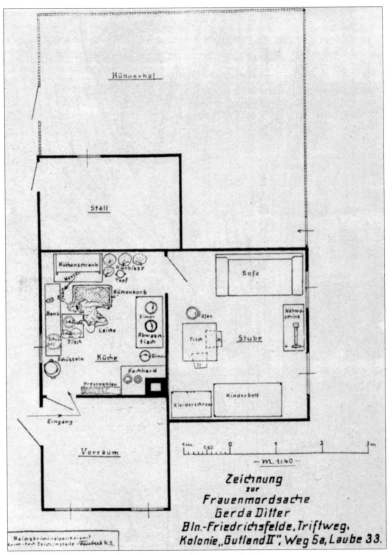

Police drawing of Ditter crime scene.
*Author's Collection*

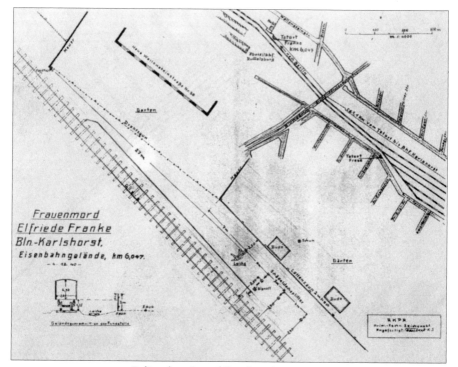

Police drawing of Franke crime scene.
*Author's Collection*

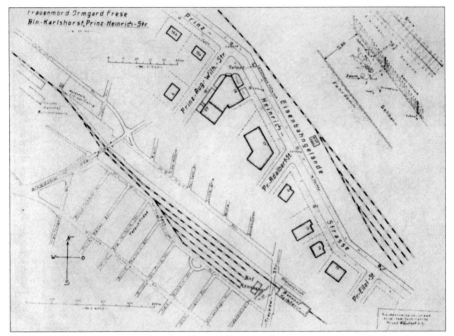

Police drawing of Freese crime scene.
*Author's Collection*

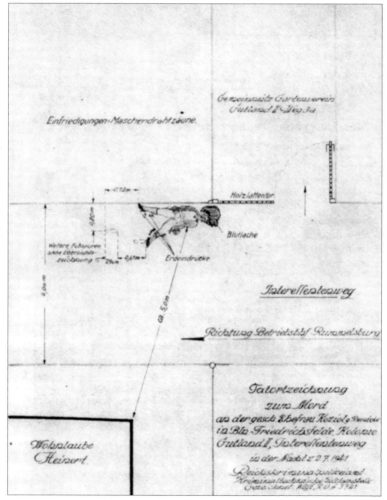

Police drawing of Koziol crime scene.
*Author's Collection*

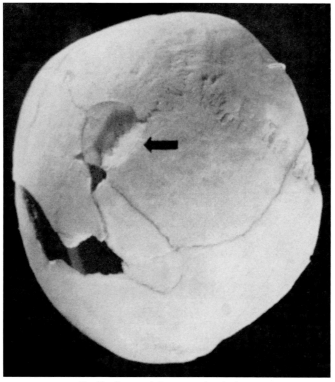

Skull of one of Ogorzow's victims.
*Author's Collection*

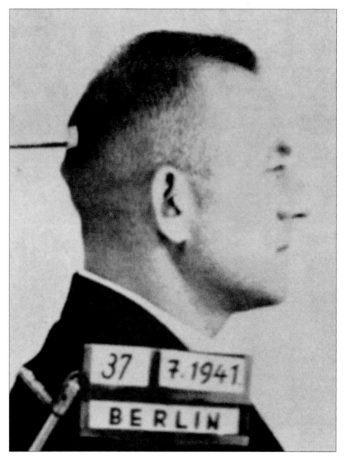

Mug shot of Paul Ogorzow.
*Author's Collection*

Police photo of Ogorzow in his uniform.
*Author's Collection*

Photo of Berlin S-Bahn class 167 built in 1938.

*Walied Schön, courtesy of "Historische S-Bahn e.V.," Berlin*

being caught. Since then, he'd learned that he also enjoyed dumping the bodies out of the train, so it now served two purposes—protecting him and the pleasure of the act itself.

He'd tried to kill on the S-Bahn twice before and failed. But now, in the early hours of Wednesday, December 4, 1940, Paul Ogorzow had committed his first successful S-Bahn murder.

## CHAPTER THIRTEEN

# Examining the Body

Just three hours after Ogorzow murdered Elfriede Franke, the police stood around her dead body. They were next to the train tracks between the Karlshorst and Rummelsburg S-Bahn stations. It was still nighttime, and the heavy-duty lamps the detectives used to light up the crime scene provided the only visible illumination in a city otherwise cloaked in darkness. The light gleamed off the gold bracelet still on the victim's wrist. Her pocketbook was nearby. There had been no robbery. The only thing stolen from her was her life.

Although the blackout was still in effect, the police were able to use their discretion in lighting up this scene. If they heard an air raid warning, they would instantly spring into action and cut all the lights they were using.

Dr. Waldemar Weimann, the well-known forensic pathologist, thought it was an air raid siren when a driver for the Kripo woke him in the middle of the night to come to this crime scene. Once he arrived, the Kripo asked him to examine the body where it was found along the railroad tracks. He was able to estimate the rough time of death, but the detective on the scene wanted more information from Dr. Weimann than he was able to provide.

After looking over Elfriede Franke's corpse, Dr. Weimann wrote in his memoirs that he was asked about the cause of death as follows:

> "Death by a blow or just by the fall?" asked Detective Zach, who was standing beside me at the accident site.
>
> "Do you have maybe an X-ray machine with you?" I replied angrily.
>
> "After all, I would be grateful if I could have your finding today," said Zach. . . . [Zach] seemed to detect my reluctance [to do a postmortem that quickly]. He pulled me aside and said, 'This is the third case of this kind . . . on this route.'"[1]

This was the first time Dr. Weimann had heard anything about this situation. Zach explained to him that two women had been thrown from the S-Bahn before and had remarkably managed to survive, one by landing in sand and the other living to talk to police despite sustaining major damage to her body.

There was more. The detective told the doctor that the first victim had strangulation marks on her neck, while the second said she'd been hit on the head. As an expert in forensic medicine, the doctor was curious what other evidence the police had beyond the second woman's word that a man had hit her. Detective Zach said that in addition to injuries related to being thrown from a train, a doctor was able to find evidence of a blow from a tool of some sort.

As Dr. Weimann recalled, he then asked, "Who was this medical examiner?"[2]

The response was a surprise: "Well, you yourself, doctor."[3]

In thinking back, it made sense to him. Dr. Weimann wrote, "First, I was angry, I remembered those ominous radiographs. They had been sent to me one day out of the Reich Criminal Police Office 'with a request for expert opinion.' Otherwise unspecified were the Who, When, Where, How and Why—the golden 'W's of the coroner. I had to the best of my expertise and knowledge expressed the judgment of: 'Flawless skull and skull base rupture by impact on a flat surface. In addition, localized fractures, possibly by impact with a blunt object.'"[4]

Dr. Weimann was a curious man, and the first question that popped into his mind after realizing that he'd already consulted on the related attack, under mysterious circumstances, was "Why the secrecy?"[5]

Detective Zach told him that it was because Joseph Goebbels, the Reich minister of propaganda, wanted this kept quiet. For Dr. Weimann, this answer made perfect sense and required no follow-up questions. He was well aware that Nazi Germany was a country in which the flow of information was tightly controlled by the government.

The doctor was thinking about what could motivate a man to throw women off the train, given that he was not stealing anything from them. He asked about it being a sexual offense, but the detective told him that the first two victims said that nothing of that sort had happened. Besides, they could see for themselves that Elfriede Franke still had all her clothes on and they were not disturbed any more than one would expect from such a terrible fall. There was nothing to suggest that any of these women had been molested.

Dr. Weimann left the crime scene to accompany the body as it was driven to the morgue.

What neither Dr. Weimann nor the police realized at the time was that the doctor had already examined a third woman, Gertrude Ditter, killed by the same perpetrator who attacked Elizabeth Bendorf and Elfriede Franke. They would not make that connection for a while to come, as Mrs. Ditter was found in her home in the garden area and had been killed with a knife, as opposed to being hit on the head and thrown off an S-Bahn train.

Dr. Waldemar Weimann was also a psychiatrist, and as this case developed, he would provide the police with assistance in understanding the possible motive and thinking of the man who did these crimes. Weimann was born in Cologne, Germany, on November 3, 1893, which meant that he was forty-seven years old when Ogorzow killed Elfriede Franke on the S-Bahn.

He looked the part of a serious man of science. Dr. Weimann's ears stuck out, and his thin, dark hair was receding. In later years, it would turn white. He had a large nose, a small chin, and dark eyes. While working, he wore a white lab coat, dress shirt, and tie.

In 1930, Dr. Weimann founded the Institute of Forensic Medicine in Berlin and became its first director. He also served as the chief medical examiner for Berlin. He later wrote of the murders committed by Paul Ogorzow, "From the myriad of large cases that I worked there, one stands out, which is one of the most interesting in criminal history."[6]

Dr. Weimann was arguably one of the best known and respected forensic pathologists in Nazi Germany. He'd dealt with high-profile cases before, including examining the body of the Nazi martyr SA *Sturmführer* Horst Wessel following his murder in February 1930. After his death, the Nazis made a song he wrote the lyrics to called "The Horst Wessel Song" their official party anthem and unofficially the co-national-anthem of Germany. The song is now banned for most uses in Germany and Austria.

At the morgue, Dr. Weimann learned that Elfriede Franke's killer had hit his victim with a blunt instrument before throwing her from the train. However, Dr. Weimann was not able to determine exactly what the weapon was.

As Detective Zach had confided in Dr. Weimann, the police had immediately put together that the individual who killed this woman was most likely the same one who had previously thrown two other women from S-Bahn trains.

So Detective Zach visited Dr. Weimann in the morgue and brought with him the heavy piece of lead cable that the police had recovered from the S-Bahn second-class train compartment after the attack on Elizabeth Bendorf. This was the same cable that Ogorzow had also used on Julie Schuhmacher.

As Dr. Weimann recalled, the detective displayed the lead object and asked:

> *"Could it have been something like that?" asked Detective Zach and hands me a piece of heavy lead wire, about two thumbs thick and fifty centimeters long.*
>
> *"Quite possibly," I said.*[7]

The doctor could not be certain that the same type of weapon had been used in this latest attack, but it was at least consistent with the newer findings. In fact, it was a different sort of blunt metal object that had been used—an iron rebar rod, not a piece of lead-encased telephone cable.

The police had not yet connected the S-Bahn assaults with the earlier attacks in the garden area. Besides the different locations, the garden attacks involved a very different modus operandi than Ogorzow used on the train—choking and stabbing versus hitting with a blunt object and throwing from a train.

Then, as now, police considered the nature of a violent crime and grouped together victims who had been attacked in a similar way. Women harassed while walking home or stabbed or strangled at their home were not seen as being in the same category of criminal offenses as women hit with a blunt object while on the S-Bahn and then thrown from the train. Also, the garden attacks often had an obvious sexual assault component, while the attacks on the train did not.

These two different areas and kinds of attack were considered by the police to be separate matters. For the time being, Paul Ogorzow had this going in his favor.

## CHAPTER FOURTEEN

# The Kripo

Now that someone had died, the S-Bahn attacks became a high-priority case, assigned to the office of the Serious Crimes Unit of the Kripo in Berlin. This office was primarily concerned with capital offenses such as homicide.

Elfriede Franke was the first person killed on the S-Bahn by Paul Ogorzow. Before her, two women had been thrown out of the moving train with only minor injuries. Franke's death changed the case and bolstered the credibility of the first two victims, so the police now felt certain that they were telling the truth and a stranger had thrown them from the train for no reason of which they were aware.

The head of this Kripo unit, Police Commissioner Wilhelm K. Lüdtke, took charge of the investigation on the same day as Franke's murder, December 4, 1940. He was then fifty-four years old.

Lüdtke held his position despite his lack of Nazi convictions. He was not even a party member until April 1, 1940, which was unusual for someone at his high level in the police hierarchy. He did not join out of political belief, but for practical reasons.

He'd joined the party exactly eight years to the day after Paul Ogorzow had. As a result of Lüdtke joining so late, he had a high party number of 8,015,159. As a point of comparison, Ogorzow's party number was almost seven million members lower at 1,109,672.

As of September 1939, the Kripo was part of the RHSA, which was short for the Reich Main Security Office (*Reichssicherheitshauptamt*). Heinrich Himmler, a very powerful Nazi official, was the chief of the German Police (*Chef der Deutschen Polizei*) and the head of the SS (*Reichsführer-SS*).

Theoretically, in regards to his running the German Police, Himmler should have reported to the Reich minister of the interior (Wilhelm Frick), but as a practical matter, his only real boss was Hitler himself. A once classified Allied document on the German Police explained: "As Commander in Chief of the SS, however, HIMMLER was directly responsible to HITLER alone, the Supreme Commander of the SS, and was, therefore, in a position to circumvent the authority of FRICK, the Minister of the Interior."[1]

Under the dictatorship that was Nazi Germany, Hitler had absolute power and reported to no one. His decisions were final.

Himmler formed the RHSA by merging various police and security organizations into one entity directly under his control. In essence, he took the intelligence agency of the SS (*Sicherheitsdienst des Reichsführers-SS*, or SD) and combined it with the Security Police (*Sicherheitspolizei*, or SiPo). The SiPo included the Criminal Police (Kripo) and the Gestapo. With the reorganization of German police forces into the RHSA, the SiPo no longer existed as an actual organization, but people continued to use the term informally to refer to those portions of the RHSA that used to belong to the SiPo.

A notable exception to the gathering of police forces into the RHSA was the Orpo, the ordinary police. Himmler ultimately controlled them as well, but through a different administrative structure. He had a trusted underling who ran the Orpo: chief of the *Ordnungspolizei* Kurt Dalüge. A historian described Dalüge as "a vast thug of a man nicknamed 'Dummi-Dummi' by his detractors."[2]

Himmler looked like a bookish bureaucrat, with his wire frame glasses, round face, and small mustache. He did not look particularly Aryan—Himmler had hazel eyes and receding brown hair. Moreover, he was terrible at sports and suffered from a variety of minor health problems.

Himmler was born in Munich on October 7, 1900, and had studied agriculture in college. He was a failed chicken farmer in the mid to late 1920s. He'd joined the Nazi Party early on, in 1923, with a low card number of 14,303. He later joined the SS (*Schutzstaffel*) with the extremely low number of 168. It was in this organization that he rapidly rose in rank. Later on, he became one of the key architects of the Holocaust, responsible for the murder of millions of people.

To run the RHSA, Himmler appointed Reinhard Heydrich as its director. Heydrich had run the Gestapo before this reorganization and been a part of the purge of SA leaders known as the Night of the Long Knives. He was a key architect of *Kristallnacht*, and later of the *Einsatzgruppen* (mobile killing squads on the Eastern Front) and the Holocaust.

Heydrich was a handsome young man, born on March 7, 1904,

in Halle an der Saale, Germany. He had an oval-shaped face, with a high forehead and close-cropped blond hair. Unlike Himmler, he fit the Aryan ideal of being tall, skinny, athletic, good-looking, blue-eyed, and blond. He was also a ruthless believer in the Nazi cause and a mass murderer many times over. His nicknames included the Blond Beast, the Hangman, and the Butcher of Prague.

As director of the RHSA, Heydrich presided over seven administrative divisions, known in German as *Ämter*, which can be translated as "offices." The first office (*Amt* I) dealt with personnel. The second division dealt with organization, administration, and law. So both of these can be understood as dealing with administrative matters for the RHSA.

*Amt* III was responsible for "spheres of German life," which included German culture, ethnic Germans inside conquered territory, and intelligence gathering within Germany. The domestic office of the SD (Inland-SD) formed the core of this new department.

A once classified Allied document on the German Police explained that this office "directs the principal functions of the SD inside Germany. . . . The main task of *Amt* III is the collection, by open and secret methods, of information concerning all events and tendencies liable to affect the maintenance of Nazi power at home and abroad. It supervises all 'spheres of German life' (*deutsche Lebensgebiete*) and gathers intelligence for the control of all religious, cultural, and economic activities, but especially for the suppression of anti-Nazi elements."[3]

*Amt* IV was the Gestapo, which this Allied document on the German police explained was "mainly concerned with investigating and crushing any opposition to the Nazi regime."[4] There were few, if any, meaningful legal limits on their power. A favored method they used to detain people was to place them into protective custody. The prisoner would sign his own request to be placed into such custody. If he refused to sign it, the Gestapo would beat him until he did.

A subdepartment of this office (RSHA *Referat* IV B4), run by Adolf Eichmann, dealt with Jewish affairs and evacuation. Eichmann would eventually play a major role in the planning and execution of the Holocaust.

The Kripo formed *Amt* V. The Allied handbook on the German Police explained that this office, "which is also known as the *Reichskriminalpolizeiamt* (RKPA), is the national Headquarters of the *Reichskriminalpolizei* (*Kripo*, Criminal Police), controlling the network of criminal police offices. . . . The RKPA developed out of the old *preußischen Landeskriminalamt* (Prussian Criminal Police Headquarters), whose functions consisted only of the combatting of crime in the normal sense of the term. The RKPA, however, under the Nazi regime, has not only expanded the concept of 'combating' to include 'prevention' in the most ruthless sense; it also plays an important part in the investigation and prosecution of what are today called 'political crimes,' but would formerly have been regarded at the most as venial offences. The line dividing cases of interest to the *Gestapo* and those within the field of the *Kripo* has in many instances become rather vague."[5]

A history of the Third Reich elaborated on this blurring of lines between the Gestapo and the Kripo: "The Gestapo was clearly the dominant partner vis-à-vis the police in general, while the twelve thousand or so criminal investigators, under Arthur Nebe, began to be indistinguishable from their political colleagues."[6]

The remaining two offices dealt primarily with matters outside of Germany itself. *Amt* VI handled "espionage, sabotage and subversion in occupied and enemy countries."[7] The foreign intelligence agency of the SD (*Ausland-SD*) formed the basis of this office.

*Amt* VII, added in 1940, mostly handled propaganda, specifically, "*Amt* VII deals mainly with occupied and satellite countries and is concerned with the preparation of political warfare material and the conduct of ideological supervision, especially in the academic field."[8]

Dr. Jens Dobler, an expert on the Berlin police during the Nazi era, discussed the potential overlap between the Gestapo and Kripo forces under this reorganization. "The Gestapo security service and the criminal investigations department (Kripo) were joined together into the Reich's Department of Security. This definitely did not lead to a bettering of the work methods. Conversely, sometimes both the Gestapo and the Kripo were handling the same cases simultaneously. Many Kripo officers who were made into members of the Gestapo attempted to get back to the supposedly 'un-political' Kripo, but, of course, the Kripo were exactly as political—supposed 'criminals,' or minorities were deported by the Kripo into concentration camps."[9]

For Police Commissioner Wilhelm Lüdtke this meant that he needed to be wary of potential Gestapo interference in his case. In addition, his ultimate superiors were more concerned about making the Nazi state look good than they were with stopping a killer of women. He was fortunate that the head of the Kripo did care about the case, but there were more powerful men whose priorities lay elsewhere.

As the head of RHSA *Amt* V, Arthur Nebe was in charge of the Kripo. Having been born in Berlin on November 13, 1894, he had fought in World War I. During this war, he experienced firsthand the horrors of poison gas attacks on two separate occasions. He survived however, and after the war he joined the Criminal Police in Berlin in 1920. He quickly worked his way up in the organization. By 1924, he'd achieved the rank of police commissioner. He joined the Nazi Party and the SS in 1931. After the Nazis seized power, the Kripo was transformed several times, first into a truly national criminal police force and later by merging with the SiPo. When that happened in 1936, Nebe was placed in charge of the Kripo. He stayed in charge of it when the RHSA was formed.

Nebe had a large nose, beady eyes, thick eyebrows, and graying hair slicked back with a part on his left. Today we might say he bore more than a passing resemblance to the actor Sir Ben Kingsley, if Kingsley still had his hair. At the time of the first murder on the S-Bahn, Nebe was forty-six years old.

Nebe's long history with the Berlin Kripo and his rising through the ranks translated into his caring about this case being solved through the application of proper police work. However, he too had to report to someone higher up than him, a consummate Nazi who couldn't have cared less about a serial killer of women, as opposed to what was in the interest of the Nazi Party.

With the creation of the RHSA, Nebe ran Office V (the Kripo) and he reported to Heydrich and Heydrich's boss, Himmler. Over the years, Nebe grew to hate Heydrich and Himmler, and secretly plotted against them and Hitler. He was very careful to hide his hatred of his superiors, as he wanted to keep his job and his life. And so he regularly lunched with both of them, making small talk about the criminal cases of the day and pretending to like them.

One history of the Third Reich contained this line describing Nebe's strange role in it: "Arthur Nebe, the head of the SS Reich

Criminal Police Office, a figure so morally challenging that he is virtually airbrushed out of many accounts of the resistance."[10] Nebe would go on to conspire against Hitler and to commit horrific war crimes, but at the start of Paul Ogorzow's attacks on women riding the S-Bahn, he was busy running the Kripo.

The Kripo detectives in this case worked out of a massive brick building informally referred to as "the Alex" in a shorthand reference to its location on Alexanderplatz. The side entrance they often used was on Dircksenstrasse 13/14.

As for the RHSA, its official headquarters were in Berlin at Prinz Albrecht Strasse 8. The cross street was Wilhelmstrasse, the street on which many of Nazi Germany's government buildings were located. The building is now in ruins and Prinz Albrecht Strasse has been renamed Niederkirchnerstrasse.

It was here at Prinz Albrecht Strasse 8 that the Gestapo had their headquarters. One writer referred to it as "the most dreaded address in Nazi-occupied Europe," owing to the well-known tendency of the Gestapo to use torture on their detainees and ultimately send many of them to their deaths.[11]

It was in the midst of this complicated relationship at the top of German policing that Lüdtke reported to Nebe about the investigation into attacks on the S-Bahn. Nebe's own office, as head of the Kripo, was located at Werderscher Markt 5/6. Nebe trusted Lüdtke and so gave him free rein over this important case.

Lüdtke was well aware that his position was a precarious one because he lacked the connections of those around him who had joined the Nazi Party early on and formed long-lasting alliances with the party elite. And he'd lost his Kripo job once before, back in 1933, over his work with the political police against the Nazis before they'd gained power. That had not stopped him from getting his current job, but it did mean that he needed to be careful. If those above him, such as Nebe and Heydrich, thought he was not properly handling a high-profile case, he could easily be fired. Therefore, he had to do well at his job, and he could not afford to have a serial killer plague Berlin indefinitely.

A June 1938 decree mandated that Kripo members join the SS, if they were not already in it, although it did not require that they join the Nazi Party itself. This meant that Kripo detectives, including Lüdtke, were at the time of the S-Bahn murders members of the SS. They were given ranks in the SS roughly equivalent to their ranks in the Kripo, which caused a great deal of confusion. Many Kripo detectives had no active duties in the SS, so they were only technically members of the SS, while continuing to carry out criminal investigations. From the perspective of some in the SS, this was upsetting as it meant that while they had worked their way up in this organization, Kripo members were being granted ranks without having started at the bottom.[12]

Lüdtke faced a very serious series of crimes against women on the S-Bahn that he needed to solve. And given his lack of job security, if he botched this case badly enough, he could find himself out of a job.

He was married to the former Amalia Bautze, who was thirty-five years younger than him. She'd been born in Frankfurt, Germany, on December 25, 1921. Lüdtke had been married once before and had two daughters from that union: Gerda, who was born on February 20, 1912, and Edith, who was born on April 30, 1915.

To relax after work, Lüdtke drank and smoked in moderation.

Those were his only known vices.[13] His home was in Berlin's Neukölln neighborhood, at Wildenbruchstrasse 77.[14]

Lüdtke had completed two winter semesters at Frankfurt University when he'd been working in Frankfurt as a policeman. He'd also taken classes at a police school. So, unlike many of his peers high up in the Kripo, he did not have a law degree, or even a university degree of any kind. Instead, much of what he'd learned came from his long years of experience as a policeman.

He had a very distinctive physical appearance that was later described as rendering him unsuitable for surveillance work "as he has a rather outstanding physical appearance" including a "jutting jaw," a "powerful build," and "bushy eyebrows."[15] After the war, he was described as five feet eight inches tall, with a weight of 187 pounds. He had an oval-shaped face, brown eyes; he wore glasses; his hair was a mottled gray-white; he had a heavy build, all his teeth, and a heavy and lumbering posture.[16] The overall impression that Lüdtke's appearance created was that of an aging thug, but he was actually a rather intelligent man. The glasses helped to temper his image, as did his graying hair.

Lüdtke faced a lot of pressure in this case, as the specter of a madman hunting the women of Berlin posed a threat to the workings of the Nazi system. The wartime economy depended on women working factory jobs, often requiring them to commute late at night or early in the morning. The regime could not afford to have them be too afraid to go to work.

Ingeborg Heidenreich, who lived near the Karlshorst S-Bahn station at the time, explained how as a twenty-year-old woman in 1940, she was afraid to ride the train home from work. "It was so that you just didn't trust yourself to go home alone. I also rode on the S-Bahn every day. At that time, I was working . . . and took the midnight train. I worked nights until ten and there was hardly anyone in the train. My mother thought it was important for me to take second class on the train—because of the cushions and so forth—and so no one was there. Of course I was always afraid."[17]

Ironically, she knew the killer, as he shopped at her father's butcher shop and lived in the same neighborhood. Decades later, she still remembered him: "Ogorzow lived here with his wife and children. I didn't know them well. I just thought of them as normal citizens—as a family man with two children, who was nice and loving to his family. That's how I perceived him."[18] She had no clue that the mysterious killer she feared every time she rode the train was the same man she saw playing with his children and tending to his cherry trees.

If she had ever found herself riding the S-Bahn late at night, she would have been happy to see her neighbor Paul Ogorzow. That way she could ride with a family man she knew from the neighborhood, and so feel safe from any predator who might strike on the train. She was lucky that never happened.

Another woman who was afraid to ride the S-Bahn was then thirty-year-old Gerda Busch, who worked at a telegraph office. "People were also talking about this, so of course everyone was afraid to go home at night. Sometimes I would work till 9, 10, 12, sometimes 12:30. And then almost no one was riding on the train and everything was dark. No lights. Nothing. And people told me to always just ride in the first car of the train."[19]

Hitler spoke of this problem after Ogorzow had been caught: "Now we have the war, we have the blackout. Women workers make up the majority of the workforce. . . . To mention one example: the [blackout killer] made many women afraid to leave the factory at night for fear that something could happen to them. There is something monstrous: the man is fighting at the front while the woman cannot dare to go home!"[20] Hitler was referring to Paul Ogorzow but did not use his name while doing so.[21]

Joseph Goebbels, the Reich minister of propaganda, picked up on this issue long before Ogorzow was caught. He also realized that having a serial killer on the loose made the police, and thus the state, look weak. A totalitarian regime depends on fear to stay in power. As such, the last thing Goebbels wanted was for people to doubt that the state could apprehend them if they didn't follow its rules. So he ordered Lüdtke to keep the fact that a serial killer plagued the S-Bahn out of the papers.

Goebbels had the power to give this order to Lüdtke despite the fact that Goebbels was not part of his chain of command. He effectively controlled the mass media in Germany in his position as minister of propaganda. The dissemination of information to the public regarding a serial killer operating in Nazi Germany fell within his jurisdiction.

Paul Joseph Goebbels was born on October 29, 1897, in Rheydt, Germany. He married Magda Ritschel and eventually had six children. His right leg was deformed, for which he wore a metal brace and special shoe. Even with these items, he still had a noticeable limp. He was short and unattractive. Although he had a doctorate, he'd written his thesis on a little known nineteenth-century writer and playwright, and he himself was a frustrated novelist and playwright until he gained power in the Nazi Party.

Among his other additional positions, he was the gauleiter of

Berlin, which meant he was in charge of the Nazi Party for the political district of Berlin. In effect, this was the rough equivalent of being the leader of this area. In addition, he was the *Reichsleiter* (national leader) of the Nazi Party. The only higher position in the Nazi Party was held by Adolf Hitler—*Führer*. So when Goebbels told Lüdtke the limits on the Kripo's ability to publicize this case, Lüdtke had to follow his directives.

A major reason as to why Goebbels did not want news of this case spread was that he wanted to project an image of Nazi Germany, and its capital of Berlin, as a place free from such problems as the predations of a serial killer. As historian Dr. Jens Dobler explained, "In the Nazi society there weren't supposed to be any more crimes, especially not rape-crimes. The news was blocked, which significantly aided the fact that no proper approach to cases could be established. Many details were first released after the war. You can definitely say that this block of the news had a big role in leading to the success of the S-Bahn Murderer."[22]

There was a strong utopian element to Nazi ideology, and now that they had their Third Reich, they believed that such crimes should not be happening. Or if they did, outsiders, such as gypsies, foreigners, or Jews, would the ones committing these crimes and the police would quickly capture the offenders. At this point, the police had no real idea who the killer was and whether he was an Aryan or not. And they certainly were not quick to catch him.

There were also many in the Nazi leadership and in the Kripo who believed that crime had a strong basis in biology. While this theory incorporated the non-Aryans already hated by the Nazis, it also included Germans who came from a background of crime, who had committed a number of crimes over the years, and whose own ancestors had been criminals. Under a racial and biological theory of crime fighting, known as preventive crime fighting, the Kripo would monitor and detain people it considered to be potential criminals.

Arthur Nebe believed in these theories, as did his deputy, Paul Werner. Werner worked on the December 14, 1937, decree of the Reich Interior Ministry on this subject. Called "Preventive Crime Fighting by the Police," it stated, "If a criminal or asocial person has ancestors who also led a criminal or asocial life. . . . the results of hereditary research have shown that the person's behavior is hereditarily conditioned. Such a person must . . . be dealt with differently than a person who . . . comes from a respectable family. . . . The criminal is no longer regarded as an individual person, and his crimes are not regarded as individual crimes. Instead he is considered the descendant of a clan, and his crimes the crimes of a clan member."[23]

Nebe's belief in preventive policing meant that many in the police force had strong preconceived notions regarding the background of a criminal, such as someone who would throw women from the train.

Given the government's interest in concealing the fact that they had a serial killer on the loose, who despite their theories about criminality they were unable to catch, there would be very limited press about this case.

In practice, this meant that the regime would try to keep news of a serial killer under wraps. While the women of Berlin still learned of this case eventually, as gossip spread and they put together for themselves what these "isolated" attacks meant, Lüdtke still could not reach out to the public for the sort of help that he could have requested if he'd been allowed to make this series of attacks public.

This blackout on press about a serial killer riding the rails in Berlin enabled Ogorzow's attacks to continue. Perhaps even with a massive publicity blitz, he would have been able to keep killing women on the S-Bahn, but such press would have made things much harder for him, as for instance women likely would no longer have traveled alone in the second-class compartments. And perhaps tips would have come in from the public. Just as the blackout that kept Berlin dark at night to protect it from British bombers enabled Ogorzow to attack women in the dark and get away with it, so too did he benefit from the press blackout.

When Ogorzow picked up a local paper to check to see what was written about his attacks, he found little to worry him. Given all the fear of getting caught that he felt immediately after killing a woman, it was a tremendous relief for him to see little to nothing in the papers.

From the perspective of the German authorities, there were two different goals in conflict here: the desire to solve this case versus the desire to control the flow of information in a way that was beneficial to the party.

The Nazi state, as represented by Heydrich, Himmler, and Goebbels, didn't want to alert people that a serial killer was able to kill women in the capital of Nazi Germany. The fact that they could not protect German women while their men were away fighting threatened to impact the morale of soldiers from Berlin who would want to be back home protecting their loved ones. Moreover, like all authoritarian states, they wanted to create the impression of being very powerful, to deter people from opposing them. So even if someone hated the Nazis, they would be afraid to resist them, as they feared the authorities would quickly capture them.

But if Nazi Germany could not keep a madman from killing the women of Berlin, then their police force looked ineffective.

Professor Dr. Christian Pfeiffer, director of the Criminological Research Institute of Lower Saxony, spoke of these limitations facing the police during the S-Bahn Murderer case: "This demonstrates exemplarily the limits that the police had at the time. If they could have worked as they did, for example, in the Weimar Republic, or as they do now, where it goes without saying that the police will work with the public and the media in a case where it is evident that the criminal who attacked is unknown to the victim, then it would have been more quickly resolved. One can justifiably assert that this serial murder case was so long-winded because the police themselves were not free to act as they had learned to do so."[24]

This was different than the case of Mrs. Gertrude Ditter, who was killed in her home in the garden area. At the time the police publicized a reward for that case, they believed it to be an isolated murder, and even Goebbels understood that people would not be alarmed that a murder occurred in Nazi-run Berlin. A serial killer preying on women taking public transportation to and from work was a different story as far as Goebbels was concerned.

Lüdtke also suffered from the Kripo having lost many of its experienced detectives. Those who were Communists or socialists had been fired. Any Jewish detectives were long gone as well.

And yet, despite these limitations, Lüdtke faced pressure from Nebe and Heydrich to solve this crime as fast as possible.

## CHAPTER FIFTEEN

# A Killing on the Ground

The same night that he attacked Elfriede Franke, Paul Ogorzow would strike again. This time, though, it would not be on the train.

After he threw Franke's dead body off the train, he rode the S-Bahn to the Karlshorst station. Even now, after having felt the thrill of attacking Franke, he felt frustrated. He still had a burning desire to sexually assault a woman, a desire that had not been quenched by his killing only minutes before.

Once he arrived at his destination, he disembarked from the train and exited the station. This time he would attack on the ground, where he would have more time if things went right. Perhaps he was not as afraid that a potential victim might scream out for help now that he had killed a woman in a single blow. Regardless, it was clear that he'd grown bolder. Committing two such attacks in one night was unprecedented for him.

Ogorzow stayed on the south side of the S-Bahn tracks between Karlshorst and Rummelsburg. When he was about halfway between these two stations, he came to a stop on Prinz-Heinrich-Strasse, where he found a place to hide. Unlike his other attacks on the ground, this one did not take place in the garden area, which was closer to the Rummelsburg station and north of the train tracks. The location was only about half a mile away, though, which was close enough for the police to make a connection between this attack and the others.

Here, Ogorzow waited in the dark for a woman walking alone from or to the S-Bahn station to pass by his position. In the quiet of the night, he could hear the distinctive sounds of the S-Bahn coming and going.

The train made a loud clickety-clack sound as its wheels rolled on the railroad track. This sound came from the small gaps in the track, called expansion joints, which had been put there on purpose. The metal tracks would expand in the heat of the summer and contract in the cold of the winter. Without these gaps, thermal stress would cause the tracks to buckle in the heat. Modern trains produce much less sound because they mostly use continuously welded rail, which avoids buckling without the need for expansion joints.

The trains of the Berlin S-Bahn also made a distinctive sound because the drive gear of the electric traction motor (GBM-700) produced ascending and descending tones. As the train came into the station, Ogorzow could hear the motor, the clickety-clack wheels on the rail and then the application of brakes. As the train left the station, the accelerating electric motor created tones instantly recognizable to anyone who has spent time in Berlin.

These sounds enabled him to prepare for the moment that someone disembarking from the train might walk past his position.

He didn't have to wait long. It was only twenty to thirty minutes after he'd killed Elfriede Franke that he found a new victim. It was now in the early hours of Wednesday, December 4, 1940.

He saw a woman walking on the other side of the street from him. No one else seemed to be around. It was hard for him to be certain of this in the dark, but he listened hard and did not hear anyone else out at this hour.

Her name was Irmgard Freese and she was nineteen years old.

Paul Ogorzow didn't say anything to her, but simply removed the iron rod he'd used earlier that night to kill Franke. He raised the rod and hit Miss Freese in the head, knocking her out. She fell down on the ground. Now that she was knocked out, he ripped off much of her clothing and raped her.

Afterward, he hit her again in the head, a total of three more times, crushing her skull and damaging her brain. Although he was trying to kill her, she was somehow still alive. She didn't feel a thing during these final moments of the attack, though, as she did not regain consciousness. Otherwise, she would have felt excruciating pain with all the serious damage that Ogorzow had done to her.

The police later characterized her status during the final stages of this attack as near death.

Paul Ogorzow never checked his victims' pulse or breathing to see if they were dead or still clinging on to life. He seemed to assume in such circumstances that if they were not dead, they would be soon enough given how badly he had injured them.

Ogorzow left Freese's body out in the open, returned to his place of work at the S-Bahn train signal station, and went to sleep there. It was an isolated building on the outskirts of the train station, and he sometimes slept there when he didn't feel like returning to his wife and two children in their apartment.

Miss Irmgard Freese's body was found around 4:30 A.M. She still was alive, but just barely so, when people walking by discovered her. She was rushed to the hospital. A detective was there the entire time just in case she regained consciousness and could give a statement. From the damage done to her clothing, it was obvious to the police that this was a sex crime. Unlike with the women thrown from the train, the motive here was clear.

Despite the policeman's vigil, Irmgard Freese never said a word. She remained unconscious from the moment she was found until she died at the hospital.

## CHAPTER SIXTEEN

# Connecting the Garden and Train Attacks

Dr. Waldemar Weimann conducted the autopsy on Irmgard Freese's body right away. His report concluded, "Death by brain hemorrhage due to a severely fractured skull. The injuries originated from a blunt, non-edged object."[1]

This was the second woman's body he'd autopsied that day with blunt weapon injuries to the head. And he'd reviewed photographs of a prior victim as well. So it was very much in his mind that the weapon used, as well as the body being found close to an S-Bahn station, suggested there could be a connection here.

He wasn't the only one thinking this. Wilhelm Lüdtke was also puzzled, as it appeared to be the same killer, but this killing had not taken place on the train—though it had occurred around the time that Elfriede Franke was thrown from the S-Bahn.

Dr. Weimann told Lüdtke that he could not be certain that the same weapon had been used on Elfriede Franke and Irmgard Freese, but that their injuries were consistent with this. He also couldn't confirm in any other way that it was the same attacker.

Despite this limitation, he was asked repeatedly about this by the police, including Zach, Lüdtke, and late that night, by Arthur Nebe himself. The head of the entire criminal police force for the Third Reich wanted to know if the man throwing women off the train was the same one who had sexually assaulted and killed a woman near an S-Bahn station around the same time.

Later in life, Dr. Weimann reflected on this moment as follows: "I knew I disappointed my friends in the Kripo. I could imagine the kind of pressure they are under: Goebbels accuses Himmler that the criminal investigation was not in a position to ensure safety on the vital train systems. Himmler blames Heydrich, the chief of the Reich Security Main Office and supervisor of the criminal police. Heydrich makes Nebe crazy and so on. I knew how much prestige was at stake here. But I also knew that criminal investigation rarely gets done well when prestige issues play a role."[2]

With these two attacks on women in different places—on the ground and on an S-Bahn train—within a short time period, the police faced the question of whether these were the work of the same criminal or if there were two different attackers of women prowling in the darkness of this Berlin night. Either way, it seemed ominous.

If it was the same perpetrator, then this was a huge escalation for him to attack two women in the course of less than an hour. Before this night, there had been a substantial time period between attacks. Also, the attacks on the train did not appear to involve sexual assault, while this attack on the ground clearly had.

If there were two separate men—one attacking women on the train and one attacking them on the ground in an area adjacent to a train station—then it seemed like a huge coincidence for these two different attackers to both strike within such a short time of each other and in such close proximity. Also, there were some similarities in the most recent attacks, such as the use of a blunt object.

In looking back on this moment in the case, when it was unclear if the police were dealing with one man or two different offenders, Professor Hans-Ludwig Kröber of the Institute for Forensic Psychiatry at Freien Universität Berlin, recently said, "When analyzing the cases, both options seemed possible."[3]

While it was far from certain that the police were dealing with a single offender, they came to believe that this was more likely than the possibility of there being two different attackers.

One of the main detectives on this case, Georg Albert Wilhelm Heuser, later wrote about this in an article he jointly authored with Lüdtke. Born February 27, 1913, in Berlin, Heuser had studied law and then applied for police work. He pretended to have a Ph.D. in law and used a "Dr." in front of his name, but he had not actually earned his doctorate.

Georg Heuser never joined the Nazi Party, but he did later commit war crimes. For now, though, he was a Kripo detective assisting Lüdtke with trying to catch the S-Bahn Murderer.

Heuser and Lüdtke wrote regarding this moment in the case: "Two murders by the same perpetrator at almost the same time in different crime scenes seemed somewhat far-fetched."[4]

The attacks on the train seemed to lack a motive, as there was no sexual assault or robbery, and the victims appeared to be chosen by circumstances. The women's sole connection to their attacker was that they both were traveling on the S-Bahn, while it was dark out, and they were the only ones in their compartment.

In sharp contrast to these mysterious assaults on women riding the S-Bahn, the attacks on the ground, for the most part, had a clear sexual component to them. If it were only one perpetrator, his actions during this one evening suggested a whole new motive to his past crimes, which meant that how the police had been thinking about this suspect was wrong.

This was the first victim the police were aware of who had been sexually assaulted. An examination of her body had found semen inside her. Ogorzow had committed prior sexual assaults, but they had all taken place in the garden area and not been connected by the police to the activities of the S-Bahn Murderer.

The killer's prior victims had been attacked on the S-Bahn and left for dead with no motive that the police had been able to determine, and it was strange to have someone killing women for no other reason than the pleasure of killing itself. Ogorzow had not had time to molest the first or the third victim, and while he did touch the second victim, there was no evidence of it, given the damage to her clothing sustained by falling from the train. And she was unconscious at the time, so she had no idea what had happened to her between her passing out on the train and her waking up on the ground. She did not know that Ogorzow had touched her after he'd knocked her out. Since she didn't know this, neither did the police.

Wilhelm Lüdtke wanted to talk to Dr. Weimann about what motive there might be for a man to hit women on the head and then throw them from a moving train. As Dr. Weimann recalled, "Commissioner Lüdtke asked this question [of possible motive] to me the next day on the phone. It was pretty late in the evening. I had spent the whole day dissecting bodies and longed for my home. 'If you have the time and inclination, we can discuss it over a glass of wine,' I suggested to Lüdtke."[5]

Lüdtke took him up on his offer and came over that evening to Dr. Weimann's home. Weimann invited him into a room that he'd turned into his home library. Amidst his large collection of books, they sat down and talked about these recent attacks on women.

The main question they grappled with was the nature of the train killer's motive, if there were two separate killers acting simultaneously. If they removed the recent attack on the ground from the equation, they were left with the question of what would motivate a man to throw women from the train. Sexual assault and robbery were both out. People often kill out of jealousy, revenge, hatred, and so forth, but it seemed to them that might explain a single case but not multiple cases. Especially as the cases appeared to be opportunistic, where the killer did not know his victims before they encountered each other on the train.

If such attacks happened today, police might think of the possibility that there had been a single crime with a typical motive, like jealousy, that was being covered up by having it appear to be part of a string of random murders. There was a famous case like that in the United States in 1986, when Stella Nickell killed her husband by adding poison to his over-the-counter painkillers and then tried to cover it up by killing a stranger with the same kind of poisoned product. In this way she tried to make the murder of her spouse look like part of a random product-tampering case, like a recent case involving a well-known pain reliever. Ogorzow's attacks on the train, however, were novel, so this copycat element was not present.

Police Commissioner Lüdtke had already given a lot of thought to this matter of motive. He'd developed a theory that the killer was mentally ill, someone who was very aggressive and enjoyed killing for its own sake. In accordance with this possibility, the police had been looking for someone who got into fights and hurt people at the slightest provocation.

During their meeting, he and Dr. Weimann considered this possibility, as well as related ones, such as a killer with various mental or physical health problems—schizophrenia, severe epilepsy, or a brain injury. This fit into the world of the Nazis, with their belief in eugenics and their institutionalized disdain for people with these sorts of health conditions.

Finally, Lüdtke brought up the possibility of these attacks being sexual in nature, even though the women on the train were not sexually assaulted, as far as they knew.

This made sense to Dr. Weimann. Given his background in psychiatry, he understood that something could be sexually motivated even without any overtly sexual act occurring. He thought of Szilveszter Matuska, who blew up two trains—near Berlin in August 1931 and close to Budapest in September 1931. He killed more than twenty people and injured around two hundred. Dr. Weimann believed one version of this criminal's motive—that he did this for a sexual thrill.

Given this example, Dr. Weimann answered Lüdtke's question in the affirmative—there could be a sexual motive here, even for the train attacks. This was the right answer as far as Lüdtke was concerned. He hadn't wanted to predispose Dr. Weimann to answer this way, but now that Weimann had given his expert opinion, Lüdtke had something to show him.

Lüdtke opened his briefcase and took out a detailed map of the garden area where Paul Ogorzow had been harassing and attacking women. "Now see and be amazed," Lüdtke said.[6]

This map was covered in all kinds of notes and symbols. Lüdtke explained that they marked where thirty-two different offenses against women had occurred recently: "It began when women walking alone were lit with a flashlight and harassed with obscene yelling. The dirty phrases gradually became fisticuffs, which grew to abuse and eventually to attempted and completed rape. In some cases the perpetrator choked victims, others were stabbed, but most of them received heavy blows on their head, with a blunt object."[7]

With these two attacks in quick succession, Lüdtke had seen the possibility of a connection between the attacks on the train, the very recent attack on Irmgard Freese near a train station, and the attacks on women in the garden area.

He had also made another key connection. Lüdtke had been on the scene at Mrs. Ditter's death, so he explained that case to Dr. Weimann as well. Geographically, it was in the same garden area as the attacks on women detailed in his map, but the pattern was different, as it took place inside the victim's home and not on the dark trails of the garden colony.

Mrs. Ditter's case had grown cold, but connecting it with the other attacks could give the police a new take on their investigation.

Dr. Weimann was not yet convinced that this was the same man, especially when they looked at the map and took into account the activity on the S-Bahn and where the lead telephone cable originally came from. It all seemed too spread apart to him.

Now Lüdtke shared the one small detail that would change Dr. Weimann's mind: "One fact makes me suspicious," the commissioner said, "Since the first woman was thrown from the train, [the police] have not heard of any more attacks in the garden area."[8]

This all made sense to Dr. Weimann. He knew how sexual attackers escalated over time, so it made sense to him that an offender would start by flashing a light on women walking in the dark and eventually graduate to rape and murder.

Now that Wilhelm Lüdtke had confirmation from an expert that he was onto something, he put his detectives to work learning more about the garden attacks and Mrs. Ditter's murder. Assuming that the same attacker was behind these crimes and the S-Bahn attacks, the police now believed that the train killings had some kind of sexual motive behind them.

Dr. Weimann was concerned that if this was the work of one man, then the short interval between the recent attacks suggested that the high the killer felt from attacking women was wearing off more rapidly, so he needed to kill more often. In this respect, Dr. Weimann viewed a serial killer in much the same way as a drug addict, as someone who needs more and more of a given stimulus in order to experience the same high he did when he started this activity.

One of the first things the police did on December 4, after having found two bodies, was to put up posters in S-Bahn stations with details of the murder of Elfriede Franke. The posters called for anyone with information to talk to the police. They did not mention the other murders. The police were treating this call for information as something limited to a single, discrete crime.

The police were torn because they wanted to ask the public for information, which might provide useful leads, but they did not want to alarm people with the news that a serial killer was on the loose. Nor did they want to advertise that the Nazi state was unable to protect the women of Berlin while their men were out fighting on the front.

Paul Ogorzow read the poster, which included a generous reward offer of ten thousand reichsmarks. This was a large amount of money. For comparison, a single reichsmark would buy five third-class S-Bahn tickets good for one-way trips in the city center fare zone. Another way to understand how much money this was is to consider the fact that Mr. and Mrs. Ditter had bought their garden house for a mere one hundred and fifty reichsmarks.

After seeing this poster, Ogorzow worried that the police were going to all this effort to try to catch him. He was well aware that ten thousand reichsmarks was a lot of money. Although he had no accomplices and he had not confided in anyone about his crimes, it still concerned him that someone might have noticed something about him worth reporting to the police. In addition, the reward meant that the police considered catching him a high priority and would not skimp on resources when trying to solve the murder and the attempted murders that he'd committed on the train.

He was relieved, though, to find that the police had a vague description of him that lacked any specific detail that would single him out from the masses of other men in Berlin it could describe. From the information contained in the reward posters, they did not appear close to catching him. So while these posters and the high reward they announced worried him, this was not enough to frighten him into giving him up his murderous ways.

Meanwhile, Lüdtke ordered that a new kind of suspect be pursued. He had his men look through crime reports for incidents where a man aged somewhere between his mid-twenties and his forties (there was no need in Nazi Germany to focus on the white part) violently attacked women in Berlin and sexually assaulted them. His theory was that this criminal would have started with assaults, then progressed to rapes, and only now escalated to murders.

The only crimes that this approach discovered were two sets that he was already considering—the man who had committed a number of attacks on women in the garden areas of a Berlin suburb and the man throwing women from the S-Bahn. Both men were in the same age range, wore a uniform during their attacks, and were known to use blunt objects to hit their victims on the head.

The garden attacker took advantage of the blackout to approach women alone in the dark and often assaulted them from behind so they could not later identify him. Only two of the garden victims were able to give a description of their assailant—they both said that he was wearing a uniform that appeared to be consistent with a railroad uniform. Although the garden attacker mostly choked his victims or hit them with a blunt instrument, he had occasionally used a knife, which the police did not see in the S-Bahn cases.

The rail tracks between two S-Bahn stations—Rummelsburg and the similarly named, adjacent stop of Betriebsbahnhof Rummelsburg—bordered the south of the garden area. The Betriebsbahnhof Rummelsburg station, however, was not accessible to the public. It had been opened in March 1902, but only for the use of railroad personnel. There was a large workshop nearby it run by the *Reichsbahn*, and so they occasionally used this station. This stop would only be made available to passengers on the S-Bahn starting on January 5, 1948.[9]

All the garden attacks took place within walking distance of these stations, and these stations were also along the route that the S-Bahn Murderer used for his attacks, which further suggested to the police that there could be a connection between the attacks.

However, the police were far from certain about this connection. Lüdtke still had some doubts that same man would engage in attacks on both the train and on the ground at almost the same time. These back-to-back criminal offenses struck him as highly unusual.

## CHAPTER SEVENTEEN

# The Wrong Kind of Suspect

Thinking about who might be carrying out these attacks did not take place in an ahistorical vacuum. Instead, the police were influenced by the beliefs of the Nazi Party. The racist ideology of Nazism suggested that the perpetrator was likely to be a non-Aryan.

Jews, of course, were the great scapegoats of the Third Reich, and so there was some speculation that it could be a man of Jewish heritage behind these attacks. There were still German Jews in Berlin. They had not yet been sent to concentration camps to be murdered.

Despite the racist depictions of Jewish people in the omnipresent Nazi propaganda, it was not yet possible simply to look at a man and tell if he was Jewish. But Jews could be identified by their paperwork, and later the German government forced them to wear yellow stars of David on their clothing.

If someone of Jewish descent were committing these crimes, then the victims would likely have noticed that their attacker was particularly skinny. Jews received much worse food rations than non-Jews and so were unlikely to fit the limited description that the police had of the man committing murders on the S-Bahn.

There was another major problem in considering Jewish suspects. In Berlin, there was a curfew of 8 P.M. for Jews. It had started in September 1939, so if someone Jewish was committing these crimes, he was doing so while violating the curfew. This seemed unlikely, especially as the police presence on and around the S-Bahn had increased in the wake of the attacks, making it virtually impossible for someone Jewish not to get arrested for a curfew violation. Ironically, the very restrictions placed on Jewish people protected them from being likely suspects in these crimes.

Jewish people were forced to work in menial jobs in Berlin, including jobs related to the S-Bahn. As a book on Jews in Nazi Berlin explained, "In May 1939 all Jewish men in Germany between 18 and 55 and all women between 18 and 50 were ordered to register for labor deployment with the appropriate department of their respective Jewish Communities. Eyewitness reports confirm that Jews were consistently deployed in work alien to their own profession. Doctors, lawyers, writers, and academics were often forced to perform the dirtiest tasks: trash collection, toilet cleaning for the Reich Railways, clearing snow in winter, cleaning jobs in the chemical and textile industries, and so forth. Or they were relegated to physically exhausting tasks such as quarrying and construction work or to strenuous and monotonous jobs in the metal and electrical industries."[1]

So one avenue of investigation was to look at any Jewish people who worked for the railway, which at this point in time would mean a low-level menial laborer, such as a cleaner. However, the police did not find anyone within this labor pool that they believed to be a viable suspect.

If the Kripo were merely looking for a scapegoat, all they needed to do was pick up a German Jew and frame him for it. Perhaps one who worked cleaning toilets at S-Bahn stations. But it was important to Lüdtke to catch the actual killer. Besides, the perpetrator of these crimes would probably kill again, and that would make the police look bad if they already had someone in custody for the crimes.

The idea also took root that the attacker could be a foreign spy trying to sabotage the Reich. Gossip spread among the police that the perpetrator was working for the British to undermine morale in Berlin. It was true that women were growing afraid to ride the S-Bahn to and from their factory jobs, and these factory jobs were essential to the German war effort. Also, this theory was built on the idea that men who'd left Berlin as part of the military would grow upset when they learned of the attacks and would wish to return home, where they could protect their female loved ones. As such, these crimes would hurt morale among soldiers from Berlin.

Other police officers leaned toward the theory that the attacker was a foreign laborer. Even though it did not explain how the perpetrator spoke perfect German or had a uniform, this angle was carefully investigated. One possibility was that the attacker knew German, despite being a foreigner, or knew a little German and so could fake his way through the language for limited interactions. In many, though not all, of the attacks, the perpetrator did not speak at all. As for the uniform, in this scenario, perhaps a foreign laborer had stolen one or made a fake uniform that looked real enough in the dark.

Citizens of conquered countries, such as Poland, were forced to work in factories in Berlin. The German authorities investigating the S-Bahn killings paid particular attention to slave laborers from Eastern Europe, as they believed them to be racially inferior to Aryans. And so the police looked into whether anyone from the labor camps could have been unaccounted for during the time of the attacks. They also took a careful look at any non-Jew not of Aryan descent working for the railroad.

This suspicion toward foreigners posed a problem for the authorities. Foreign laborers formed an essential part of Germany's war effort, and a growing fear of them on the part of Berliners could potentially disrupt the important work they did. Although Germany fought this war in the name of creating more living space for pure Aryans, it ironically decided to import large numbers of foreign laborers into Germany to do the work that the war required. German men were already mobilized to fight, and women were increasingly doing factory work as well.

The technology of the time required large amounts of manual labor to move earth and work machines. There was a wide spectrum of foreign laborers who did such tasks, ranging from those imprisoned in camps, who were worked to death, to those who came from countries allied with Germany and had many more freedoms.

The investigation was necessarily limited to those workers who were not imprisoned and who had access to the trains. Many laborers had curfews and were not allowed to ride on public transportation such as the S-Bahn. Others lived in barracks or similar group accommodations that enabled the authorities to keep track of their comings and goings.

These racially motivated approaches to solving these crimes did not lead anywhere. While these lines of detection did waste police resources, they did not stop the investigation from going forward, and Lüdtke stayed focused on other ways to try to catch the killer.

## CHAPTER EIGHTEEN

# The Rummelsburg S-Bahn Station

While the police investigated the garden assaults to see if they were connected with the attacks on the S-Bahn, they also took another look at the October 4, 1940, murder of Mrs. Gertrude "Gerda" Ditter.

Commissioner Wilhelm Lüdtke realized that if the garden attacker and the train killer were the same person, he might also have killed Mrs. Ditter. And since this murder had occurred between the first two attacks on the S-Bahn, before the third one, which marked the first actual murder on the train, then Mrs. Ditter would have been the perpetrator's first homicide.

The murder took place inside of a house, which varied from the garden attacker's usual pattern of assaulting women outdoors. So the police were not even certain that the garden attacker and the killer of Mrs. Ditter were one and the same, let alone that this same man was the S-Bahn Murderer. Even so, they decided to take a second look at her case.

They had no witnesses to the attack on Mrs. Ditter, but they did have survivors of attacks in the garden area. Lüdtke put the information he had about the garden area attacks together with what he knew about the S-Bahn attacks. The eyewitness descriptions of the attacker roughly matched up, but these were so vague that they fit a huge number of the men in Berlin. Given the darkness of the blackout, the descriptions provided to the police did little to help. The witnesses didn't notice any distinctive marks, such as tattoos or scars.

While Ogorzow had neither of these, he did have an improperly set broken nose that resulted in an oversized right nostril. No one had noticed this yet, at least no one who had lived to describe her attacker. His ears stuck out a bit, and his hair was thin, but these details too went unnoticed in the confusion of the attacks and the darkness of the blackout.

All the police had to go on in terms of a physical description from the garden attacks was an age range of thirty to forty, but even that had to be considered rough, as it was hard to tell someone's age in the dark. So his age could have easily been twenty-five or forty-five for all the police knew. As to height, the police had descriptions of around five feet four inches to five feet six inches.

A major difference between the description of the attacker in the garden area and the description by the S-Bahn victims was that on the S-Bahn the perpetrator always had on a uniform, while only two of the many victims in the garden area reported that their harasser was wearing a uniform. And these were two of the most low-level incidents, where Ogorzow had flashed a light at women to startle them during the blackout and yelled crude things. All the other attacks in the garden area so far had involved a man who appeared to be wearing civilian clothing. Again, given the darkness, Ogorzow could have been wearing his uniform during many of these attacks and his victims did not notice it.

So while it was a breakthrough that Lüdtke made a connection between these two different areas of attack, the S-Bahn and the garden area, including the killing of Mrs. Ditter, for now it added little actionable intelligence to his operation to catch this killer.

The fact that none of the attacks happened on the U-Bahn provided the police with a possible clue as to the attacker's identity. Different companies ran the U-Bahn and the S-Bahn. So this might mean that the killer had a connection to the company that ran the S-Bahn, the National Railroad. Of course, the police could not be certain of this. There could be other reasons why the killer chose to use the S-Bahn for these attacks.

The police were able to narrow down the killer's hunting ground even more because it was only along one part of a single S-Bahn route. He preyed on women in otherwise empty second-class carriages between the Rummelsburg and Friedrichshagen stations. Back then, this line was called *Schlesische Bahn*. Two experts on the S-Bahn explained that it had this name "as it was the suburban line near the main line to the former part of Germany called Schlesien. From 1930 on all lines had internal 'names,' that were not shown to the public. For example after reconstruction of the route to Erkner it got the internal name 'train group E.'"[1] The *Schlesische Bahn* is still in use today. After the reunification of Germany, it was named S3.

Lüdtke realized this was the route for him to monitor. He posted at least one officer at all times on each of eight stations along this line. He started with Rummelsburg followed by Karlshorst, Wuhlheide, Köpenick, Hirschgarten, and Friedrichshagen. He then went a bit beyond the killer's normal route to include two additional stations past Friedrichshagen. These were Rahnsdorf and Wilhelmshagen. (These eight stations did not include Betriebsbahnhof Rummelsburg as that station was not then open to the public.)

The detectives that Lüdtke placed on the train stations wore railroad uniforms so people would assume that the company that ran the S-Bahn employed them and they were not police officers. Detectives also worked ticket booths at S-Bahn stations while wearing *Reichsbahn* uniforms. While checking people's tickets, they would try to observe if there was anything suspicious about a passenger that suggested he might be their suspect.

However, this got the police nowhere. Without a decent description of the suspect, they could not hope to find him just by looking at train riders.

Lüdtke decided to take an active approach to this investigation—instead of waiting for the next victim to be discovered, he set out bait to tempt the killer. There were policewomen in the Kripo, which provided Lüdtke with the opportunity to try to trick the killer into attacking a police officer.

While the Gestapo in Berlin had women working for it as well, they held purely administrative positions. So when the Gestapo needed a woman for a job, such as to try to seduce a heterosexual male spy or some other gender-specific task, they were forced to use someone without proper training for such activities.

The Kripo, however, had actual police officers that were women.

In 1927, Miss Friederike Wieking organized a small number of female police into a unit of the nationwide criminal police force. She retained her authority when the Nazis gained power, and her female police department became the Female Criminal Police (*Weiblichen Kriminalpolizei*, or WKP). Of the many section heads in the RHSA, she was the only woman.

Lüdtke approached Wieking to find out about using her female police as part of his plan to catch the S-Bahn Murderer. She agreed to assign some of her policewomen to this task. But when Lüdtke wanted to arm these women with handguns so they could protect themselves if they did run into the killer, Wieking refused. She did not believe that women should be armed. Instead she saw the role of women policemen as assisting male police with gender-specific tasks, but not to be their equals.

This was yet another frustration for Lüdtke, as it meant that he needed to make sure that a policewoman riding the S-Bahn had male backup close enough to be able to help her if she were attacked, but far enough away and out of sight so as not to deter the killer from striking. Lüdtke was well aware that the killer only attacked women traveling alone, so his inability to train these women in how to use firearms and provide them with handguns was a serious problem.

Despite this limitation, he elected to go ahead and try using policewomen as decoys on the train. He had policewomen dressed in fashionable civilian clothing ride the S-Bahn, accompanied at a distance by a male police officer. A policewoman would ride the second-class compartment alone while a male companion would try to keep watch from the adjacent third-class compartment.

On this route, there were two different types of railroad cars used by the S-Bahn in the 1940s. Only one of these types could be used with female decoys, for with the other kind it would not be possible for them to have male backup. The cars built in the 1920s had doors between the second-class compartment and the adjacent third-class one. These trains used "engine cars" and "control cars," with the final control car featuring a second-class compartment connected by doors to a third-class compartment. With this setup, a female police officer could ride in second class, the only class in which Ogorzow ever attacked his victims, while an armed male police officer would be waiting in the adjacent third-class compartment. He would be ready to burst through the door between compartments at the first sign of trouble.

The newer trains, built mostly in the late 1930s, had "engine cars" with "trailer cars." The trailer car with the second-class compartment had no door connecting it to third-class or any other part of the train. There were solid walls on each end of the compartment. The use of female decoys would not work with these trains as there was nowhere for male help to be waiting. Even with the darkness in the train, it would be very difficult to hide a male cop in the second-class compartment, and if anything looked off, the criminal would not strike. It's possible that Ogorzow favored one kind of train over the other, but the police were not aware of any such preference and so they used female police in the older kind of train.

If Wieking had granted Lüdtke's request to train and arm the female police, this might have worked. At one point, it almost did anyway. Using a female police officer, the Kripo narrowly missed catching Ogorzow. He was riding the S-Bahn, looking for a woman to attack. He entered a second-class compartment and saw that there was a woman already riding in it. She was alone and no one else boarded this compartment with him.

As the train started moving, he walked toward this woman, while mentally and physically preparing to attack her. What he did not yet realize was that this woman was a female police officer in disguise. She was not dressed in a uniform, but instead was traveling undercover in fashionable civilian clothing. She did not have a firearm, but did have a male police officer riding in the adjacent third-class compartment, waiting by the door between compartments for a signal that he should rush through to her aid. It was hard to communicate between compartments and it would take time for her to get help, so this was a serious flaw in Lüdtke's plan.

Somehow, just as Ogorzow was close enough to attack the woman, he realized that she was a cop. He knew already from his own observations, his friends in the SA, and his fellow railroad workers that there were female police officers riding the S-Bahn, waiting for the killer to strike.

The inside of this train compartment was not pitch-black. There was some minimal lighting, and it was enough as he got close to her for him to see something that scared him. Perhaps it was that she was not afraid of him, or maybe there was something about her posture that suggested she was in the police force. Whatever the reason, he quickly aborted his approach and turned around, walking back to his starting position near the train's door.

He knew that police officers kept an eye on the various stations along this line during the blackout, so he worried that he would be detained when the train came to the next station if he was right that this woman was a cop. His behavior in going up to her and then abruptly turning back was suspicious. Even if he were caught, he could make some excuse, and this was not enough to prove he was the S-Bahn Murderer anyway, but at the very least the police would hold on to him while they investigated him. And perhaps they would then find something that convinced them that he was their man.

Ogorzow decided that he would risk jumping off the moving train instead of seeing what awaited him at the next station. He opened the door, looked out into the darkness, and instead of throwing a victim out of the train, he himself hopped out. He managed to land without seriously injuring himself and then ran toward the Rummelsburg S-Bahn station. He needed to disappear before this woman could raise the alarm at the next station and police swarmed the tracks looking for him.

The woman looked out and was able to tell in what direction he was heading. This had all happened too fast for her to do anything else. Without a gun, she would have had trouble safely stopping him from fleeing anyway. And it took time to get help from the male cop in the adjacent third-class section.

Paul Ogorzow's intuition was right. He had almost attacked a female police officer and she alerted her colleagues at the next station. They did mobilize, but by the time police arrived to look for him, he was gone. If he had been unfortunate enough to have broken a leg or otherwise seriously injured himself during his jump from a moving train, they would probably have found him. Also, the very act of jumping out of a train in motion made him look guilty. If he were not the S-Bahn Murderer, he would have to be insane to do such a thing. This jump combined with his strange behavior in regards to the undercover policewoman would have almost certainly resulted in the police arresting him for the S-Bahn attacks if they had caught him.

Because he got away, the police then turned toward finding out as much as they could about this suspect from the policewoman who had encountered him on the train. Given the poor lighting in the compartment, the only details she could report were that the suspect wore a black jacket that looked like it belonged to some sort of uniform, that this jacket appeared to not have any buttons, and that he was wearing a hat of some sort. She thought he was probably around the same height as her. Even though the police had almost caught Ogorzow, they learned almost nothing of value from this incident. The details the policewoman recalled added little to what they already knew.

This incident provided a real-life example of how quickly things could happen in the train compartment and how long it would take a male policeman to come to the rescue of a woman in another compartment. It became apparent to Lüdtke that it was impossible to safely balance the need to draw out the killer with a woman alone and the need for a male policeman to be close enough at hand to intervene if an attack did occur. And so he stopped using female decoys to try to catch the killer.

Despite this close call, Ogorzow continued to hunt for women to attack on the S-Bahn trains. As dangerous as the S-Bahn was becoming for him with all the police attention on it, it still felt safer to him than the garden area. While he could take the time to sexually assault his victims in the garden area, he did enjoy the process of throwing women from the train. As scary as it had been for him to jump from a moving train and have to run away, it was not as bad as the time that he had been caught by two men in the garden area who came to the rescue of their loved one. Those two had beat him up and would have handed him over to police if he had not managed to get away and escape them in the darkness of the garden area.

The smart move might have been to find a new hunting ground entirely, but these were the two areas that he felt secure in and knew well. Police attention could get him to change his method of attack in small ways, like timing. But given his compulsion to attack and murder women, it was not enough to get him to stop.

A contemporary expert on serial killers, Düsseldorf detective Chief Superintendent Stephan Harbort, described this aspect of the hunt for the S-Bahn Murderer: "In order to catch the serial murderer, maybe even while in the act, all S-Bahn stations which were relevant to the investigation were being monitored by officials of the *Reichsbahn* and the homicide division . . . as well as all commuter traffic on selected days between 8 P.M. and midnight. However, the murderer showed himself to be completely unfazed by all of these security measures."[2]

As a National Railroad employee, Paul Ogorzow had a uniform and a free pass to ride the S-Bahn as much as he wanted. In terms of enabling his attacks on the train, however, his work provided him with more than this. He heard official word from the police and the train company regarding the police investigation and the posting of officers along the train line. Moreover, his fellow train workers would gossip about this case, giving him even more information about what the police were up to.

Most importantly, his job provided him with the opportunity to ditch work, while on paper it would appear that he was there. This meant that when police were looking for an S-Bahn employee who could have committed these attacks, Ogorzow had what appeared to be a solid alibi for the times he committed crimes while he was supposed to be at work.

While the police caught on to the importance of this train route, they did not realize that one of these stations was more important than the others. In fact, the attacks took place along a route that passed through the S-Bahn station at Rummelsburg where Paul Ogorzow worked.

His tasks for this job included a large amount of outdoor work, such as checking on the tracks and on the signals. Thomas Krickstadt and Mike Straschewski, experts on the history of the S-Bahn, explained why Paul Ogorzow was able to leave work so often without being noticed: "The sum of the above mentioned [outdoor] tasks are the reason why Ogorzow often was not at the signal tower. Another reason for his not being noticed was that the signal tower was a bit outside of populated areas. A lot of weekend houses were nearby, so on weekdays the area was uninhabited."[3]

It was here near the Rummelsburg S-Bahn station that Ogorzow reported to work. When he was not out checking on and fixing things on the railroad tracks nearby, Ogorzow was supposed to be in a signal tower designated "Vnk." The name was painted on the side of the tower and used in maps of the railroad facilities surrounding this station.

An S-Bahn expert explained, "'Vnk' was the official abbreviation for the name of the signal station. It meant '*Verbindung nach Küstrin*' ('Junction to Küstrin') because the signal station was at a junction where a line to Küstrin (since 1945 a Polish city) led."[4] During the time Ogorzow worked in this signal station Küstrin was part of Germany.

This same expert described how the train switching technology of the time worked: "In the 1930s there were two basic techniques in German signal towers. The older technology was purely mechanical with big levers. . . . In the new version, small levers have been used through which an electrical pulse is triggered electro-mechanically. Thus, the switches and signals were detected [through this machinery]. This technique was the one used in the Berlin signal tower 'Vnk.' The guard in 'Vnk' received his instructions by phone or by telegraph from the dispatcher."[5]

The building Paul Ogorzow worked in, Rummelsburg S-Bahn signal tower Vnk, was an ugly, redbrick building bordered by the train tracks on two sides. It had two stories aboveground and a basement below. The front of the building faced train tracks with two stories visible, while on the other side, it looked like a three-story structure with its basement at ground-floor level. Although it was only a few feet from the tracks on the front and back it was built on a steep drop-off so that the back was built into a retaining wall to keep the hillside from eroding away onto the train tracks. In other words, the front of the building appeared to have two stories, while the back looked like three stories as the basement level merged into the retaining wall.

Inside, there was a fireplace to heat it. There were two entrances on the front side, one at the same level as the train tracks and the other up a flight of metal stairs. The backside was bricked up, without any means of entering or exiting the building. It was a small building, the sort of place that could make one feel claustrophobic after a while. This tower was located in the far northwest corner of the various facilities at this station. It was an isolated outpost on the outskirts of the Rummelsburg station. Paul Ogorzow was often working alone, so he could sleep in the signal tower or come and go from it as he pleased.

Ogorzow's job at this signal tower provided him with an alibi, while actually allowing him to generally come and go as he pleased. There were times that he needed to actually be in the tower, but much of the workday he was free to leave without anyone noticing.

## CHAPTER NINETEEN

# Uniforms, Decoys in Drag, and Another Murder

Police Commissioner Wilhelm Lüdtke focused in on the attacker's uniform. His men interviewed two women from the garden attacks who saw their assailant wearing a uniform, along with the women who had survived being attacked on the S-Bahn.

However, due to the darkness, the speed of the assaults, and the problems with eyewitness testimony generally, the police were not able to pinpoint who the attacker was from his uniform. For example, the two women who survived being thrown from the train said different things about what their attacker wore. One said that it was a blue uniform; the other said it was black. They both testified that he wore a hat pulled forward to partially conceal his facial features, but they could not agree on what kind of hat it was.

The police found this incredibly frustrating, as they desperately wanted to know more about their suspect. A basic fact like whether his uniform was blue or black could point the investigation in a totally different direction. The last thing the police wanted to do was interview thousands of people who had blue uniforms if the killer actually had a black uniform.

As much as the police wished it was otherwise, it was to be expected that there would be so little useful information that their witnesses could agree on. Eyewitness evidence can be problematic under the best of conditions, as people are nervous when they are victims of a violent crime, and the human mind generally does not retain as many useful details as we think it does. As such, it is not surprising that the police did not gain much useful information from those whom Paul Ogorzow attacked.

The police had a pool of five thousand active train workers whose uniforms could match their composite description. And this did not even include someone with a similar-looking uniform who did not work for the railroad, or someone who only impersonated a railroad employee, or a former railroad employee, for that matter. Checking out all these potential suspects and whether they had alibis for the times of the crimes would be a huge undertaking.

Besides, Nazi Germany was awash in different kinds of uniforms, many of them in dark colors that would look the same in blackout conditions.

If it was not an S-Bahn-related uniform, then the other main possibility the Kripo considered was that the uniform belonged to a member of the SS paramilitary organization. The SS had a number of uniform changes over the years, most notably going from all-black uniforms to a field-gray color.

If it was an SS uniform the assailant wore, then the accompanying hat was not part of it. Although it was dark, and witnesses had not seen much that could help the police, what they had noticed of the perpetrator's headwear did not match an SS cap. The SS had a peaked cap with an eagle and an ominous-looking skull and crossbones insignia, known as a death's head, on it.

The National Railroad hat Paul Ogorzow wore looked similar to many other German uniform caps during World War II. While they might look the same from a distance or in the dark, a major difference between these hats was the varying emblems used by different organizations. Ogorzow's hat featured the eagle clutching a swastika, but with a slightly different version of the eagle that was specific to the National Railroad Company. In addition, his hat had a white circular badge with a large red dot in the middle affixed to a wraparound black band. Taken together, this created the black, white, and red color scheme that represented Germany at the time.

It would be hard for one of Ogorzow's victims to see this in blackout conditions. Plus, after suffering a traumatic event, such as being attacked and then thrown off a moving train, it is understandable that one would not remember the exact details of what the eagle looked like on Ogorzow's hat or that it had a white circle with a red dot on it. There were other details specific to a given kind of hat, such as the colors on the braiding, but since more noticeable branch-of-service indicators went unnoticed, these smaller details were not relevant to the investigation.

If a member of the SS were riding the S-Bahn and throwing German women off the train, toward what he believed to be their deaths, then Lüdtke could be in for a hard time. It was one thing for him to question civilians working for the state railroad company, and quite another to cast aspersions on members of the SS.

Going after the SS would be a major problem for a number of reasons, not least of which was the fact that the director of the Reich Main Security Office, Reinhard Heydrich, reported directly to the head of the SS (*Reichsführer-SS*) Heinrich Himmler. Heydrich and Himmler were close; Heydrich was widely considered one of Himmler's most trusted aides.

Lüdtke realized that the best approach for now would be to put the SS issue on the side and focus in on the railroad. He flooded the S-Bahn late at night with decoys, using men in drag that in the darkness of the blackout a killer could mistake for lone women. Other police would travel in the adjacent compartment as backup, so that if they heard a struggle, they could rush in to assist. The idea was that these men would not need immediate backup in the same way that a female police officer would, the big difference being that these men would be carrying guns, while the female police Lüdtke had used before did not.

Young, skinny men who might pass for women in the dark were called to this highly unusual duty. A photo taken at the time showed a group of these policemen dressed as women. They looked ridiculous. All of them wore tall leather boots that ended just below the knees. They had on leather gloves, maybe to fit in with the winter clothes worn by real women, or perhaps to conceal their manly hands and spare them the indignity of putting on nail polish. Common accessories included knotted head scarves, wide-brimmed hats, and brooches. One policeman had a fur stole around his neck, while the others had silk scarves. These were attempts to conceal their large Adam's apples.

They were all clean-shaven and wore a dark, possibly red lipstick. Some might pass as women in a poorly lit environment. Others would appear to be men if there were any light to expose them at all. Unfortunately for these cross-dressing policemen, there was some light on the S-Bahn trains even during the blackout, although the platforms themselves were shrouded in darkness.

Male agents dressed as women were an unusual occurrence in Nazi Germany, a country whose government persecuted those it identified as homosexual.

Their target, Ogorzow, knew of these police actions, so he did not fall for them. As mentioned previously, he had two main sources of information about the police investigation—one, as a railroad employee he heard gossip about activities on the train, and two, as an active member of the paramilitary SA, he had friends in the police force who mentioned this use of decoys.

The police primarily rode the rails late at night, as most of Ogorzow's prior attacks had been around midnight. Ogorzow simply adapted to this fact and began attacking during the early morning hours, while it was still dark.

Early on Sunday, December 22, 1940, Ogorzow searched on the S-Bahn for a woman traveling alone that he could attack. Sometime before seven in the morning, he found her. The sun would not rise that day until 9:15 A.M., so there was little light out.[1]

Thirty-year-old Mrs. Elisabeth Büngener was riding the S-Bahn to see her husband. He was a military recruit in a town near Berlin called Fürstenwalde. Christmas was only days away and she wanted to see him before the holiday.

Germans celebrated Christmas Eve the way Americans did Christmas morning. So for her, it was only two days until the holiday during which she normally would exchange presents and eat a large meal with her relatives.

In the second-class compartment of the train, the only passengers were Ogorzow and Büngener as the train pulled out of the station at Friedrichshagen. If someone else had happened to travel second-class as well, Mrs. Büngener would have been safe. But with just the two of them in this section of the train, Ogorzow felt comfortable attacking her.

He stuck to his modus operandi on the train—he hit her on the head with a blunt object, and while she was out of it, he pulled the train door open, felt the wind blow on his face, and then dragged her body to the door. She was still alive.

He then felt the rush that came with throwing a woman off the S-Bahn while it was in motion. She tumbled off into the night between the Friedrichshagen and Rahnsdorf stations. He threw her things off after her, as he always did. The train was still in motion, so these items landed a good distance from her.

This marked his first attack in the early morning hours of a Sunday. It was a time to which he would soon return. It was still dark in the early morning, so he could take advantage of the blackout while avoiding the heavy police presence that evening now brought to this part of the S-Bahn. Moreover, the trains tended to be relatively empty early on Sundays as many people had that day off from work and were still asleep at home. Fewer people on the train meant there was more of a chance that Ogorzow would be able to find a woman traveling alone.

Five hours later, around noon, workers for the railroad stumbled across Mrs. Büngener. By then, she had died from her injuries. The workers had to be careful as she was lying near the third rail, which had 750 volts of direct current flowing through it to power the

S-Bahn trains. As such, it posed a serious electroshock hazard. These workers contacted the police immediately.

At first, the police thought that this was a suicide, given that such events were common right before Christmas, and the victim had on her person a piece of paper that declared her psychologically unfit to work. This note was an attestation from a doctor.

Upon examination of the area around her body, however, investigators found her belongings approximately one thousand feet down the railway. It was not possible for her to throw herself off the train to commit suicide and then somehow throw her belongings afterward. Someone had to have tossed them out of the moving train.

If Mrs. Büngener had committed suicide and someone had been in the same train compartment, the police wondered why they would throw her stuff away, rather than leave it on the train or keep it. There was tobacco, which was a valuable commodity during this time of wartime rationing and shortages. There was also money.

Paul Ogorzow never stole from his victims. Perhaps he felt bad about what he had done and wanted nothing to do with their bodies once he had finished attacking and sexually assaulting them. He had a good working-class job, but he was not so well off that the money in his victim's handbags would have meant nothing to him. If he had taken their money and valuables, it would have had the added benefit, from his perspective, of possibly leading the police astray as to his motive. They might have then believed that someone was throwing women from the train not out of a sexualized compulsion, but for the far more mundane reason of wanting to rob them. The violence might then be seen as an attempt to avoid having a witness that could go to the police.

So if he had stolen from his victims, not only would Ogorzow have been able to spend his victims' money and smoke their tobacco, but the police might have been wasting time looking into muggers and purse snatchers instead of a more productive path of investigation.

Unlike some other serial killers, Paul Ogorzow never kept souvenirs or trophies of his kills. He never took anything from them, even something of no economic value, such as a torn bit of clothing or lock of hair. He did not take anything from the scene of his crimes either, like a bit of dirt or foliage from one of his garden area attacks. Nor did he revisit crime scenes to relive the memories of his attacks. He returned to the same general area to hunt again, but he did not return to the exact locations of his past crimes.

It would have been better for the police if he had taken souvenirs. If he had taken, say, an item of clothing from each victim, it would not have confused the police as to motive, but it would have given them something concrete to search for when they finally did have a suspect. Distinctive souvenirs mean that the police will someday have an easy case if they find this collection in the possession of the killer.

Given the discovery of the victim's tossed out belongings, it was clear to the police on the scene that this was no suicide, despite the doctor's note about Mrs. Büngener's mental state.

This meant that it was a case for the Kripo, which quickly linked it to the other women attacked on the S-Bahn.

Lüdtke came down to the scene and examined the body as best he could without moving it. His initial thought was that the attacker had choked Mrs. Büngener by grabbing her neck and then thrown her still-living body off the train. While her body remained lying on the side of the tracks, it was hard to tell what injuries she had sustained from the attack on the train and what damage had come from the fall off the train.

Dr. Weimann arrived at the scene after Lüdtke. Weimann took a look at Mrs. Büngener's body and was able to determine that she had been hit in the head. Lüdtke's initial thought that she had been choked was wrong. Dr. Weimann determined that she died from injuries to her skull and internal damage to her body caused by the fall from the train. All of this suggested to both men that this was the work of the S-Bahn Murderer, as the man who attacked women on the train had come to be called.

Furthermore, the police speculated that the change in this criminal's time of attack from late at night to the early morning suggested that he was aware of the hours that the police monitored the trains. Lüdtke mentioned that the S-Bahn night shift had ended at six that morning. This fact, he reasoned, might explain the timing of this attack.

Regardless of the reason for this change in the killer's pattern, it meant the police needed to stretch their resources even thinner to cover this time on the train as well as the late night shifts they had focused on until now.

## CHAPTER TWENTY

# The Attacks Continue

Wilhelm Lüdtke had the two women who survived attacks on the S-Bahn look through photos of thousands of S-Bahn workers. These were Gerda Kargoll and Elizabeth Bendorf. They did not recognize anyone. He also ordered his officers to monitor the S-Bahn and use decoys not just at night, but also in the early morning hours. This used a great deal of manpower, but he felt that he had to do this given that the latest attack had occurred in the morning.

During the early morning hours of Sunday, December 29, 1940, Paul Ogorzow again took to the S-Bahn to hunt for a victim. He had the same iron bar hidden inside his uniform's jacket sleeve so he was ready to strike when he had the opportunity. Near the Karlshorst S-Bahn station, he had his chance when it was just a female passenger and him traveling in the second-class train compartment. Her name was Mrs. Gertrud Siewert and she was forty-six years old.

Ogorzow released his iron rod from where he was concealing it inside his jacket sleeve. He then walked over to Mrs. Siewert, raised the iron rod up high, and brought it down hard on her head. He was now careful to conduct his attacks in such a way that his victim had no idea what was coming until she felt the blow to her head, or at most saw it coming a split second beforehand. Either way, she was unable to defend herself. And by now Ogorzow had become skilled at hitting women in the head with blunt metal objects, so one hit would be enough to stun if not kill them. As the saying goes, practice makes perfect.

With this hit to Mrs. Siewert's head, she went limp. Ogorzow thought she was dead. As in other attacks, he did not take the time to actually check if she had a pulse, was breathing, or had any other sign of life.

He opened the train door and dragged her body over. The dim illumination on the train meant that only a small amount of light bled out into the night. With this bit of backlighting, Ogorzow savored this moment as he felt his victim's body and then hurled it out onto the side of the railroad tracks.

He had thrown Mrs. Siewert off the moving train around six-twenty in the morning. It was about three hours before sunrise. Although Ogorzow believed he had been handling a corpse, Mrs. Siewert was still alive. She'd survived Ogorzow's blow to her head. She even survived the fall from the train, but just barely.

That morning, Mrs. Siewert was found alive on the side of the train tracks between the Karlshorst and Rummelsburg stations. The police also located her belongings strewn along the railway. As in prior S-Bahn attacks, they'd been thrown out after her.

The authorities rushed her to the hospital for medical attention. She arrived there alive but died later that day. While the fall from the train caused serious injuries to her bones, Dr. Weimann ruled that the initial blow to the head was the cause of her death. This was the third murder on the S-Bahn. Including the attempted murders, Mrs. Siewert was the fifth woman to be attacked and thrown from the train so far. It was also the second time that the killer had struck on a Sunday morning.

Paul Ogorzow felt the overwhelming urge to kill again soon. It is common that serial killers accelerate like this and have less and less time between attacks. It was only a week later, on Sunday, January 5, 1941, that he returned to riding the S-Bahn looking for a woman traveling alone.

During the early morning hours, he found twenty-seven-year-old Mrs. Hedwig Ebauer. She was five months pregnant, although Ogorzow would later claim that he had not noticed this detail in the darkened conditions on board the train. This time Ogorzow did not have a weapon with him, such as the lead cable or iron bar he'd used in previous attacks. He used his hands to choke her with a strong grip around her neck. Mrs. Ebauer fought back though. She damaged her hands with her punches to Ogorzow. He reacted by punching and kicking her. Despite her struggling against him, Ogorzow succeeded in choking her into unconsciousness.

He opened the train door and felt the rush of cold winter wind as he looked out into the darkness of a blacked out Berlin. He then dragged Mrs. Ebauer's inanimate body to this opening and threw her from the train while it was in motion between stations.

That morning Mrs. Ebauer was found, still alive, by the side of the train tracks near the Wuhlheide S-Bahn station. Like Ogorzow's prior victim, she arrived at the hospital alive but died there that same day. She never regained consciousness. Her death was determined to be the result of head injuries sustained during her fall from the train, and not from Ogorzow's attack on her while they were on board. That she had not died from the actual attack on the train, unlike some of Ogorzow's victims, was probably the result of his not hitting her with a weapon but instead using his hands and feet to attack her.

This was Ogorzow's third attack in the early hours of a Sunday morning. Based on their knowledge of the train system, when and where Ebauer was found, and the fact that the killer appeared to exclusively attack in the second-class section, the police were able to determine in which train compartment she had probably been attacked. They came to the conclusion that the assault had likely occurred in train compartment number 6439.

For a moment, it seemed like this could be a promising lead. Perhaps there would be evidence in this compartment that would lead the police to the killer. Once the detectives made this determination, they quickly tried to track down this train compartment.

When the detectives located the compartment and entered it for an inspection, they were bitterly disappointed. It had been cleaned since the attack. This meant that any evidence the killer might have left behind had been destroyed.

The body count on the S-Bahn was adding up. Including his

latest victim, Hedwig Ebauer, Paul Ogorzow had now attacked six women while riding the S-Bahn, killing four of them. This figure did not include those women he had attacked on the ground.

By now, many Berliners had heard rumors that a killer of women rode the S-Bahn during the blackout hours. Even without Lüdtke making a public announcement that a serial killer prowled the trains, word leaked out eventually.

Lüdtke pushed hard to be allowed to publicize this case in order to obtain tips that might enable him to find the murderer. He wanted to make a radio announcement of the case and its associated reward, to reach out to the people of Berlin. Reich Minister of Propaganda Joseph Goebbels refused his request.

Goebbels used films, radio programs, speeches, posters, newspapers, magazines, and more to spread the messages that he considered to be in the Nazi Party's best interest. Stories that he believed made the Reich look bad, such as that the German Police could not stop a serial killer from murdering women in the heart of the Reich, went nowhere.

While Lüdtke did not get from Goebbels the kind of press exposure for this case that he wanted, he did get something. Goebbels approved the use of up to two thousand flyers announcing a reward. Lüdtke wanted permission to print more information sheets, as this seemed a small number to him. In response to this request, Goebbels told Lüdtke no.

Somehow, Lüdtke eventually managed to get an article on this case placed in a Berlin newspaper called *Das 12 Uhr Blatt* (the *12 O'Clock Journal*). On January 7, 1941, this paper ran an article with the headline "Attacks on the S-Bahn" and the subtitle "Who knows the criminal?" The article explained the case as follows:

For some time, a man has been making trouble on the S-Bahn line between Rummelsburg and Erkner—he has tried in different ways to attack women who use the S-Bahn and throw them out of the trains. Repeatedly, he has abused women with rough physical violence. Mainly, women have been endangered who were riding alone in the second class. Up to now, the criminal has not stolen anything from the victims.

He is described as follows: 1.6–1.65 meters tall, medium-strength physique, drooping shoulders, a forward-inclined head, and a sloppy gait. He was wearing a dark coat—maybe a shunter's coat, as used by the railway—and a cap belonging to a railroad employee, which he wore pulled down.

The possibility must be considered that not all crimes committed by this criminal have been made known to the police. All fellow Germans who may have already made useful observations or may continue to do so on the aforementioned S-Bahn line, or who know a man similar to the afore-described individual, are being asked to immediately report to the criminal investigations department in Berlin, Alexanderplatz, Dircksenstraße 13/14— room 902, phone number 51 00 23, extensions 699 or 738—or with any other police department.[1]

While this article did give specifics on what was known about the perpetrator of these crimes and included speculation that his uniform was, in fact, a railroad uniform, it was light on the gruesome details of his crimes. It also omitted specifics such as the names of his victims or even how many of them there had been. Still, this was a rare bit of press that Lüdtke hoped would result in useful leads that would enable him to solve this case.

## CHAPTER TWENTY-ONE

# Volunteer Duty

On Tuesday, January 28, 1941, Lüdtke distributed a document to the police working for him to catch the S-Bahn Murderer. It let them know that his attempts to get approval from Goebbels for a radio announcement related to this case had failed. As a consolation, he stated that approval had been granted to use the resources of local party organizations as needed to try to catch this killer.

Manfred Woge, a now elderly resident of the garden area near the S-Bahn tracks where Paul Ogorzow attacked women, recalled that even as a ten-year-old boy he knew that there was a killer of women hunting in the garden area. "There was a general uneasiness among the people here—especially, of course, among women. Every-where there were rumors about what actually was happening—

where the man was coming from, where he was always headed. This area was full of trees—everything was shadowy . . . dark . . . narrow alleys . . . little lighting . . . blackouts because of the war. A person could really hide himself very easily."[1]

Although news of a serial killer on the loose, attacking women on a train, would dominate the news in a society with a free press, here there was only minimal coverage that Lüdtke managed to obtain despite Goebbels's express orders not to publicize the case, except in very limited ways.

Rumors, however, had spread, down to the level of even ten-year-old boys like Manfred Woge.

Commissioner Wilhelm Lüdtke pushed hard with Joseph Goebbels to be allowed to do more to involve and protect the public. The killings appeared to be escalating, as the perpetrator had gone from around a month and a half between murders to a week. The police were well aware that acceleration was common with such offenders, and they found it worrisome. Unless they caught this offender soon, he would kill again.

While Joseph Goebbels got in the way of this investigation by limiting press coverage of it, he did try to protect the women of Berlin through another office he held in the Third Reich. In his capacity as gauleiter of Berlin, Goebbels organized a program for unaccompanied women to be able to travel with a trusted man during their nighttime commute.

Not just any man would be used for this job; the call for volunteers was not made to the public at large. It was not even made broadly to Aryan men without criminal records. The only people that Goebbels trusted to protect women traveling alone at night were party members and Brownshirts (as SA members were informally called). Goebbels's decree on this matter referred to this volunteer task as a service of honor.

Ironically, Paul Ogorzow volunteered for this program of traveling with women on the train and then walking them home. His activities in the SA qualified him as a trusted German in the eyes of the authorities, and so he was eligible to be a part of this endeavor. Because records were kept for this program, Ogorzow could not attack these women and get away with it. As Lüdtke later wrote, Ogorzow accompanied women, "of course without harassing them in the slightest way."[2]

Although he could not safely use this program as a way to find victims to attack, it did provide him with certain benefits. Being a part of this volunteer duty would help him blend into the background of the case and look like someone the police should trust. A second benefit was that by being part of this group, he might be privy to information from the police and gossip with his fellow volunteers about the investigation into his crimes.

On Tuesday, February 11, 1941, Ogorzow spent the early evening accompanying women who would otherwise have been riding the S-Bahn alone. Unlike all the other volunteers, he had no fear that the S-Bahn Murderer might attack while he rode the train protecting a lone woman. It must have been a bizarre feeling for him to be a part of a program protecting women from himself.

He would go out at night on a volunteer shift and have to pretend that he was keeping an eye out for the killer. Riding the train and walking a woman home from the S-Bahn station in the dark of the blackout, he would need to look around to make sure it was safe. If he seemed too casual and not at all concerned, as if he were protecting a woman from a threat that did not exist, he risked her saying something to the police or the organizers of this service. The last thing he wanted was for anyone to become suspicious of him.

The women that he walked home at night had no clue that they were accompanied by the very killer they feared.

Just in case he did have the opportunity to use it, he often carried his iron bar with him. He wouldn't use it on one of the women he was assigned to protect, though. He was well aware that if he were to do so, then the police would quickly catch him.

If he came across an opportunity that night to attack a woman who was not assigned to him, then he could use his hidden iron bar without this same fear of being caught. So while was he was serving volunteer duty protecting women, he brought with him this weapon that he'd used to kill before. It must have been frustrating for him to feel the weight of the iron bar while alone with a woman and yet know that he could not safely use it to attack her.

Odds were that he would be arrested within a day of such an attack. Someone would find the body and alert the police. The police would then look into the woman's movements and find that that she had used this volunteer program and been assigned to Mr. Paul Ogorzow. Although he was a party member in good standing, a family man, and an employee with a good work record, he would have a tough time convincing the police that he was not the killer. And even if the police believed it possible that he'd delivered the woman safely to her desired destination and someone else had killed her, they would still look at Paul Ogorzow very closely and maybe find evidence tying him to his other crimes.

As strong as the desire was in Ogorzow to attack and kill women, he was able to control it. So he never attacked when he thought it was too dangerous, no matter how much he may have wanted to do so.

His volunteer shift ended without incident at ten on the night of February 11. Afterward, he was waiting on the platform of the Rummelsburg S-Bahn station, which was the same station that Lüdtke had earlier deduced to be a central location for the killer, when a woman came up to him.

Thirty-nine-year-old Mrs. Johanna Voigt was a mother of three and was three months pregnant. She was worried about the S-Bahn Murderer, so when she looked around the platform and saw Paul Ogorzow, she walked over and asked him if he would be willing to accompany her on the train to the Karlshorst station. This was a spontaneous request by Mrs. Voigt and not part of the organized accompaniment program. She either trusted Ogorzow because of his uniform, or did not understand that she needed to check in with someone to be a part of the volunteer program authorized by Goebbels.

So no one knew that she was with Ogorzow. Unlike the women he'd accompanied earlier that night as a volunteer, if something happened to Mrs. Voigt, he would not be a suspect.

From Ogorzow's perspective, a wasted night suddenly had potential. And he was ready to take advantage of this opportunity. He told Mrs. Voigt that he would ride the train with her to Karlshorst, which was only one station away.

Once the train arrived, they entered the empty second-class compartment together. As the train left, Ogorzow pulled the iron bar he'd used in prior attacks out from his jacket sleeve. He needed to attack now, as Mrs. Voigt was only riding the train to the next station. Ogorzow slammed the iron rod down hard on Mrs. Voigt's head. He didn't want to take any chances that she might still be able to function despite this blow, and so he quickly hit her again and again.

Sometime during this attack, she lost consciousness. Paul Ogorzow now opened the train door and dragged her body to it. With the train still in motion, and the wind blowing past him into the compartment, he threw Mrs. Voigt's body off the train.

Although Mrs. Voigt had been alive when Ogorzow threw her from the train, she did not survive long afterward. By the time she was found she was dead. Dr. Weimann concluded that she'd died as a result of a combination of the blows to her head from a blunt object and injuries resulting from being thrown from a moving train. Of course, her three-month-old fetus did not survive either. This was the second pregnant woman that Ogorzow had killed on the train.

While the police did not find any clues on Mrs. Voigt's body, Kripo commissioner Wilhelm Lüdtke did notice the absence of something. As he later wrote, "It was striking that in several cases the ticket of the victim was missing. It was concluded that the offender, in order to approach his victims quietly, may have been known as a ticket inspector."[3]

The police were thinking that the killer might be a ticket inspector or merely be pretending to be one. They believed that the S-Bahn Murderer might have used this as an excuse to approach women on the train without scaring them. These missing tickets could have been evidence of that, or it could be that some of his victims had boarded the train without tickets, or that their tickets had been lost in the struggle on the train and the ensuing tumult when their attacker threw them and then their belongings off the moving train.

In the case of Mrs. Voigt, the police were wrong. Paul Ogorzow had not approached her. She had approached him, and it had nothing to do with her ticket. Although Lüdtke's theory made sense given the absence of a ticket in some of the cases, he was mostly wrong. Paul Ogorzow had not needed to pretend to be a ticket inspector when approaching women on the train. Instead, he had used his uniform to reassure them while they were alone and then suddenly attacked them.

He had discussed tickets with Gerda Kargoll when she accidentally traveled past her destination. Also, he had invited her and later Elizabeth Bendorf to ride in a second-class compartment even though they had tickets for third class. But he had not impersonated a ticket inspector in either case.

All the police work to date and the creation of a volunteer service to accompany women home had not been enough to prevent Mrs. Voigt's violent death.

## CHAPTER TWENTY-TWO

# Push to Catch the Killer

With the murder of another woman on the S-Bahn (Mrs. Voigt), the pressure on the police to catch the S-Bahn Murderer increased. Joseph Goebbels, Heinrich Himmler, and Reinhard Heydrich all wanted this case closed. And so Arthur Nebe, as head of the Kripo, was well aware that it was a priority to stop these killings. And he in turn pushed Lüdtke to stop this killer before he threw another woman from the train.

As part of this effort, the police regularly visited the Rummels-burg and Karlshorst S-Bahn stations in the hopes of finding the killer there. They also rode the rails, often while wearing the uni-forms of regular S-Bahn staff.

Given that the police had little to go on to catch their killer, other than a general description that could fit a huge percentage of the male population and the possibility that he worked for the railroad company, Lüdtke thought that their best hope lay in catching the killer in the act. As this was an important case, he was able to use a large amount of manpower to pursue the S-Bahn Murderer.

In addition to deploying men to train stations, Lüdtke orchestrated massive roundups of train riders at key times. Ogorzow had established a recent pattern of attacking women during the early morning hours of Sunday on a single S-Bahn route. So around six in the morning on a Sunday, Lüdtke had his detectives and large numbers of uniformed police round up everyone riding the train and waiting on the platforms on this route. This took hundreds of policemen, as all eight stations that Lüdtke focused on needed to be checked simultaneously. The S-Bahn was halted at the platform and the police went through and checked for any signs of foul play and anyone that they found to be suspicious. They also looked for men carrying weapons, especially the heavy blunt instruments that their suspect favored.

Nothing of substance resulted from this search, other than a bunch of inconvenienced train passengers and tired policemen. Lüdtke tried a second time the following Sunday, and then again a third time, on another Sunday. Each time took a few hundred police officers and shut down a huge part of this subway line. The police found only minor offenders who did not interest the Kripo investigators. Despite these carefully planned searches of train riders, Lüdtke failed to locate his killer among the Sunday morning riders on this stretch of the S-Bahn.

In addition, Lüdtke obtained permission from higher-ups to place a newspaper article that gave more details on this case and the latest attack of February 11, on Mrs. Voigt. On February 14,

Valentine's Day, 1941, the German newspaper *Der Westen* ran an article about the S-Bahn Murderer:

### WOMEN THROWN OUT OF S-BAHN TRAINS
#### Four Dead to Date—
#### Who Knows the Criminal?—
#### 13,000 Mark Reward

As was made known by the press at the beginning of January, since late-autumn 1940, there has been an unknown man causing trouble on the S-Bahn line between Rummelsburg and Erkner, mostly near the Karlshorst area; he has attacked lone women and thrown them out of moving trains. Four of these women have died from their injuries. Mostly, women have been endangered who were riding alone in the second class. To date, the criminal has committed the crimes in the late evening or early morning, as well as on Sunday mornings.

On the 11th of February, 1941, shortly after 10 P.M., the body of . . . Mrs. Johanna Voigt of Berlin-Friedrichshagen, Friedrichs Straße 37, was found about in the middle of the Rummelsburg-Erkner line between Rummelsburg and Karlshorst, lying right next to the S-Bahn tracks. On this same line, about 300 meters from the place of her discovery and about 50 meters from one another, a woman's hat and an empty market bag, as well as a bundle of lingerie, and a wash cloth wrapped in cellophane were found. Near the body, there was a glove; the other was missing.

The woman was most likely also thrown out of a moving S-Bahn train. According to the external circumstances, the incident must be related to the aforementioned ones, which have occurred on this line since last autumn and resulted in death for lone women.

The motives out of which the criminal is acting are not yet known. Despite an emphatic manhunt, he has not yet been identified. However, because he must be rendered harmless—in order to prevent future events—all German people are being asked to help in his capture. Every piece of information, even things which seem unimportant, could be decisive in solving this crime. All news which leads to the identification or capture of the criminal will be rewarded with 13,000 RM. The reward is only for people from the public and not for officials whose job it is to solve punishable deeds. The deployment of the money will follow the conclusion of the legal process.

Women traveling alone, namely those who use the second class, are being urgently asked to continue being careful. Description of the criminal: 1.60 to 1.67 meters tall, middle-physique, shoulders and head tending forward, sloppy (slouchy) gait, wrinkled face. Clothing: dark coat, and presumably a railway employee's cap. There is also the possibility that the criminal was wearing a railway-employee uniform or a similar uniform.

**Answers to the following questions are of special importance:**
  a. Who knows a person who fits the above description? (It might be that the criminal is now wearing civilian clothing)
  b. Which people are illegally wearing railway or similar uniforms (dismissed/laid-off railway employees etc.)?
  c. Who saw the above-described man on the line [meaning Rummelsburg-Erkner]– in particular, when and where?

d. Who has been harassed in the last few months by a man on the named railway line who did not report this to the police?

Written or verbal news, which will be handled completely confidentially if desired, is being accepted by the criminal commissioner's office M I, 2 in the police headquarters, Alexanderplatz, entrance Dircksenstraße 13/14, room 902, phone number 51 00 23, extensions 699 and 738. However, also all other police headquarters are able to accept notifications with reference to these announcements.[1]

As highlighted by this article, the already very substantial reward of ten thousand reichsmarks had gone up to thirteen thousand reichsmarks. This was in addition to the thousand-reichsmark reward still unclaimed for leading the police to Mrs. Gertrude Ditter's killer.

With the high amount of money on offer, it's not surprising that the police received a large number of tips from the public, despite the many limits the police faced in publicizing these rewards. In all, the police received about fifteen hundred tips. Investigating these possible leads would use a tremendous amount of manpower.

Ironically, the police publicizing the fact that the killer struck in the second-class compartments may have worked in Ogorzow's favor. The more aware the public was of the dangers of riding in second-class during the blackout, the fewer people would do so. While this would protect those travelers who changed their plans from traveling second class to riding in third class, it meant that second-class compartments would be even emptier. Ogorzow only struck when second class was empty of everyone other than his female victim and himself.

While Ogorzow might have to wait longer for a woman to ride in second class than he had before his attacks began, there still were women in Berlin who did not know that they should avoid riding in second class by themselves.

Another plus from Ogorzow's perspective was that fewer people riding second class meant that he was less likely to have someone enter the train as he was leaving it after one of his attacks. If someone boarded a second-class S-Bahn compartment just after Ogorzow had attacked a woman and thrown her from the train, then there was a small chance that even in the darkened conditions they might notice something amiss, perhaps some sign that a bloody struggle took place. And they might apprehend Ogorzow, or at least report what they saw to the police, along with a better description of him.

The description the police had so far was not a good one. The details listed in this news article could be any one of thousands of men who worked for the railroad company. And the police were not even certain that the killer actually worked for the S-Bahn. As they noted in a question in this article, they were looking into the possibility that he could be someone who was not supposed to have a National Railroad uniform, such as a former worker who had kept his uniform. They did not even know for certain that it was a genuine railway uniform—it could have been a fake that someone made. It also could have been stolen; during the blackout, thefts had become more common. And with the bombings of Berlin by Britain's Royal Air Force, when someone's house was bombed, sometimes those clearing the rubble or passing by stole things like clothing.

The police hedged their words regarding this uniform, as they were well aware that it might not be an S-Bahn uniform at all. They knew it could belong to another civilian or military service. It was a dark-colored, not particularly distinctive uniform, and the conditions in the train were not ideal for noting details.

As for harassment on the train, that was a good question, but it did not generate usable leads. Ogorzow did not harass women on the train other than when he was attacking them. And even then, he suddenly attacked; he did not spend time first bothering them. He was very focused on the tight timetable on which the S-Bahn forced him to operate. He only had a few minutes to attack his victims and then throw them from the train before it entered the next station.

Ogorzow continued to serve as a volunteer who escorted women to and from the S-Bahn during blackout hours. He never bothered any of these women. So he clearly was able to control himself enough not to harass women other than when he was actually attacking them.

In addition to responding to any other leads that came in on this case, the Kripo proceeded to investigate the possibility that the killer worked for the S-Bahn. Detectives interviewed thousands of S-Bahn workers—there were five thousand of them, in twenty-eight departments. Roughly a quarter of these could be eliminated based on their age, height, and other factors. The rest had to be questioned in person—a process that started in February 1941 and ended that July.

The police examined time cards to see who would have had the opportunity to commit these crimes. They had difficulty finding a viable suspect who was free to ride the rails for the times of the attacks. Going through all these records by hand was a huge task—most workers had irregular shifts, which made it hard to determine who could have committed these crimes.

Many of the attacks happened around the change in shifts, either from eleven at night to midnight, or from six to seven in the morning. So that seemed to suggest that the killer might be a train worker who was either starting or ending his work then.

According to his time card, Ogorzow worked during some of these times at a fixed location, so it appeared that he could not have been on the S-Bahn. When the police combed through the S-Bahn workers for potential suspects, he was eliminated as a possible perpetrator because, according to his work records, he could not have been present when these crimes were committed.

Although Nazi Germany generally kept very thorough and accurate records that were of tremendous use to the police during investigations such as this one, the paperwork for workers kept by the *Reichsbahn* was a mess.

Professor Laurenz Demps discussed the nature of this problem in relation to the investigation into the S-Bahn Murderer: "The structure of the *Reichsbahn* office in Berlin was complicated. At the beginning of World War II, the *Reichsbahn* was ordered to send employees into the occupied areas of Poland. These employees needed to be replaced and so employees from other duty stations were relocated—specifically, they were also relocated to Rummelsburg. So, what is complicated about this is that the displaced train worker had a new post, but his original post headquarters had his personnel file."[2]

It would take time to access all these records, which were kept in different locations, and try to find viable suspects within the large pool of men who worked for the S-Bahn in Berlin.

The police also talked with people who lived in the garden area. This population included roughly eight thousand people who needed to be interviewed. And the police also searched inside of people's residences there. It was an overwhelming and slow task.

Manfred Woge, a longtime resident of this area, remembered when the police came to his home to ask about this matter when he was a child. He recalled a ring of the doorbell and a family member opening the door, "and there was a detective who wanted to ask about a murder. In these times, if the police were at your door, even if they seemed to be harmless, it was a reason to be uneasy."[3]

With all the police activity on the trains, the killer stopped his attacks. Commissioner Lüdtke became convinced that he knew of their activities. He did not believe it to be a coincidence that just as they stepped up their surveillance on the S-Bahn, the murderer stopped killing women on it. Lüdtke later said, "Now I could not allow myself to be distracted from the fact that the perpetrator has a detailed knowledge of all our operations."[4]

## CHAPTER TWENTY-THREE

# A Dangerous Gambit

The very fact that Wilhelm Lüdtke was expending tremendous amounts of police resources on this case—with thousands of interviews, police staking out the train system, and so on—had resulted not in catching the killer, but in driving Ogorzow to wait to commit more attacks until he believed it was safe to do so again. This was a massive undertaking made all the more difficult by the limitations placed on Lüdtke's ability to reach out to the public for help in this matter.

Wilhelm Lüdtke held a secret meeting with his top detectives and shared his belief that the killer knew all about their work to catch him on the trains, which suggested that the killer worked for the railroad. This looked like an inside job. Until now, Lüdtke had coordinated his activities with the railroad company. He explained that the police would have to "continue the investigation even more intensively than before" while trying to conceal key details from railroad personnel.[1]

With all the police activity on the S-Bahn line that Ogorzow used and also, to a lesser extent, in the garden area near the train where he also victimized women, Ogorzow had stopped his criminal activities. Since he'd killed Johanna Voigt on February 11, 1941, he had not attacked any more women in the first half of 1941.

While there was a large police presence, Ogorzow decided to try to suppress his desire to kill women and wait the authorities out. There were hundreds of policemen spending an inordinate amount of time patrolling the trains and otherwise trying to catch him. Under any conditions, a state can only afford to use so many of its resources trying to catch one criminal. Each policeman riding the S-Bahn waiting for something to happen was one more cop that could have been tasked with something else.

And these were not normal times. The strain of this use of police resources was tougher with the many demands of the war, criminals taking advantage of the blackout conditions and bombings, and the Third Reich using police resources against their perceived enemies and those who did not fit into their white supremacist vision for Germany.

Ogorzow knew that this could not last forever. Eventually the police would ratchet down the resources they dedicated to catching him. This meant that he only needed to control himself until then. Time was on his side.

He continued to report to work, spend time with his wife and children, tend his cherry trees, and volunteer to accompany women who were too afraid to ride the S-Bahn alone. It was difficult, but the days turned into weeks. Weeks became months.

Lüdtke later wrote that as he "had very little evidence that could be used to convict the perpetrator, he had to try to catch him in the act" of attempting to attack a woman.[2] While the massive police presence on the trains did not result in the police catching the killer, he believed that it had "achieved a preventive effect" since the attacks had stopped.[3]

This was not a workable solution though. Lüdtke could not afford to indefinitely use all these policemen to prevent a single killer from striking again.

Police Commissioner Lüdtke now decided to take a bold move to try to flush out the killer. He felt confident that the killer was a train employee with a high-level of awareness of police activity, and he engaged in a dangerous gambit based on that belief.

He had his officers spread word in June that, as of July 1, 1941, "police monitoring [of the train and garden areas] will cease as it is obviously futile."[4]

Germany had just broken its treaty with the Soviet Union in a surprise invasion that started on June 22. With more than four million military men now fighting their way east as part of Operation Barbarossa, it seemed believable that the German Police needed to reallocate their resources. Having police out in force to protect the women riding this S-Bahn line and walking though this garden area was not something that could be sustained long-term, and recent events had made everyone in Berlin aware that Germany had use of men elsewhere.

On the date of this invasion, Lüdtke turned fifty-five years old. He could not afford to wait until his next birthday to catch this killer. He wanted the perpetrator of these crimes to return to the S-Bahn, in the belief that it would be safe to do so. And then the trap would slam shut, as the police still present on this rail line would catch the killer in the act. The police would not be gone, but would be deployed in new and less conspicuous ways.

Lüdtke was using hundreds of policemen to keep one part of the S-Bahn and one small area of land safe for women to travel alone at night. It was way too great a strain on resources already spread thin by the demands of a police state and the need for men in the German military. This entire investigation was a huge drain as well on the homicide division—they had been concentrating their attention on this single criminal and doing all they could to try to catch him.

The risk of this new plan was substantial. The intentional spreading of this rumor could be seen as giving the killer a green light to return to his old ways of hunting and killing women. And, of course, the risk would be borne by the women of Berlin and not by Lüdtke himself. If this went wrong, and the killer started attacking women again, they would be the ones to suffer.

The rumor reached Ogorzow's ears. He believed it and had no idea the Kripo had purposefully spread the story. He now felt free to attack again, although he believed that the garden area would be safer than the train line. Even with the false information that Lüdtke had put out, Ogorzow believed there to still be some police presence on the S-Bahn, if perhaps diminished.

He now returned to the S-Bahn, but not to kill there. This time he would kill on his old hunting ground of the garden area near the Rummelsburg S-Bahn station. It had been five months since his last attack.

During the early hours of July 3, 1941, Ogorzow left his work at the train company signal station. He was having an affair at this time with a woman whose husband was away in the German military. After leaving work, he stopped by her house in the hopes of having sex with her, but she was not home. He then returned to the S-Bahn and took the train to the Rummelsburg station. Despite the late hour eleven people besides Ogorzow got off the train at this station.

As Ogorzow looked out in the dim light that dispersed from open train doors, he saw ten women and one man exiting the train and walking on the platform. He watched the lone man and observed that he was walking with one of the women. The other nine women were alone. Ogorzow lingered behind as they passed through the ticket inspection area and exited the station.

Once out of the station, these people took different paths home. Ogorzow needed to think quickly here—he had to determine a target and follow her. He had no interest in the couple; he only attacked women whom he believed to be alone. Even when selecting lone women to attack, he was careful to pick petite women, as he did not want to risk a struggle with a larger, stronger woman who might be able to fight him off.

Of the nine potential victims, one walked down a path in the dark that Ogorzow thought would be the best place from which to attack. Her name was Mrs. Frieda Koziol, and she was thirty-five years old. None of the other women headed in this direction. Since he had followed her from the train, Ogorzow felt confident that she was alone. Unlike with a woman he randomly found walking around, he did not have to worry that there was anyone she knew following behind her.

Now that he had selected a target, Ogorzow increased his speed to catch up to her. He had needed to walk slowly before so he could see where everyone went and make his decision. He was wearing his work uniform, which often inspired women to trust him, and he tried to talk to Mrs. Koziol, asking if he could accompany her.

She rejected this offer. She did not stop to converse with Ogorzow. Instead, she kept walking. Despite his wearing a uniform, Mrs. Koziol was not about to chat with a man she did not know in an isolated and dark place late at night.

Ogorzow had his iron bar with him. He gripped it and raised it up in the air, then without warning slammed it down on the back of Mrs. Koziol's head, behind her ear.

She fell to the ground, and he then hit her in the head with the iron bar over and over again. He used so much violence that her skull caved in. He then stopped hitting her and ripped the clothing off the lower part of her body and tore her shirt. The only things she now had on below her waist were her knee-high boots. In a photo of the crime scene, a mass of pubic hair can be seen.

As she lay there dying, Ogorzow raped her. She may even have already been dead. Ogorzow was not sure. He left her body where it was, naked below the waist. She was lying on her back on a dirt path with small plants all along her right side.

Afterward, Ogorzow disposed of the iron rod by throwing it near the train tracks leading into the Rummelsburg station. He did not bother trying to hide Mrs. Koziol's body. He'd never tried burying or otherwise concealing the bodies of his victims, beyond throwing the ones on the train off of it.

Mrs. Koziol's body was found around four-thirty in the morning on July 3. The police quickly moved to pursue all leads related to this new murder.

Although she was divorced, Mrs. Koziol's ex-husband was not

a suspect for long. The police were interested in him, as they always look at a victim's current and former romantic partners. He lived near the crime scene, in the garden plot area, with his girlfriend. That proximity to where his ex-wife was attacked intrigued police, but Mr. Koziol had an alibi, which the police decided was a valid one.

They determined that whoever had attacked Mrs. Koziol had also raped her, based in part on the semen recovered from her body.

The police came to view this as the work of the S-Bahn Murderer. Lüdtke felt like this attack made it even more likely that he was right about the earlier killing of a woman in this area—Mrs. Gerda Ditter—being the work of the same man who attacked women on the S-Bahn.

The commissioner had blood on his hands. If he had not made a show of lifting the police monitoring of the S-Bahn and the adjacent garden area, Ogorzow would probably not have attacked Miss Koziol. Lüdtke tried to justify this later on by writing, "The course showed that this consideration was correct but unfortunately the way the criminal responded was highly unlikely and it was not foreseen."[5]

Commissioner Lüdtke was right that the killer was aware of the police activity and changed his own actions based on it, but Lüdtke should have given more consideration to the possibility that his ploy would result in the killer striking again. And in a way that resulted not in him being caught, but in a woman dying.

Later in life, Lüdtke explained this decision by pointing out that he'd expected to catch the perpetrator in the act of trying to assault a woman, even though it did not work out that way. His main rationalization was that by allowing the killer to feel free to attack, a new avenue of investigation was opened up, based on this most recent crime. He wrote in an article, "It is so very unfortunate that yet another human life fell victim to this criminal, yet the harshness of this fateful event can possibly be alleviated by the fact that this new murder led to new ways to investigate these crimes."[6]

## CHAPTER TWENTY-FOUR

# A Red Herring

Near the corpse of Frieda Koziol, the police found clear shoeprint impressions in the dirt.

They tried to track the prints, but lost the trail about fifty meters from the body. They concluded that the trail disappeared because the person in question had been running, which made it harder for the police to track him.

Wilhelm Lüdtke believed that these shoeprints belonged to the killer. The body had not been there long. As best the police could extrapolate from the scene, whoever had left the prints had bent down on both knees by the body and had then gotten up and run away from the scene. The footprints barely showed this person's heels, which indicated that he began to run after kneeling by the body.

Weather conditions resulted in a tight time frame for the creation of these prints. They could not have been old prints that somehow, miraculously, happened to be in a place that fit the narrative of someone standing by this body, inspecting it, and leaving it. It had rained around midnight that night, and the crime itself had occurred one or two hours later. So the rain would have destroyed any footprints created before then.

The police took photographs of the prints next to an L-shaped wooden ruler to document their size and features. In addition, they made a plaster mold of one of the shoe prints. They could tell that the sole was a rubber one with a very distinctive tread pattern. One side of the sole had rubber tread in a solid line, while the other had it in small box-like figures. The front of the sole had a shape like a collapsed tower, while the inside pattern had small boxes on top of solid lines.

From this mold, they later determined that whoever had made these prints had been wearing a shoe manufactured by a company called Salamander. The brand name was *Fußarzt*, which means "podiatrist." The size was a men's thirty-nine and a half.[1] This was a specialized shoe, with extra thick rubber soles, and German businesses kept extensive records, especially with a complicated system of rationing in place.

Rationing had started in Germany on August 26, 1939, with gasoline. This rationing was another reason why the S-Bahn was so important a form of transportation in Berlin. During World War II, with civilians having very limited access to fuel in Berlin, such public transportation helped alleviate the disaster that gas rationing would be in a large city without such a system.

The day after the gas rationing started, the government

announced that a host of consumer items, including shoes, would require rationing cards. This was shortly before Germany invaded Poland. When the full rationing went into effect on Monday, August 28, 1939, people in Berlin could see signs of the impending war everywhere around them. The city was congested with soldiers traveling through on their way east toward Poland.

One could still get food at restaurants by paying the bill, or buy a Christmas tree for the holidays, but most everything else required that one clip a small box on a ration card. These ration cards were issued by the German government.

As for shoes, the meager rations provided to Jews in Berlin did not include shoes. So that suggested that it was highly unlikely that a Jew would have a new pair of specialized shoes such as this suspect wore.

Lüdtke thought that these shoes would be the clue to solve this case. His detectives followed up on this print, going to shoe shops in the area and finding out the names of all the men who had bought this size and model. Out of this group, they were hoping to find the man who had left the shoeprint behind at the crime scene. They believed that this man was likely to be the S-Bahn Murderer.

Once they gathered these names, they eliminated those who were not in the Berlin area during the time of the crime. Since many men were not at home, having been sent to the far reaches of German-controlled territory as part of the war effort, this eliminated a large portion of the potential suspects.

Of those remaining, many lived in areas of Berlin that were far from the scene of the crime. However, the police did have one purchaser of these shoes who lived in the garden area, within walking distance of the murder scene.

A carpenter named W. Heimann had bought a pair of these shoes in the same size being sought by the police. And he lived three hundred feet from the crime scene, in the garden colony Gutland I.

The police checked to see if he had a criminal record and found that he had a prior conviction for a sex crime, albeit a relatively minor one of spying on a couple having sex. Still, that did mark him as a pervert in the eyes of the law, and so the police were optimistic that they might have found their man.

They picked Heimann up and interrogated him. He denied knowing anything about this crime or even being at the crime scene. Meanwhile, they searched his home and took the clothing items they found there and on his person to the forensics lab. The police hoped to find blood spatter on his clothes that matched the blood types of the various victims of the S-Bahn Murderer. They also hoped to find a uniform, perhaps from the National Railroad, that would be consistent with reports that the killer wore a dark uniform.

They found no such uniform and did not find any other incriminating evidence that would tie the suspect to the crimes. They did however compare the tread on Heimann's shoes to that of the plaster mold made of a shoeprint at the Frieda Koziol crime scene. Although new shoes of this size and model would have matching treads on the bottom, as the shoes were worn, the treads would develop a new pattern based on how the wearer allocated his weight, little bits of gunk and stones that caught in there, scuffs, and other signs of wear and tear.

The National Institute of Justice recently explained that a shoeprint creates an impression that in turn can be checked for a pattern: "Impression evidence is created when two objects come in contact with enough force to cause an 'impression.' . . . Pattern evidence may be additional identifiable information found within an impression. For example, an examiner will compare shoeprint evidence with several shoe-sole patterns to identify a particular brand, model or size. If a shoe is recovered from a suspect that matches this initial pattern, the forensic examiner can look for unique characteristics that are common between the shoe and the shoeprint, such as tread wear, cuts or nicks."[2]

The Kripo properly documented this three-dimensional impression evidence and looked at the pattern to determine the kind of shoe they were after. They collected the shoes of the suspect and carefully checked them against the photos and mold of the prints found at the scene. They had a match.

Although the suspect denied it, the police were now certain that he had been at the scene of the crime within the tight time frame dictated by the weather. And he had a record, which marked him in their eyes as a sexual deviant who might have escalated to more serious crimes against women.

However, he had no connection to the S-Bahn system, other than occasionally riding it, the same as almost everyone else in Berlin. He was a carpenter, so even in Nazi Germany, where uniforms were rife, he did not wear one to work. And he did not have outside activities, such as involvement with Nazi groups, that would provide him with a uniform. Of course, he could have stolen a uniform or created one himself, but the police could not find anything like that in their search of his residence.

Although he denied knowing anything about this crime at first, the police continued to question him. They held him for three days and interrogated him eight times before he admitted to being at the crime scene. This confession occurred when he was confronted with the shoe pattern evidence. He told the police that he had stumbled upon the body in the dark and then fled when he realized that this woman was dead.

This man was another kind of criminal who prowled Berlin during the blackout to hunt women, but he did not attack them. He was a Peeping Tom who took advantage of the darkness to sneak up on houses and peer through any uncovered portions of the windows. He also stole things at night, small things, such as the occasional purse or clock.

He'd already been arrested for such a crime before, and so he panicked when he found a dead body. He was afraid that as a sexual offender, who took advantage of the blackout, he could be facing very harsh penalties, including being shipped off to a concentration camp and/or being castrated.

He had an even bigger worry than that, though. He understood that the police were under pressure to solve this case, and he would make a good scapegoat because there was evidence tying him to a crime scene. He had a history as a sexual offender, and he had no faith at all in the judicial process of the special courts used by Nazi Germany to try such crimes. They moved fast, had little in the way of protections for defendants, and their death sentences were carried out swiftly.

It took a while for Lüdtke to believe him, but Heimann had solid alibis for the times of some of the S-Bahn Murderer's crimes. Lüdtke and his detectives were disappointed that this promising clue had led to a dead end, but they did have the consolation prize of having caught a Peeping Tom.

If they had been tempted to pin the crimes on this man anyway, the biggest deterrent from doing so would have been the fact that the real killer was still out there. So even though it would have been simple to frame Heimann and thus reassure the public and their superiors that the matter was solved, it would have blown up in their faces if the crimes continued to occur. And serial killers rarely quit on their own, so it was unlikely that the killer would stop, even if he heard that someone else had been caught for his crimes.

## CHAPTER TWENTY-FIVE

# In Police Custody

About a week after this last murder, the police experienced their big break in the case, although they had no idea at the time how important this new lead would be. They had been questioning thousands of railroad employees in order to see if any of them were suspect in any way or could provide any information that might help in the investigation.

After having determined that a particular railroad worker they were interviewing was not a suspect, the Kripo detectives would conclude their interview with this now standard question: "Have you noticed anything suspicious about any of your coworkers?"

This particular worker replied that while he did not know the identity of the killer, he had seen a coworker ditch his job by climbing a fence. Then, much later, this coworker returned to the job before anyone in charge had noticed that he'd left his post. When he asked this man where he was going, he replied that he was going to see a woman. He did not know the man's name, but he could describe him. He also told the police that the work site in question was the signal tower Vnk at the S-Bahn Rummelsburg station. These were enough details for the police to be able to follow up and determine the identity of this mystery railway employee.

This coworker turned out to be Paul Ogorzow, who had worked for years near the Rummelsburg S-Bahn station. The police looked at Ogorzow's work record and saw that he had a certificate for good service issued by his superiors and that there were no complaints against him. And the vast majority of the criminal acts the police were investigating occurred during times that he was at work. They had talked with him before, as they had talked with most railway workers and people who lived near the garden area.

The police had cleared him on the basis that he was working at the time of some of the attacks. They noted three different times that he was on duty when attacks occurred, including one time he was manning a telegraph, a task the police thought it would be impossible for him to leave without getting in trouble with his superiors.

Ogorzow had not looked to the Kripo like whatever they imagined a serial killer would be like. He appeared to be a happily married family man, a loyal party member and Brownshirt, whose only interest outside his work and family was tending the fruit trees in his garden. His superiors gave him high marks for the quality of his work. There was some grumbling by his coworkers that he said offensive things about women at times, but nothing that suggested he hated women so much that he killed them.

Now the police took another, much closer look at him. When

the detectives looked in detail at his work records, they realized that the activities that provided him with alibis for certain murders could not be corroborated.

During these times, Ogorzow was working alone, with duties that he could have temporarily abandoned without being caught by his employers. The police now knew that he would sometimes climb over a fence to ditch work. They also realized that he could simply walk to the S-Bahn station closest to his workplace and ride the rails from there.

This made him a potential suspect; although the police were far from certain that he was their man. This was simply another lead to be investigated—one of many generated by the extensive interviews with thousands of railroad personnel.

At six-forty-five in the morning on Saturday, July 12, 1941, Kripo Detective Georg Heuser went to Ogorzow's apartment with two lower-ranked officers for backup. They picked up Ogorzow without incident and brought him back to their station for questioning.

This same day the United Kingdom and the Soviet Union signed a formal agreement, the Anglo-Soviet Agreement, to fight together against Germany. This was a huge turning point in the war, as until Germany had attacked the Soviets three weeks ago, a nonaggression pact had been in place between Germany and the Soviet Union.

Lüdtke studied the file he had on Paul Ogorzow. It showed a married man with kids, a Nazi Party member in good standing, and a sergeant in the SA. He'd been employed by the railroad for a long time and worked his way up to his current position. Lüdtke thought that the description that they had, as conflicted and vague as it was owing to the blackout conditions, did not particularly match Ogorzow, other than that he was the right general size. Most noticeably,

Ogorzow had a striking nose that no one had mentioned in their descriptions of the S-Bahn Murderer.

As for his criminal record, Ogorzow's only entry did not suggest a sexual predator or murderer. It was for a break-in he'd committed with two others in 1932. He'd committed this crime in the town of Königs Wusterhausen, which was at the end of the line for one of the Berlin S-Bahn routes. He and his two accomplices had broken into an inn to steal things. He'd been unemployed at the time. For this crime, he was tried in the district court of the town of Nauen. The Nazis had not yet gained power, and the German government of the time was known as the Weimar Republic. Ogorzow's trial took place under their laws, and this court sentenced him to nine months in prison.

However, with Hitler and the Nazi Party gaining power in early 1933, things changed for Ogorzow. On March 21, 1933, Adolf Hitler handed President Hindenburg two documents to sign. One was for a full pardon of party members such as Paul Ogorzow. As a result of this amnesty, Ogorzow was a free man. Others who were set free that day included numerous other Nazis who'd been convicted of violent crimes.

Often sexual predators will have past crimes in their record that indicate their progression from relatively small-time crimes such as harassing women to the much more serious crimes of raping and killing. While Ogorzow had such an escalation in his criminal activities, it was not reflected in the paperwork the detectives had in front of them, as he had not been caught for any of his prior crimes against women.

Moreover, Ogorzow did not fit the preconceived notions that the police had developed early on in their case. A family man was not thought of as a serial killer—instead the image police generally associated back then with such crimes was a single man. Also, the racial ideology of the Third Reich meant that many of the detectives had focused on the usual suspects of their warped belief system— Jews, who had yet to be deported from Berlin to concentration camps, and foreigners, who were used as forced labor.

But Lüdtke had kept an open mind and come to believe that his suspect had to be someone who worked at the railroad company. So seeing Ogorzow's file did not result in Lüdtke letting him go. Instead, he had his men follow through on this possible break in the case.

When questioned by Detective Heuser, Ogorzow at first denied that he had ever left his workplace while he was supposed to be on the job. He also denied ever climbing the fence there. So for the moment, the police only had the word of one railroad employee against another.

Although the forensic science of the time was primitive compared to what we have now, there still was a great deal of evidence that could be gathered by examining Ogorzow's belongings. Though the police found nothing of interest in his home, they did confiscate his clothing and submitted it to their lab for inspection.

The police sent to the lab a combination of the clothes Ogorzow had been wearing when they brought him in and items they took during the search of his home. They later put together a list of these items as follows:

### ITEMIZATION. THE SECURED PIECES OF CLOTHING OF THE ACCUSED, PAUL OGORZOW:

1. a pair of ripped, blue pants,
2. a dark work-coat,

3. two terry-cloth towels, dirty,

4. a light-gray suit, complete (pants, vest and jacket),

5. a uniform-coat of the German State Railways,

6. a pair of uniform-pants of the German State Railways,

7. a uniform jacket of the Imperial German Forces with a white collar,

8. two uniform-caps,

9. a blue visor cap,

10. a pair of blue sports pants,

11. a silk sports shirt,

12. a pair of socks.[1]

In gathering these items, the police concentrated on things that Ogorzow could have been wearing during his various attacks on women, as well as anything he might have used to clean himself up afterward. As the police were not certain of exactly what uniform he'd been wearing, they took anything that was a uniform or resembled one. The towels were taken as well, as they were still dirty, and so if he'd wiped off blood or other evidence on them, it might still remain. If the towels had been laundered, they would not have bothered with them, as their forensic technology could not pick up usable evidence from washed items. Even today, that would be difficult to impossible, depending on what one was looking for. The most one could hope for in such a scenario would be fibers that might match something or a suspicious stain.

The uniforms, even if washed, would be potentially useful for determining if they looked familiar to any of the reports from witnesses in this case.

During his interrogation, the police refused to believe Ogorzow when he claimed that he had never abandoned his work post. As long as he was believed to have been at work at all the times he was supposed to be there, then he had an alibi for the time of many of the S-Bahn Murderer's crimes. He didn't need solid alibis for the times of all the crimes. It would be enough if his alibis held up for some of the crimes, as the police believed that one man had committed all of these attacks on the S-Bahn and in the garden area.

When confronted repeatedly by his coworker's statement that he'd seen Ogorzow ditch work, Ogorzow eventually admitted to leaving work by climbing the fence, but claimed that he had done so in order to secretly meet with a woman who lived nearby. According to Ogorzow, they had been carrying on an affair and he had lied to the police because he did not want to get in trouble for leaving work; nor did he want anyone to know of this sexual relationship, as they were both married. Her husband was away in the military.

When brought in by the police, this woman admitted to the affair. Ogorzow now had a credible explanation for ditching work and lying to the police about it, but he still had two problems. One was his demonstrated ability to leave work without being caught, which meant that he could no longer use his job as a meaningful alibi. If it had been just this, the police would have let him go. Lacking an alibi was not enough, even in Nazi Germany, for the Kripo to close the case. Besides, with thousands of railroad workers interviewed, there were bound to be some who did not have alibis for key times.

The second, and much more pressing problem for Ogorzow, was that the police lab found blood on his uniform. While the police were interviewing him, they had sent his uniform for a rush examination by the lab.

A microscope was needed to see this blood, so Ogorzow had not been aware that it had stained his uniform—both his jacket and his pants. A particularly incriminating, and disgusting, detail was that a large amount of blood was found in and around the crotch area of his pants, especially the zipper region. He'd already cleaned up anything that he could see himself, but there was enough blood remaining for the examiner to determine that it was of human origin, although not enough to run tests to establish blood type.

Again, Ogorzow tried to explain away the evidence against him. He had yet another plausible story: his wife had been very sick three days before, and in caring for her, he had gotten blood on his work clothing. The police then questioned his wife, who had no opportunity to consult with her husband. She confirmed that she had been sick, that she had bled on him, and that all this had happened on the same date that Ogorzow claimed it had.

As DNA testing did not yet exist, and there was not enough blood evidence to see if it was the same blood type as his wife's, the police now had no way to disprove Ogorzow's version of how it came to be there, given his wife's corroboration of his story.

Because Ogorzow did not know that blood type was a nonissue, he also provided a second explanation for any blood that did not match his wife's. He claimed that he'd injured his finger recently and wiped it on his clothes.

The problem for Ogorzow was that the forensics lab believed the bloodstain on his jacket to be the result of a struggle. The blood spatter on the jacket, in particular, did not fit a narrative of either wiping a bloody finger or helping his injured wife. Neither situation would explain why the blood found on his jacket appeared to be in a pattern consistent with him having violently attacked someone.

So the police viewed Ogorzow as a strong suspect. If it were not for this bloodstain pattern analysis, they would have probably let him go. Instead they detained him for on ongoing process over a period of days. The police were holding on to Ogorzow until they either were convinced he was their man or until they cleared him of involvement in this gruesome case.

## CHAPTER TWENTY-SIX

# The Interrogation

The police did not give up, and next they asked Ogorzow about the route that he took to get from work to his home. Until this line of inquiry, Ogorzow had answered questions quickly. He now took his time to answer, seeming to suspect a trap.

If he had been in the United States, this is the time when he might have invoked his Fifth Amendment right to silence and his Sixth Amendment right to a lawyer, but this was Nazi Germany, and as a practical matter, he had no such rights. He felt compelled to answer the questions being posed to him.

The police carefully got Ogorzow to admit that he took the S-Bahn home and then often walked through the garden area on the way to his apartment building. They then pointed out that a number of women had been harassed by a man wearing a railroad uniform along that route during the time that he would have been going to or from work.

The police were also interested in the bicycle that he often rode to and from the S-Bahn. This bicycle had a powerful dynamo light on it. Dynamo lights produce current from the usage of the bike itself. They were particularly practical during the wartime conditions in Germany, as they did not require that the user purchase batteries; instead the bicycle rider made his own power just by riding the bike around.

Ogorzow tried to deny that he had anything to do with the harassments in the garden area, but under intense questioning regarding the light on his bike and the women he would pass on his way home, he eventually admitted to the most low-level incidents along this route, ones where he had said something inappropriate, used a flashlight or his bike light to scare someone, or at most, grabbed a woman.

The police now felt increasingly confident that they had their man.

While the police investigated him, Ogorzow stayed in their custody. He was locked up at night and still held out hope that he would be able to survive this investigation and convince the police that they were on the wrong track. It was a frustrating and scary process for him, though. He had to go through a cycle of being interrogated and then being locked up and waiting to be interrogated again. As the time passed, it wore on him. And the police were using this time to investigate him further and so prepare to better interrogate him.

One day, during daylight hours, they took him from the station to the garden area. The Kripo demanded that Ogorzow show them the exact locations of the minor crimes to which he had confessed.

Ogorzow was confused about where each crime had taken place. He had committed so many crimes in this area, when one included all the flashlight attacks as well as the more serious offenses, that he had trouble keeping the different scenes straight in his head.

While he thought that he was admitting to very minor charges, the police were getting details out of him that placed him near serious attacks. He mistakenly admitted to an attack on a woman at the location of a felony assault—a local underpass of the railway Kaulsdorfer. He'd become confused and thought he was taking the police to a place where he had merely scared a woman by shining his flashlight on her.

Over the course of three hours, Ogorzow showed the investigators four locations that had been the settings for minor incidents, as well as mistakenly showing them a total of two locations where he had committed violent attacks that the police classified as attempted murders.

The police now had a connection between Ogorzow and two of the scenes where violent attacks occurred. He would have a hard time arguing that he'd engaged in minor harassments in the same exact place where such attacks had transpired. So the police were slowly and thoroughly building a case against him.

Next the police wanted to have two of the women who'd been assaulted in the garden area identify Ogorzow as the man who'd attacked them. The police had a long list of women who'd been attacked in the area, but they settled on these two as the best ones to possibly identify their attacker.

The police did not arrange a physical lineup of men in railroad uniforms who resembled Ogorzow in terms of height and build. Nor did they put together a collection of photos of such men, with one of Ogorzow added into the mix. The identification process they used did not reach that level of reliability.

Instead the police brought two women who had survived Ogorzow's garden attacks to confront him directly in the same area. The police pointed him out, while asking the women if this was the man who attacked them. Even with this highly suggestive process, while one woman said that she was certain Ogorzow was her attacker, the other one said that she could not tell.

For the one that did recognize him, the police had done the identification in a very dramatic way. This witness was Mrs. Gertrud Nieswandt, whom Ogorzow had stabbed in the neck in front of her parents' garden home.

The police started with Mrs. Nieswandt facing Ogorzow's back and then commanded Ogorzow to turn around. He had no idea why he was supposed to turn around, as the police did not tell him that someone was waiting to identify him. When he turned and was face-to-face with Nieswandt, she yelled that he was the one who had attacked her. She then spontaneously showed Ogorzow the long scar on her neck that he had made with a knife.

The police had taken Mrs. Nieswandt back to the area where the attack occurred in the garden allotments, and pointed out a single suspect, so there must have been a strong psychological desire in her to pick out this person as the one who had committed the crime.

In this case, he actually was the one who had attacked her, so it is entirely possible that Mrs. Nieswandt did genuinely recognize him, although that begs the question of why she had not been able to provide a more accurate description before this. His broken nose, for instance, was a very noticeable trait that none of the witnesses had ever mentioned. It's possible that she had subconsciously noticed details that her conscious mind did not have the ability to remember. In which case, the shock of seeing this person could have revived those subconscious impressions. Or perhaps she did not recognize him at all, but merely thought she did based on how this was set up.

If the police wanted a more meaningful identification, they should have done a lineup of similar-looking men wearing the same kind of clothes. Even that can be problematic, though, and these days, the preferred method of eyewitness identification is to use a sequential lineup or sequential photographs.

However, if the point of this process was not to make sure that the eyewitness had identified the right man, but to spook someone that the police were already confident was their man, then it was played just right.

Ogorzow behaved as if Mrs. Nieswandt identifying him as her attacker did not concern him at all, but it was just an act. He could see that he was in serious trouble.

On the way back to the station afterward, Ogorzow asked to speak to the man in charge of the Serious Crimes Unit. Commissioner Lüdtke agreed to this request and handled the interrogation himself. Ogorzow made this request because he was scared, and he mistakenly assumed that a high-level official like Lüdtke would help him out because of Ogorzow's status as a party and SA member.

## CHAPTER TWENTY-SEVEN

# The Confession

Ogorzow and Lüdtke sat together in an interrogation room. Even in Nazi Germany, Lüdtke still wanted a confession from Ogorzow in order to give prosecutors enough to convict him of the S-Bahn murders. Right now, he had enough evidence to arguably make a decent case for some of the garden attacks, but he had no real evidence tying Ogorzow to the S-Bahn attacks.

Lüdtke needed Ogorzow to confess. In order to do this, Lüdtke used a few props. He had the skulls of five of Ogorzow's victims sitting on a table. Dr. Weimann had previously cleaned them, so they were bleached white. Each skull had a decent sized hole in it from where it had been struck by a heavy blunt object.

Lüdtke kept the room darkened, but turned on a bright light so it illuminated this macabre exhibit.

Ogorzow and Lüdtke spent some time sitting there in silence. Suddenly, Ogorzow pleaded with him, saying, "You gotta help me!"[1]

Ogorzow explained that he was asking this as a loyal party member and SA *Oberscharführer* (senior squad leader). Given the violence Ogorzow had taken part in as a member of the SA, when he and his fellow brown-shirted thugs beat Jews and smashed up Jewish places of business and worship, he desperately hoped that his loyalty to the party might be enough to excuse his killings.

Lüdtke manipulated Ogorzow's pleas as a way to obtain a confession. Just as modern-day police may pretend to sympathize with a suspect so as to elicit the suspect's version of events, so did Lüdtke take advantage of this opening that Ogorzow had given him.

He told Ogorzow that before they could discuss what could be done to help him, Lüdtke needed to know what exactly he had done. Of course, Lüdtke had no intention of helping Ogorzow. His crimes were horrific, and the justice system in Nazi Germany would not let the murder of Aryan German women go unpunished merely because the perpetrator was a party member and Brownshirt.

For Lüdtke, his career was potentially on the line. His superiors knew that he had a likely suspect in custody, and his performance was being monitored.

Lüdtke bore primary responsibility for the investigation into the S-Bahn Murderer. He had demanded and employed large numbers of men and women on this case. Even with all these resources, and the large rewards, he had yet to solve this crime. He'd had an embarrassing moment when he'd believed the case to be solved with his arrest of the man whose shoes matched the shoeprints found by the body of Frieda Koziol. After all the excitement that had generated, it had been a huge letdown for all involved when the arrested man turned out to be not the killer, but just a carpenter who took advantage of the blackout to peep on women.

The pressure on Lüdtke to close this case came not just from those above him, like Arthur Nebe, the head of the Kripo, and his boss, director of the Reich Main Security Office Reinhard Heydrich, but also from the public. Lüdtke later wrote, "Rarely has the work of the Berlin criminal police, particularly homicide, been of such strong public interest in Berlin, as in the handling of the S-Bahn murders. There were often bitter words one heard from the public, especially those of East Berlin, which was most threatened by the actions of the S-Bahn Murderer, which grew worse, the longer they were kept waiting on the clearance of these crimes. This was understandable given the severity and the accumulation of crimes."[2]

While some in positions of power in the Third Reich could screw up at work and not worry about repercussions because of their longtime loyalty to the Nazi Party and connections within the party and government, Lüdtke had to succeed on his own merits. So the pressure was on for him to make sure that Ogorzow had indeed committed these crimes and to get an airtight confession from him to close the case.

For Paul Ogorzow, his life was on the line. He knew that he was fighting to keep his head on his shoulders. If he did not manage to find the right words to get out of this, he understood that the German government would quickly try, convict, sentence, and execute him. And just like the poor souls in the French Revolution, he would die under a blade falling in a guillotine.

He still had hope that he might figure out a way to not only save his life, but also mitigate the damage this arrest would cause him.

If he denied everything, maybe he would be able to walk out of the police station a free man. He could return to his wife and kids and cherry trees. Or if there was too much evidence against him, perhaps as a party member, Lüdtke would cut him a break and let him go, or arrange for him to be convicted of a lesser offense.

Paul Ogorzow would never take full responsibility for his attacks on women. Even as he was pushed into a corner and made to feel like he needed to admit certain details of what he'd done, he continued to hold out hope that there was a way he could survive this.

Lüdtke stuck to the line that if Ogorzow wanted his help, then Ogorzow would need to tell him in detail exactly what he'd done. Ogorzow was torn because he did believe that Lüdtke had it in his power to help him and that he might do so on the basis of Ogorzow's loyalty to the party and rank in the SA, but he did not want to further incriminate himself.

Lüdtke used all the evidence at his disposal to try to convince Ogorzow that the Kripo already had more than enough to connect him to these crimes. Lüdtke was hoping that this argument, combined with his suggestion that he would help Ogorzow once he admitted what he'd done, would result in a confession.

Paul Ogorzow fell for this, but with a twist of his own. Ogorzow admitted to the attacks. However, he had yet another trick up his sleeve. He decided to confess to the attacks in a manner that contradicted the evidence. Ogorzow hoped to say enough to get Lüdtke to help him, but also have a way out if there was no help and the state tried to use this confession against him. He could see from the skulls that it was obvious that he had used a blunt instrument to damage the heads of some of his victims; he would lie and say he had used something else.

So Ogorzow falsely claimed that he used a knife in one of the attacks, in which he'd actually used a heavy blunt instrument. He lied about the rest of his attacks by saying that he'd punched his victims with his bare hands. A confession has to match up with the facts of the case. One in which Ogorzow's claims are contradicted by the evidence would be problematic, at the very least. Like a game of cat and mouse, a back-and-forth occurred wherein Lüdtke kept trying to get a proper confession out of Ogorzow, and Ogorzow attempted to weasel his way out of trouble.

When Lüdtke pressed his suspect on the method of death, Ogorzow said it could have been strangulation or punching with his fist or stabbing.

Only by carefully and thoroughly going over the evidence, including the skulls, did Lüdtke finally get Ogorzow to admit the truth. Lüdtke used the skulls to explain that it was impossible that fists or a knife caused the holes in them.

At this point, Ogorzow was physically reacting to the dire situation he was in. The blood had gone out of his face and he was shaking. He no longer had the energy to tell an obvious lie with the evidence of the truth right in front of him. It did not occur to Ogorzow to try to tell a new lie, that this damage must have been caused by injuries related to falling from the train. It was beyond his expertise to tell if these injuries could have been caused in that way, although unbeknownst to him, Dr. Weimann had already ruled that out based on his examinations of where the bodies were found and the nature of the injuries to these skulls.

When Lüdtke asked Ogorzow directly, "What did you beat these women to death with?" Ogorzow finally answered him truthfully. "With a lead cable."[3] In Lüdtke's opinion, this was the moment that Ogorzow broke. Lüdtke described Ogorzow looking "ashen" and "trembling" when he answered this question.[4] Afterward, he freely admitted to all of his murders, in both the garden area and on the S-Bahn. He even wrote up an account of his crimes in his own words.

The police learned that he had gone back to visit only one of his victims. After he'd killed the first woman on the train, he'd gone to work. Then, when he was off duty, he'd returned to her body. Instead of getting the rush he'd expected, he'd felt sickened by being confronted with what he'd done. Since then, he'd avoided seeing his handiwork. This was why it was so hard for him to see the two living victims in the garden area and the five skulls in the interrogation room. While many serial killers enjoy visiting their victims' remains, Ogorzow could not handle it.

As for his two modi operandi—one, attacking women on the S-Bahn and then tossing their bodies off the train while it was between stations, and two, attacking women in the garden area adjacent to the S-Bahn—he explained that he switched between them based on where he believed it to be safer for him to operate. The train had the advantage that no one could sneak up on him, he could see that a compartment was empty before he attacked, and he could dispose of the body en route, while the garden area had the advantage that he could take his time with his victims.

Serial killers are generally thought of in terms of a single modus operandi, and this made things harder for the police. For example, his moniker as the "S-Bahn Murderer" only referred to one of Ogorzow's two hunting grounds. Of the eight murders he committed, five were on the S-Bahn and three had been in the garden area.

Now that the police had their man, the limits imposed by Minister of Propaganda Joseph Goebbels regarding the press were lifted. From his perspective, this case no longer made the Nazi state look bad. Instead, it showed the resourcefulness of the German Police in being able to solve a difficult crime.

On July 18, a major Berlin newspaper, *Berliner Morgenpost*, ran a front-page article with the definitive headline of THE BERLIN S-BAHN MURDERER CAUGHT![5] The article stated, "No previous crime had occupied the Berlin public as completely as the series of murders committed by the 28-year-old Paul Ogorzow."[6]

## CHAPTER TWENTY-EIGHT

# Excuses

Even while making a full confession in writing, Ogorzow still had one last idea for how to avoid being executed for his crimes.

He thought that if he somehow blamed all his attacks on a Jew, this combined with his party and SA membership might be enough to obtain some leniency from the Nazi criminal justice system.

If convicted for his various crimes, he faced the death penalty. So he desperately needed a compelling reason for the German state not to take his life. He was in a tough position, as he had murdered eight women. And not just any women, but German housewives and young women who were working in factories that produced the goods needed to keep the war going. Some of these women had men serving in the German military machine. In Nazi Germany, these were victims the state would feel the need to avenge.

Ogorzow had also taken advantage of the blackout to commit his crimes. This alone was reason enough for the state to take his life. In November 1939, the Berlin Special Court had sentenced a man to death for committing a single, nonviolent property crime during the blackout. The defendant had snatched a woman's purse and been caught. The prosecutor in that case successfully argued to the court that it "had to set an example" as "the Special Court was a kind of drum-head court on the home front, with responsibility to protect it from criminals. . . . The front soldier must absolutely be assured, that the solid wall of the inner front cannot be worn down by sub-humanity."[1]

With such a decision in the case of a purse-snatcher taking advantage of the wartime darkness in Berlin, Ogorzow faced a near certainty of death for his own much, much worse blackout misdeeds.

The Reich minister of justice wrote an open letter to all German judges that discussed blackout criminals. Although this letter was written about a year after Ogorzow's trial, the reasoning in it regarding how to treat those who took advantage of the blackout conditions was not a new development. It articulated sentiments that the Special Court in Berlin already held regarding the need to protect the home front through the use of the death penalty.

Reich minister of justice Otto Thierack wrote in this letter:

At a time when the best of our people are risking their lives at the front and when the home front is tirelessly working for victory, there can be no place for criminals who destroy the will of the community. Those in the administration of justice must recognize that it is their job to destroy traitors and saboteurs on the home front. The law allows plenty of leeway in this regard. The home front is responsible for maintaining peace, quiet, and order as support for the war front. This heavy responsibility falls especially to German judges. Every punishment is fundamentally more important in war than in peace. This special fight is targeted especially against those designated by law as "pests." Should a judge decide after conscientious examination of the criminal act and of the perpetrator's personality that a criminal is a "pest," then the seriousness of this determination must also be firmly expressed in the harshness of the verdict. It is a matter of course that a plunderer, who reaches for the possessions of another after a terror attack [bombing] by the enemy, deserves only death. But every other culprit who commits his crimes by exploiting the circumstances of war also sides with the enemy. His disloyal character and his declaration of war [on the German people] therefore deserve the harshest punishments. This should especially be applied to criminals who cowardly commit their crimes during blackouts. "I don't want," the Führer said, "a German woman to return from her place of work afraid and on the lookout so that no harm is done to her by good-for-nothings and criminals. After all, a soldier should expect that his family, his wife, and relatives are safe at home."

The majority of German judges have recognized the immediate needs of the moment. The death sentence that the Special Court handed out to the 18-year-old assailant of the defenseless soldier's wife, and to the "work-shy" purse-snatcher, placed the protection of the people above all other interests. There are, however, still cases in which the personal circumstances of the culprits are placed above the interests of the necessary protection of the community. This is shown in the comparison of the judgments listed above. The cunning, nighttime handbag robbery perpetrated by a culprit with prior convictions and the 21 thefts committed by the 19-year-old worker were wrongly punished with four years in prison. The decisive factor [in sentencing] is not whether stealing the handbag was legally theft or robbery (which, by the way, does not depend upon whether the bag was carried tightly or loosely); it is not whether the sex offender caused a specific damage with his offense. That he cowardly and cunningly attacked a defenseless woman, and endangered the security of the darkened streets, makes him a traitor. The protection of the community, above all, requires that punishment in such cases serve as deterrence. Prevention here is always better than reparation. Every sentence given a "pest" that is too lenient sooner or later damages the community and carries in itself the danger of an epidemic of similar crimes and the gradual undermining of the military front lines. It is always better for the judge to quell such epidemics early than to stand helpless later against an infected majority. In the fourth year of his prison sentence the criminal should not get the impression that the community's fight against him is waning. On the contrary, he must always feel that German judges are fighting just as hard on the home front as the soldiers are with the foreign enemy on the military front.[2]

While some purse snatchers who committed their crimes during the blackout received death, others received a few years in prison. As this open letter to German judges explains, the government wanted judges to focus on the impact of crimes on the home front as opposed to the personal circumstances of the perpetrator. As the German state had Ogorzow dead to rights for these crimes, his only hope was to try to get the court to overlook the danger he posed to the women of Berlin and instead contemplate his personal circumstances.

And so Ogorzow wrote in his confession, "A few years ago I had sex with a stripper and then went to a Jewish doctor. The Jew, who knew that I was a party member, has, out of hatred of the Nazis mistreated my gonorrhea. The consequence of which affected my state of mind. I would like this considered for sentencing purposes. Therefore, I am not responsible for my actions. Also, please bear in mind that I'm a party member."[3]

By his own account, Paul Ogorzow contracted sexually transmitted diseases on three different occasions. Each time occurred during his marriage but involved consensual sex with a woman who was not his wife. The first time had been in Berlin in 1934. The second occurrence was in Poland in 1940, during the German occupation of that country. This third, and final, incident happened in German-occupied Paris in 1940.

The German authorities took Ogorzow's multiple infidelities and related contractions of sexually transmitted diseases as reflecting poorly on his moral character. They noted that he was only away for short times, a matter of weeks, in Poland and France, yet managed to contract venereal disease during both trips. Combining this with his earlier STD, they felt that he did not care about keeping his marriage vows and was unable to control his sexual impulses.

Ogorzow claimed to have first contracted gonorrhea in 1934 and, when he noticed that he was sick, to have been referred to a Jewish doctor by the name of Wilhelm Schwarzbach.[4] According to Ogorzow, he did not know this doctor was Jewish when he first went to him. When he found this out six months later, he had already undertaken expensive treatments that the doctor had promised would cure him and he'd felt that it was "unfortunately too late to let go of him."[5]

In Ogorzow's self-serving recounting of these events, the doctor prescribed injections and pills that not only did not cure his gonorrhea but also made his health worse. He claimed the doctor intentionally treated him poorly because he knew Ogorzow was a party member, and this then caused his various hospital stays for all sorts of different conditions.

Gonorrhea is an ancient and very common sexually transmitted disease. Commonly known as "the clap," it produces symptoms that Paul Ogorzow probably noticed when he went to urinate and felt a tremendously painful burning sensation. The disease is now usually treated with a course of antibiotics. However, in the 1930s, German doctors commonly used a form of colloidal silver, sometimes in conjunction with other forms of treatment. Antibiotics were in use then, but they were not at the point of easily curing this disease.

While gonorrhea does cause terrible damage to the human body, this does not include creating in someone an irresistible compulsion to kill women. Perhaps this excuse would have worked better if Ogorzow had had an advanced case of another sexually transmitted disease, syphilis, which can make someone crazy. Even tertiary-stage syphilis, however, while it is commonly referred to as turning brains into Swiss cheese, does not result in someone becoming a highly organized serial killer.

In addition to blaming this doctor, Ogorzow also brought up various head injuries he'd sustained over the course of his life while suggesting that they could have contributed to his compulsion to attack and kill women. These included suffering a blow to the head from a fall on the ice in his youth. He claimed to suffer from bad headaches, which he now interpreted as signs that there was something wrong with his brain. He also brought up a stomach condition that had been attributed to nerves. And so, according to Ogorzow, his criminal actions toward women were the result of a drive, a compulsion, arising from an untreated derangement.

He asked in writing for placement in a mental hospital: "The offenses which I committed and admitted to in protocol are all based in this unendurable sickness. I remorsefully acknowledge that I was not supposed to do it, but an impulse arose and during the situation I had a sudden blackout because of the sickness. I ask to please be taken to a psychiatric clinic. Signed, party member Paul Ogorzow."[6]

Ogorzow hoped that his various medical excuses, blaming a Jew, and his party membership would combine to save his life.

The authorities did not care about these excuses. They did however have a doctor examine him to see if he was mentally ill or if this claim of an STD making him attack women had anything to it. The doctor reported that Ogorzow was physically and mentally fit and that there was nothing to his excuse of an STD treatment gone wrong having caused him to stalk and murder women. Of course, this doctor may not have been a disinterested expert. He may have been inclined to produce the result that the authorities wanted to hear. But even a completely objective doctor would have had a hard time believing Ogorzow's self-serving excuses.

Ogorzow also claimed to have desired not to kill women, but only to stun them so he could sexually assault them. He wrote in a short addendum statement to the police, "I would add that I have not beaten the women in my mentally ill state (that I have already put on record) with a piece of lead wire and a piece of iron with the intention to kill them but for the purpose of sexual intercourse."[7]

He tried to make use of the blackout as part of his excuse, saying that he could not see if the women he attacked were "young, old or pretty." He somehow thought this might make him appear more sympathetic to the court and perhaps persuade the judges that his actions were those of someone who was not mentally well and not the actions of a normal sexual offender.

He also tried blaming women as a whole, saying that "he had a certain hatred of women" owing to his having contracted sexually transmitted diseases from them. While he referred to his wife as "a little frigid," he did not blame her for his attacks. And he did point out how much he loved his son. It appears he was trying to play the family man card as well.

Paul Ogorzow would find out soon what the court thought of his excuses. Justice, such as it was in Nazi Germany, moved swiftly in this case. Ogorzow's trial was scheduled for only two weeks after his initial arrest.

## CHAPTER TWENTY-NINE

# The Trial

On July 20, 1941, the Nazi Party officially revoked Ogorzow's membership. The next day, the Kripo mailed to the NSDAP office for Berlin, on Hermann Göring Street, Ogorzow's party member book (NSDAP card number 1,109,672). Also on July 21, the Kripo transferred Ogorzow from their direct control to a detention center in Moabit, Berlin.

On July 22, the Kripo concluded their work in this case. They named it after the final victim in the case, so it became "Homicide Koziol." Lüdtke and his detective Georg Heuser signed their final report and sent it by messenger to the prosecutor's office.

The Berlin Special Court (*Sondergericht*) would try Ogorzow. Ironically, the general amnesty decree for imprisoned Nazis that freed Paul Ogorzow from prison back in 1933 was followed by a decree that set up the special court that would now try him. On March 21, 1933, Chancellor Adolf Hitler and Vice-Chancellor Franz von Papen signed into law the special courts. Unlike with the amnesty decree, then-President Paul von Hindenburg did not sign this document.

The idea of the special courts was to try political offenses, as opposed to purely ordinary criminal offenses. Inspired by the brutal efficiency of military court-martials, these courts were to proceed quickly, without the use of juries. The need of the Nazi-controlled state to quickly deal with what its organs considered to be internal threats greatly outweighed the rights of the accused.

The jurisdiction of these courts continued to expand as the Nazis solidified control over the state and, later, as they waged war throughout Europe. Those accused of committing crimes generally were much better off if they were able to appear before more traditional criminal courts. Unfortunately for Paul Ogorzow, although he'd committed what we would now consider to be ordinary crimes, as opposed to political crimes, his terrible deeds fit numerous criteria used to determine if the special courts should handle a case. These included crimes that threatened the public order, took advantage of the blackout, or involved violent assaults, among other criteria.

There were no appeals from this kind of court, so whatever judgment and sentence the court handed to Ogorzow would be final.[1] The judges would decide his fate, not a jury of his peers. The court would appoint a defense attorney without input from the accused, and his powers would be extremely limited. As one author put it, "The characteristics of the [special courts] thus violated the legal principle of due process and fulfilled the desire of National Socialist authorities for pronouncing harsh sentences rapidly."[2]

Moreover, unlike in the contemporary American criminal justice system, a death sentence meant a life measured in a matter of hours or, at most, days. There would be no long stays on death row, for years or even decades, while appeals worked their way through the court system.

The attorney general at the Court of Justice, as the prosecutor at the Special Court, indicted Paul Ogorzow on July 23, 1941. The prosecutor for the case would be Deputy Prosecutor Neumann. The prosecutor indicted Ogorzow for crimes "in Berlin in the years 1939 to 1941 by 14 independent acts in serious acts of violence, namely, eight murders and six attempted murders by dangerous means."[3] The specific charges were from "§ 1 of the regulation against violent criminals from 5 December 1939 in connection with § 211, 43, 73, 74 of the Criminal Code."[4]

In a press statement released by the chief of police in Berlin on the same day as this indictment, the police explained why Ogorzow was only being tried for these fourteen crimes and not for any of the many sexual assaults and other crimes he'd committed in the garden area near the Karlshorst S-Bahn station before he started attacking women on the S-Bahn.

The press release stated, "Countless further criminal offenses of the murderer, in particular the moral offenses committed by him, are not being considered for the accusation because the punishments expected for these deeds hardly carry any weight."[5] By "moral offenses," this statement meant the attacks on women that did not rise to the level of violence required for an attempted murder charge, or the death required for a murder charge. There were serious punishments against such crimes, including long terms in prison if all the punishments for all these offenses were added together. However, such punishment paled in comparison to the death penalty that was a potential punishment for the attempted murder and murder charges that Ogorzow faced. As such, it was a practical decision for the German criminal justice system to focus on these fourteen crimes.

On July 24, 1941, Ogorzow's trial was held at the Special Court III of the Berlin Regional Court. The trial lasted only about six hours, with the judgment issued at 4:40 that afternoon.

Ogorzow's wife spoke to the court to ask for mercy on the grounds that he was good to her and his family, other than his bouts of jealousy. This plea for Ogorzow's life fell on deaf ears.

The first words of the court's decision, underlined and on the top of the page, said, "In the name of the German people!"[6] This court was very much an institution of the Nazi government, and it believed that its right to judge a man and to sentence him to death flowed from the German people via the Nazi Party.

The court considered Ogorzow's defense of mental disease or defect, also known as an insanity defense. Courts around the world had and continue to have very different tests for what mental capacity means in regard to whether a person is responsible for his actions. Some common tests include whether the defendant, at the time of his actions, knew the difference between right and wrong. Another, much stricter, test is whether someone would have done the same action even if a policeman had been standing nearby watching him.

For instance, if a mentally ill person thought he was fighting off muggers when he was actually kicking innocent passersby, would that person still do this even if a cop were there? But Paul Ogorzow would have failed this insanity test, since he would not kill a woman if a cop were watching him. He would control himself and wait until it was safe to commit the crime.

The German law regarding this issue was contained in the German Criminal Code (*Strafgesetzbuch*, or *StGB*), section 51, paragraphs 1 and 2. If Ogorzow had any chance of not being sentenced to death for his heinous crimes, it would have to come down to one of these two possible defense pleas detailed in German law. If he fell into either category, he might survive.

The first possibility was one of his being considered as not having committed an offense at all. Paragraph 1 stated, "An act does not constitute an offense if the actor at the time of the commission of the act was either unable to realize the forbidden nature of his act or unable to act in accordance with proper understanding because his consciousness was impaired or because he has suffered either pathological mental derangement or mental infirmity."[7]

The second plea mentioned in the German law was one of a reduced punishment insofar as the court finds that paragraph 1 does not apply, but that there still should be some consideration given to a defendant's excuses. Paragraph 2 sets forth, "If the ability to realize the forbidden nature of the act, or the ability to act in accordance with its proper understanding, was considerably diminished due to one of the above stated reasons, the punishment may be reduced in accordance with the provisions for the punishment of attempt."[8] By "above stated reasons," Paragraph 2 means the reasons contained in Paragraph 1 above. So for example, if a mental infirmity was not severe enough to fit the criteria of Paragraph 1, it could still mitigate the punishment given to a defendant.

While other aspects of the law catered explicitly to Nazi Party ideology, as a U.S. Army commentary explained after the war, this version of the "text of Section 51 was introduced at the very beginning of the Nazi regime and was derived from the drafts of a new

Criminal Code prepared earlier and is rather in line with pre-Nazi European penological doctrine."[9] This commentary summed up the two provisions as follows: under "a condition of complete irresponsibility, the perpetrator must be acquitted; in case his responsibility is diminished he must be convicted, but a lighter penalty imposed."[10]

In order to determine whether Paul Ogorzow's claimed reasons for mental incapacity fit either of these two paragraphs, the court relied on the report of an expert, Dr. Freiherr von Marenholtz, regarding Ogorzow's mental health.

In regards to his headaches, the doctor attributed them to a chronic nasal disease resulting from the damage to Paul Ogorzow's improperly set broken nose. As such, the doctor explained to the court, "the headaches are therefore not the result of a disease of the brain or otherwise damage to the central nervous system."[11]

The doctor informed the court that the accused lacked any inherited diseases. The doctor also did not find any "serious diseases which could have a bearing on the central nervous system."[12] Although this doctor may have been under pressure to produce findings in line with what the court wanted, there is no reason to doubt his conclusions. The health problems that Ogorzow complained of, the headaches, the sexually transmitted diseases and associated treatment, would not explain away his attacks on women.

In analyzing this issue, the court took a closer look at Paul Ogorzow and his criminal and sexual activities. The judgment states, "The defendant had a very strong sex drive."[13] It goes on to detail his gonorrhea infections and that he lost his virginity at sixteen. The court also claims that he "masturbated too much" but what amount of masturbation a German special court considered to be just right, as opposed to too much, it did not say.

The court went on to note that Ogorzow had a history as an exhibitionist—before he escalated to actually attacking women, he apparently flashed them. This was not in his criminal record, though. The court perceived him as having variations in his sex drive as compared to normal people, and that it was this that led him to attack women. In fact, he derived sexual pleasure from the process of attacking women, even without sexually assaulting them. Ogorzow told the police that he ejaculated once while throwing a woman from a train, and the court referred to this detail.

Step by step, the court tore apart Ogorzow's attempt to use a section 51 mental capacity defense. It found no medical basis for Ogorzow's claim of some sort of psychological drive or mental noise compelling him to attack women. As for alcohol, he was never drunk enough to not remember in detail his attacks. And so Ogorzow's detailed confession was used against him, as "the accused had for almost all his deeds an accurate memory, which is a sign that he was sane when he committed the deeds themselves."[14]

The court looked at the nature of how the accused committed his crimes. This is the same strategy that a modern American prosecutor would use when confronted with a mental capacity defense— break down the details of the crime to show the elaborate forethought and planning that went into it and how the accused was careful to avoid being caught.

The court wrote that "the defendant had acted according to a plan, as is particularly apparent from the fact that he was often on the train a long time back and forth, until he met a woman traveling alone. Had he acted in a 'frenzy,' such a scheduled execution of the act would not have occurred. The accused can also control his perverse instincts, because if he did not find a suitable victim on the rails, he did not commit a crime."[15]

The fact that Ogorzow was very picky when choosing his victims, in the sense that he made sure that he only attacked women traveling alone, during a time and place such that he felt secure he could get away with the attack, suggested to the court that he did have control of his actions. Having perverse sexual desires was not enough to satisfy either paragraph of section 51, otherwise no one would be fully punished for committing sexually related crimes.

In sum, the court's expert informed the court that there was nothing to Ogorzow's claims: "According to the expert report of Dr. Freiherr von Marenholtz the Defendant did not meet the requirements of § 51, paragraph 1 or 2 of the Criminal Code. This means that the defendant does not suffer from a mental illness or mental deficiency. He was not at the time of the acts disturbed in his mind . . . in accordance with . . . section 51 paragraph 2 of the Criminal Code."[16]

The special court agreed with the expert's opinion and ruled, "The defendant is therefore fully sane and responsible for his actions."[17]

Since Ogorzow's mental capacity defense was not valid, the next issue became whether he in fact violated the laws the court charged him with breaking. Some of the laws Ogorzow was charged with breaking, most notably the murder charge of section 211, had been changed since Ogorzow had committed his earlier crimes, but the court decided to retroactively apply the new laws to all of his offenses, regardless of whether they had occurred before the law had been amended.

This would not have happened in the United States, as the U.S. Constitution prohibits ex post facto ("after the fact") laws in article 1, section 9, clause 3. The idea is that people should be charged with the laws in force at the time of their alleged actions, not the laws in place when they are facing trial. Although there was a significant change to the murder charge, even if the court had used the earlier definition, Ogorzow would still have been in very serious trouble.

The court convicted Ogorzow of all the charges against him— eight counts of premeditated murder and six counts of attempted murder. The special court sentenced him to death and ruled that he now had no civil or political rights.

The judges did not care that he had a past as a party member or that he was an SA man, nor that he blamed his crimes on a Jewish doctor mistreating him. Even in the Third Reich, the excuse that a Jew made him do it did not work to absolve Ogorzow's many sins.

The head of the court stated that Ogorzow was "a beast in human form deservedly eliminated from the national community."[18]

That same day, the police issued a press release celebrating the fact that Ogorzow had been convicted. Under the headline OGOR-ZOW FOUND FULLY ACCOUNTABLE, it stated, "In addition to the eight witnesses who showed up to the trial against the 28 year-old, 8-fold woman-killer, Paul Ogorzow . . . a medical authority was invited to examine the mental state of the accused. His report states that the requirements of § 51 StGB (legal insanity) do not exist at all. He has been found fully accountable for his multiple crimes."[19]

## CHAPTER THIRTY

# A Date with the Executioner

The next morning, at 6 A.M. on Friday, July 25, 1941, the Third Reich executed Paul Ogorzow. It had been only thirteen days since his arrest.

The execution took place at the notorious Plötzensee Prison in Berlin. During the Nazi reign of terror, this huge brick structure would be the temporary home to many prisoners on their way to the executioner. These would include a diverse range of prisoners, from ordinary criminals such as Ogorzow to political criminals, including many Germans who took part in the July 1940 plot against Hitler.

Ogorzow was not the only person put to death in Plötzensee Prison that morning. Three political prisoners were killed as well. Two of them had been sentenced to death for "actions subversive to the defensive strength of the German people, treasonable furtherance to the enemy, and preparation for treason."[1] The third political prisoner had been convicted of "spying for an enemy intelligence service for purposes of personal enrichment."[2]

There was also a fifth prisoner executed by the German state that day. This man, Kurt Polenski, had killed his wife.

The *Chicago Daily Tribune* reported on the executions that morning with the rhyming headline of 3 NAZI TRAITORS AND 2 SLAYERS DIE ON GUILLOTINE.[3] It described Paul Ogorzow as "one of the most notorious mass murderers of recent times in Europe. For two years he is said to have terrorized passengers on late elevated trains operating in the outer suburbs, attacking women in empty compartments and disposing of his victims by pushing them out of the moving train."[4]

This article also noted the fact that Ogorzow had been found guilty only the day before his execution, which was fast, even in Nazi Germany.

The prison authorities would use a guillotine to swiftly separate Ogorzow's head from his body. That was the method used in Germany in 1941, and Ogorzow had no choice in his manner of execution. Until a few years before, the state had killed condemned prisoners by beheading them with an axe. Future executions at Plötzensee Prison would include hangings.

The guillotine was widely considered to be more humane than an axman doing the job. A man with an axe could make a mistake and require more than one swing to decapitate a condemned prisoner. An eighteenth-century French executioner, who used a sword to chop men's heads from their bodies, talked about this problem: "In order to accomplish the execution in accordance with the law

it is necessary, even without any opposition on the part of the prisoner, that the executioner should be very skillful and the condemned
man very steady, otherwise it would be impossible to accomplish
the execution with the sword."[5] He went on to talk about swords
breaking, which was less of a problem with Germany's twentieth-
century axes, but still could be a problem after heavy use.

The guillotine, as long as it was kept in working order, had no
such flaws. Adolf Hitler saw one in operation and liked it so much
that he ordered a number of them to be made and installed in his
prisons.

Kee D. Kim, a doctor and professor of spinal neurosurgery,
recently explained Paul Ogorzow's cause of death in medical terms:
"Guillotine leads to an instantaneous and complete disruption of
blood supply (carotid and vertebral arteries in the neck) and neural
connection (spinal cord in the neck) to the brain. Sudden disruption
of blood flow to the brain leads to certain death. The answer can
become more complex depending on the definition of death."[6]

A related question is the time it takes to lose consciousness.
There are plenty of stories told about people still retaining a few
seconds of consciousness after their heads are separated from their
bodies, including a number of colorful, if hard to verify, ones involving scientists beheaded during the French Revolution.

The macabre image of a dying man seeing out into the world
and his brain processing that last sensory information is a powerful
one, but the question remains of whether it is real. Would Ogorzow
have had one last look at his prison after he was just a head?

Dr. Kim went on to answer this question as follows: "Timing
of the loss of consciousness is more difficult to answer. If we define
loss of consciousness very narrowly as an inability to perceive pain,

that may be easier. One recent animal study from Holland looked at EEG tracings of rats that were guillotined. The investigators found that in approximately 3.7 seconds, the EEG readings changed to the levels that they equated to the loss of consciousness. I don't think anyone can be absolutely sure, but my feeling is that the loss of consciousness in humans also takes place in seconds."[7]

So Paul Ogorzow may have a had a few extra seconds to contemplate his fate after a fast-dropping metal blade cut his head off. Perhaps he finally did feel some regret for the things he'd done. Given his thought processes up until then, though, that seems unlikely. He never expressed regret for what he had done and all the suffering he had caused.

Now that Ogorzow was dead, the German state would not waste his remains. Instead, his head and body would be taken to the Institute of Anatomy and Biology to be dissected.[8]

After executing a prisoner, the authorities would mail a bill to the deceased's heirs. In this case, that meant his grieving wife, who was completely innocent of any involvement in his terrible crime spree. This bill sent to Mrs. Gertrude Ogorzow contained a charge for the wear and tear on the guillotine blade caused by severing Paul Ogorzow's head from his body.

# EPILOGUE

After the Berlin police had caught the S-Bahn Murderer, the regime reversed its previous ban on publicity regarding this case, since now that it was solved it would no longer generate fear in women who needed to travel alone, but would serve to highlight the effectiveness of the Third Reich in solving crime.

The day after Paul Ogorzow's execution, the police issued the following press release to highlight their work in catching him:

The Chief of Police in Berlin
Newspaper/print.
Berlin local announcements
Date: July 26, 1941. Number: 178
Karlshorst S-Bahn Murderer Executed
The judiciary press office in Berlin discloses:

Paul Ogorzow, who was sentenced to death and long-lasting suffering this Thursday by the Special Court of Berlin as a parasite to the people and violent offender of civil rights, was executed on Friday. In many instances, Ogorzow used the darkness on the S-Bahn to attack women and throw them out of the train. He also committed multiple murders and murder attempts in the garden area of Berlin-East.

On Thursday of last week, the serial woman killer, whose gruesome deeds put the people of Berlin-East in fear and dismay, was captured by the police after painstaking investigation. A week later, the trial–thanks to the commendable cooperation between the criminal police and judiciary–was able to be carried out against him. Yesterday, the death penalty of this beast in human form was carried out. The public greeted this quick execution of the law with satisfaction.[1]

This press release praised the rapidity with which Ogorzow went from arrest to trial to execution. The government was proud of the level of "cooperation" between the police and the courts. The idea was that the courts and the police worked hand in hand to eliminate those people from German society who posed a threat to the well-being of the Third Reich and the German people. There is a very different view of the role of the courts and police in a democratic society with civil rights, in which the courts serve as a protection against the police arresting the wrong person or violating a suspect's rights.

They referred to Paul Ogorzow as the "Karlshorst S-Bahn Murderer" because some of his crimes took place near the Karlshorst S-Bahn station and he lived near there. In time, though, the garden attacks faded from the popular imagination in comparison to the more dramatic attacks that took place on the train itself. As such, he became known as simply the S-Bahn Murderer.

In addition to the fleeting attention brought to this case in the news media, it occurred to the Nazi higher-ups that there was value in promoting additional awareness of the Kripo's effective work in catching a killer.

Reich Minister of Propaganda Joseph Goebbels wrote to *Reichsführer-SS* Heinrich Himmler that a series of detective novels based on the successes of the German Police could help boost faith in the capabilities of the Reich. Himmler, in his position as chief of German Police in the Reich Ministry of the Interior, approved of this project.

The first book in this crime fiction series was to be based on the Paul Ogorzow case. Nebe in turn agreed to this proposal as this case made him look good and he was a consummate lover of detective novels. The head of the Reich Chamber of Writers, Wilhelm Ihde, wrote *Death Rode the Train* (*Der Tod fuhr im Zug*) under the pen name of Axel Alt. It cost 1 reichsmark and featured a font on the cover that made the title look like a moving train. This pulp fiction version of the case was a huge best seller—the first printing of five hundred thousand copies quickly sold out.

A professor of German studies recently wrote that this "novel is representative of the dominant tendency of the period to celebrate the work of the criminal police while avoiding any portrayal of the totalitarian apparatus that surrounded criminal politics in the Third Reich."[2]

It was a work of fiction that built on the actual police file in this case. The author changed Ogorzow's name to "Omanzow," but the

German reading public knew exactly whom he was writing about, as these crimes, once solved, had been heavily publicized.

Wilhelm Lüdtke spent the rest of the war in Berlin with the Kripo.[3] He'd already served in the German army in World War I and he was fifty-five years old by the time he closed the S-Bahn Murderer case.

In April 1943, Lüdtke received a promotion to the rank of *Kriminalrat* (detective superintendent) and received additional training at a police school in Prague. He continued to run the homicide division in the Berlin Kripo, however. On February 1, 1944, he was promoted to become the Kripo personnel chief in Berlin, which involved additional responsibilities but did not require him to give up his position running the Berlin homicide division.

While he was not drafted into military service, Lüdtke was a member of the SS (number 52239) and was issued an SS uniform. He had the mid-level SS officer rank of *Hauptsturmführer*. But he was not assigned to a special SS unit, nor had he volunteered to join the SS. In 1938, everyone in the Kripo who was not already a member of the SS had been required to join it.

Although many detectives in the Kripo could stay in plain clothes, for his new duties, Lüdtke often wore a uniform. It was the same uniform worn by Kripo detectives in occupied territory, as they were not allowed to be in plain clothes there. They wore an SS uniform in field gray.

For Wilhelm Lüdtke, the SS unit he was assigned to was the Security Police in Berlin. In practice, this meant little in addition to his normal Kripo duties.

He was in Berlin until the bitter end. While others, like Hitler Youth leader Artur Axmann, fled when Hitler killed himself and the Russians came pouring in, Lüdtke stayed. When asked after the war about his work experience, in the denazification questionnaire called a *Fragebogen*, he wrote that he worked for the Berlin Kripo until "*Zusammenbruch*," which meant the "collapse."[4]

Berlin surrendered to the Soviets on May 2, 1945. It was chaos as the Red Army moved in and took control of the city. While many other Germans destroyed their uniforms and papers, Lüdtke continued to wear his. If it had been a uniform specific to the Criminal Police, he might have been fine. Instead, he was wearing an SS uniform.

On May 8, 1945, the Soviet secret police arrested him. He fell into the automatic arrest category as a member of the SS. They held him for less than two months, releasing him on July 2, 1945, as they felt that his duties as a Criminal Police officer did not merit incarceration.

Wilhelm Lüdtke stayed in Berlin, in the American sector, but was not able to rejoin the German Criminal Police. It took time for him to go through the denazification process, as he had been arrested by the Soviets while in an SS uniform. He collected witnesses to explain that his SS rank of *Hauptsturmführer* had been automatic and that while many Kripo officers in Berlin had been able to avoid wearing a uniform, there had been times that he believed it to be part of his duties to wear his uniform. The fact that this uniform belonged to the SS was a problem for Lüdtke. He went through a lengthy process before being able to persuade the authorities that he had not been a member of the SS in any meaningful way, but that it had been an automatic part of his job with the Kripo.

In addition, he was reaching retirement age, having been born in 1886. He'd been a policeman for thirty-five years, and even once he was denazified, he would be too old to rejoin the force, even if they would otherwise be willing to take him back.

While he did have a modest pension, he took supplemental work as a private detective for coffee import and export firms in Berlin and Hamburg from 1945 to 1951. The U.S. Central Intelligence Agency (CIA) described this work as follows: "[Lüdtke] is gainfully employed as an investigator by a group of coffee merchants interested in the suppression of smuggling operations involving the unauthorized import of coffee from [East Germany] to Western Berlin. He also works in an inofficial capacity for the Zollfahndungsdienst (customs investigation unit) of the Berlin Senate."[5]

In April 1951, the CIA recruited him for full-time work; before then he'd done some part-time work for them on a case-by-case basis. He'd received no punishment as part of his denazification process, so the CIA was not concerned that he had been a member of the SS, although they did research his background thoroughly. They periodically had concerns about the Soviets having held him for two months, but his account of how that happened made sense. At one point, the CIA subjected Lüdtke to a lie detector test that asked if he'd told the truth about that arrest and if he had been recruited by the Soviets as an agent. He passed.

The CIA noted in Lüdtke's file that this had been an "automatic arrest for the Soviets, since subject was apprehended in SS uniform. At the time, the German police branch of which he was a member had been assimilated into the SS, and such uniforms and rank designations were a matter of course."[6]

He worked for the CIA as an undercover asset in Berlin as part of three different Cold War operations against the Soviets and the Polish Communists. He did this out of a combination of hatred of

Communism and financial hardship. Lüdtke found it hard to live on his pension. He used this fact for his cover story to his friends and neighbors, who knew him as a retired policeman earning extra money on the side as a free-lance part-time private investigator.

In addition to paying him a tax-free salary, the CIA also promised him that if the Soviets and/or East Germans invaded Berlin, if possible they would evacuate him and his wife.

For his first job with them, the CIA gave him the cryptonym of CAUTERY-4. He was being run by the CIA's REDCAP program to encourage Communists to defect to the west. The CIA provided him with fake credentials for the "Economic Assessment Unit" under the name of "Ernst Hartmann."[7]

REDCAP eventually reassigned him from Operation Cautery to Polish operations, specifically Operation Besmirch. His cryptonym then became BESMIRCH-2.

For the Polish operations, Lüdtke received a new cover. He was now doing research for newspapers and had all the right credentials, including a counterfeit investigator's pass. The CIA described his mission for BESMIRCH as follows: "Mission: [Wilhelm Lüdtke] knows that his activities are directed toward the establishment of a support mechanism which could mount and support clandestine operations in Poland. Subject knows that we are interested in obtaining intelligence reports on the transit railroad traffic from East Germany to Poland and the USSR. [He] is also aware of our interest in the barge traffic to Poland and illegal border crossers in the East German/Polish border area of Guben to Gorlitz."[8]

When Project BESMIRCHED ended, the CIA still valued Lüdtke as an agent, so they assigned him to Project BECRIPPLE. He now had the codename of BECRIPPLE-2.[9] CIA records summarized this operation as follows: "BECRIPPLE Project (1954–60) provided Polish operations run from Berlin and other Stations/Bases with support assets such as a secure safehouse . . . ; garage for a German plated vehicle; an agent/cutout for obtaining credit investigations on persons of operational interest; an agent for monitoring local Polish emigre activity; an agent for obtaining clandestine photographs of West Berlin Polish installations and other support facilities."[10]

The CIA valued Lüdtke based on his extensive police experience and his knowledge of how German bureaucracies work. While they thought his appearance was too noticeable for more than very short-term surveillance work, they complimented his work as an interrogator, legman, and spotter. The CIA noted that he "is a good interrogator and an adept handler of people."[11] This was the same skill set that had enabled him to get Paul Ogorzow to confess.

The CIA terminated his services on July 10, 1957. They paid him a severance bonus and gave him a way to reach them that would be good for one year in case the Soviets came after him during that time. The reasons cited in his file for his dismissal were "over-use, compromise, and ill health."[12] "Compromise" in the intelligence community has a different meaning than in everyday life. They meant that his cover may have been blown, and other intelligence services, such as those of the Soviet, East German, and Polish governments may have known he was spying for the Americans. As for his ill health, he was now in his seventies so it was normal for him to have trouble with the various activities being a spy entailed. The last page in his CIA file is a short letter to the chief of the CIA Berlin base notifying him that Wilhelm Lüdtke died from cancer in August 1957 and was buried in Berlin.

Arthur Nebe, the head of the Kripo, was assigned in 1941 to be in charge of one of the mobile killing squads (*Einsatzgruppen*) that followed the Nazi advance into Soviet territory. It was common for police officials to be assigned to *Einsatzgruppen*, which carried out massacres of Jews, Gypsies, Soviet political commissars, and others the Nazi regime wanted eliminated. These groups slaughtered well over a million men, women, and children.

Nebe was in charge of *Einsatzgruppe* B from its inception in June 1941 until November 1941. There are conflicting reports regarding the extent to which he tried to minimize the murders committed by his group, as well as his personal reaction to various massacres.

Nebe played a key role in the development of the use of hermetically sealed vans to gas people to death. Until then, the Third Reich had mostly used firearms to slaughter people. Gunning down civilians, including women and children, was bad for the morale of troops, and gas was a way to efficiently kill large numbers of people without needing large numbers of soldiers to shoot them. Those placed in the back of the vans would die as a result of carbon monoxide being pumped in.

If Nebe had survived the war, there were other war crimes he could have been charged with, including selecting fifty prisoners out of those captured from the Great Escape (the famed breakout from the *Stalag Luft* III POW camp) for execution. The head of the Gestapo ordered him to pick which prisoners were to be killed.

These were just the major crimes with which he was involved. There were other very troubling events that would have been investigated if he had lived to be tried at Nuremberg by the Allies.

Nebe was executed just before the end of the war for his role in the July 20, 1944, bombing plot to kill Hitler. Nebe's job as part of this plot, called Operation Valkyrie, was to neutralize his enemy/boss Heinrich Himmler, but he never received the signal to do so. When Hitler survived the bombing, Nebe thought the Gestapo was on to him, so he ran away on July 24. He was mistaken, as they had no idea he'd been a part of this plot to assassinate Hitler.

He hid on an island in the outskirts of Berlin until his ex-mistress, Police Commissioner Heidi Hobbin, turned him in to the Gestapo. She did this out of jealousy of his relationship with another woman.[13]

On March 21, 1945, he was executed in the same Berlin prison as Ogorzow. While Ogorzow was killed by guillotine, Nebe was hung using piano wire, as Hitler reportedly wanted those who had tried to kill him hung like cattle.

Nebe's old boss Reinhard Heydrich did not survive the war either. If he had, the Allies would have tried him for his many war crimes. In addition to being director of the Reich Main Security Office, he was appointed the deputy protector of Bohemia and Moravia in September 1941. In essence, this new job meant that he was the dictator of this majority Czech territory and responsible for brutally suppressing any and all resistance to Nazi rule.

On May 27, 1942, Heydrich was riding to work when Czech and Slovak resistance fighters dramatically attacked him. An assassin stood in front of his Mercedes convertible and tried to open fire on him with a submachine gun. The convertible was open, and if the gun hadn't jammed, this might have spelled the end of Heydrich. Instead of fleeing, Heydrich had his driver stay so he could shoot back. Given this additional opportunity to attack, another assassin threw a grenade at Heydrich. This grenade mortally wounded Heydrich, and he died after a surgery to remove grenade fragments from his body.

Heydrich's old boss, Heinrich Himmler, survived the war, but just barely. The man who until the fall of the Third Reich a month before had been in charge of the German Police and the SS was reduced to trying to pretend to be a normal soldier making his way home. He was picked up at a British checkpoint, and only two days later did his captors realize his true identity. He'd shaved off his famous mustache and removed his trademark glasses. When a doctor tried to search inside his mouth for any concealed poison pill, Himmler bit down on a cyanide capsule, which caused his death.

Another high-ranking Nazi official who played a key role in the investigation into the S-Bahn Murderer, Joseph Goebbels, also took his own life. Near the end of the war, he was living in the Berlin Reich Chancellery bunker along with his wife Magda, their children, Adolf Hitler, Eva Braun Hitler, head of the party chancellery Martin Bormann, and other Nazi personnel.

As the Soviets fought their way into the government center of Berlin, Adolf Hitler killed himself on April 30. His very recent wife, Eva Braun Hitler, killed herself as well.

On May 1, Joseph and Magda Goebbels arranged for the murder of their six children. (Magda Goebbels's grown son from a previous marriage was not there.) There are conflicting versions of exactly who administered what to them, but it is clear that both parents agreed to kill their offspring. They were aged from four to twelve years old when they died in the bunker.

Unlike Himmler, Goebbels did not try to go into hiding. He and his wife walked out of the bunker to the chancellery garden and killed themselves on the night of May 1. Others in the bunker area tried to break out of the Soviet encirclement that evening, and some, including Hitler Youth leader Artur Axmann, made it out of Berlin. Goebbels did not take the chance of doing so and being caught, as he feared what the Soviets would do to him. German forces in Berlin surrendered to the Soviets the next morning.

One of Lüdtke's main detectives on the S-Bahn case was Georg Heuser. The two of them would jointly write an article on the murders for the *Journal of Criminology* in 1942. Heuser, like Arthur Nebe and many Kripo detectives, served in one of the mobile killing squads on the Eastern Front after the Ogorzow case. At first, he was in the operational subunit *Sonderkommando* 1b of *Einsatzgruppe* A, but he went on to a variety of different positions, including head of the Gestapo in German-occupied Minsk.[14]

Ironically, this meant that one of the lead detectives in the Ogorzow case would kill more innocent civilians on a particularly brutal day than Ogorzow did during his entire crime spree.

Heuser survived the end of the war by getting rid of his SS uniform and wearing civilian clothes. By that time, he'd had the same rank as his old boss Lüdtke, *Hauptsturmführer*. Lüdtke, though, had been foolish enough to keep wearing his uniform.

After the war, Heuser worked a number of odd jobs before he managed to become a policeman in West Germany, rising to the rank of police chief of the West German state of Rhineland-Palatinate. Heuser lied about what he had done during the war, and a typo, in which his last name was misspelled with an "ä," helped him in that regard. He'd concealed his past, but it eventually caught up with him. He'd committed alleged war crimes in Slovakia in 1944–45, but he was never tried for those. Instead, he was in trouble for the murders he'd committed when he'd been based in Minsk (the capital of Belarus).

He was arrested for war crimes on July 23, 1959, specifically the murder of more than eleven thousand men, women, and children. Most of these people were murdered for being Jewish. The charges were that Heuser had issued orders for these mass murders as well as taken direct part in some of them personally.

He was tried in 1962, as part of a large war crimes case, along with other defendants who had committed war crimes in Belarus. In a particularly chilling bit of testimony, he recalled one mass shooting of Jews "in early May 1942 in Minsk. I went to the pit. A shock came over me. Someone shouted, 'There is one still living.' I shot at him. Then I shot more like an automaton."[15]

The court convicted Heuser and sentenced him to fifteen years' imprisonment. However, he was released early on December 12, 1969. He died in January 1989 in Koblenz, Germany.

Another key figure in the S-Bahn investigation was the forensic pathologist Dr. Waldemar Weimann, who conducted autopsies of the bodies of Ogorzow's victims. He did a psychological character study of Ogorzow after he was caught, based on his knowledge as a psychiatrist.

Even while he worked with the Berlin police to solve and understand crimes, Dr. Weimann allegedly secretly assisted Reich doctors who euthanized hundreds of sick children. As a book on Nazi medicine explained, "in clear contravention of his professional duties, he would develop an inordinately inconspicuous, painless, and unprovable killing procedure."[16]

Despite this, he continued to work at his job in Berlin assisting the police with forensics until he retired in 1958. In 1963, Dr. Weimann cowrote a book on forensic medicine (*Atlas of Forensic Medicine*) that became a standard work in this field. His memoirs, including his thoughts on the Ogorzow case, were published in 1964 as *Diagnose Mord* ("Diagnosis Murder"). He died in Berlin on February 14, 1965.

Following the defeat of Nazi Germany, the Berlin S-Bahn train system came under the ownership of East Germany. The *Reichsbahn* controlled the trains in East Germany (the German Democratic Republic), while a new train company was formed to run the trains in West Germany (*Deutsche Bundesbahn*). The Reichsbahn however continued to operate the S-Bahn in Berlin, including in West Berlin. So the East German government controlled the commuter train system in all of Berlin. In August 1961, Berlin was physically divided with the construction of the Berlin Wall. The S-Bahn now served two different groups of passengers, those in West Berlin and those in East Berlin. With the reunification of Germany, the S-Bahn became whole again and passengers could ride it across the entire city.

In later years, the signal tower Ogorzow worked at would become covered in graffiti. In May 1998, it was retired from use. On December 5, 2005, it was destroyed to make way for the construction of a new bridge.[17]

# ACKNOWLEDGMENTS

I'd like to thank my family: my brother Todd (aka "The Selby"); my parents, Richard and Rikki; Maria Olga Vargas and her son Christopher; my girlfriend Mandy Jonusas and her mother, Kerstin Jonusas; my cousins Marc and Mitch Goldstone; and my aunt Marcy Goldstone.

Additional thanks go out to my literary agent, Scott Miller of Trident Media Group. Thanks to everyone at the Berkley imprint of Penguin, including my editor Natalee Rosenstein and Robin Barletta.

To my friends who kindly gave me advice on this project, thank you. They include Jennifer Brody, Laura Dawson, Felize Diaz, Janet Dreyer, Kikki Edman, August Evans, Catherine Culvahouse Fox, Leor Jacobi, Jordan Joliff, Michael Maggiano, Rachel McCullough-Sanden, Gabriel Meister, Annabel Raw, William Salzmann, Jeremy Sirota, Alfred "Dave" Steiner, Ryan Swanson, Nader Vossoughian, and Abigail Wick.

For help with translations: Nader Vossoughian, Ph.D.; Lee-Ellen Reed; Bettina Wirbladh; and Abigail Wick.

For help related to the research for this book: Martin Luchterhandt, Ph. D., of the Landesarchiv Berlin; Kee D. Kim, M.D., associate professor and chief of spinal neurosurgery, Department of Neurological Surgery, University of California Davis School of Medicine; Robin Gottschlag and Historische S-Bahn e.V. (Berlin)—a nonprofit organization dedicated to preserving and sharing the history of the Berlin S-Bahn, www.hisb.de;

## ACKNOWLEDGMENTS

Professor Patrick Wagner; Frank Pfeiffer; Sven Keßler; Mike Straschewski and Thomas Krickstadt from Geschichte und Geschichten rund um die Berliner S-Bahn (stadtschnellbahn-berlin.de); Roland Anton Laub (photo laub.com); Gabi Schlag, Benno Wenz, and Dörte Wustrack; and others who wished to remain anonymous.

# FOR FURTHER READING

Alt, Axel. *Der Tod fuhr im Zug, den Akten der kriminalpolizei Nacherzaählt.*
Berlin-Grunewald: Verlag Hermann Hillger k.-g, 1944.

SHAEF, G-2 (Counter-Intelligence Subdivision, Evaluation and Dissemination
Section), *The German Police*, EDS/G/10, Apr. 1945.

Weimann, Waldemar, and Gerhard Jaeckel. *Diagnose: Mord. Die Memoiren
eines Gerichtsmediziners.* Bayreuth, Germany: Hestia, 1964.

Williamson, Gordon. *German Security and Police Soldier, 1939–45.* Warrior
Series (Book 61). Oxford, UK: Osprey Publishing, 2002.

# ABBREVIATIONS

**GESTAPO** *Geheime Staatspolizei* (Secret State Police)

**KRIPO** *Kriminalpolizei* (Criminal Police)

**NSDAP** *Nationalsozialistische Deutsche Arbeiterpartei* (Nazi Party)

**ORPO** *Ordnungspolizei* (Order Police, generally handled lower-level police matters)

**RHSA** *Reichssicherheitshauptamt* (Reich Main Security Office)

**SA** *Sturmabteilung* (Storm Troopers, paramilitary force of the Nazi Party)

**S-BAHN** *Stadtschnellbahn* (City Fast Train, a commuter railway in Berlin)

**SD** *Sicherheitsdienst des Reichsführers-SS* (intelligence organization of the SS)

**SIPO** *Sicherheitspolizei* (Security Police)

**SS** *Schutzstaffel*

**U-BAHN** *Untergrundbahn* (Underground Railway, a rapid transit railway in Berlin)

# NOTES

## EPIGRAPH

1 Supreme Headquarters Allied Expeditionary Force (SHAEF) Evaluation and Dissemination Section, G-2 (Counter Intelligence Sub-Division), compiled by MIRS (London Branch), *The German Police*, April 1945, E.D.S./G/10, ii.

## CHAPTER ONE

1 Dorothy Elkins, T. H. Elkins, and B. Hofmeister, *Berlin: The Spatial Structure of a Divided City* (New York: Methuen & Co., 1988), 86.

2 Laurenz Demps, quoted in Gabi Schlag and Benno Wenz, *Tatort Berlin—Der S-Bahn-Mörder von Rummelsburg*, TV documentary program, original airdate November 26, 2012, broadcast in Germany by Berlin-Brandenburg Broadcasting (rbb).

3 Lothrop Stoddard, "People of Berlin Show Little Interest in War, Says Observer," *Calgary Herald*, December 16, 1939, 28.

4 Ellen Pastorino and Susann Doyle-Portillo, *What Is Psychology? Essentials* (Belmont, CA: Wadsworth Cengage Learning, 2011), 87.

5 John E. Douglas and Mark Olshaker, *The Anatomy of Motive: The FBI's Legendary Mindhunter Explores the Key to Understanding and Catching Violent Criminals* (New York: Simon and Schuster, 1999), 39–40.

6 Ibid., 40.

## CHAPTER TWO

1 National Archives, Washington, D.C., RC Box #082, Location (RC) 230/86/23/05, "Ludtke Wilhelm," 9. Note that the file name is missing the umlaut. Lüdtke also mentioned this in his *Fragebogen* (denazification questionnaire), which is contained in this CIA file.

## CHAPTER FOUR

1 The quotes from Paul Ogorzow's attack on Mrs. Nieswandt are from Special Court of Berlin, judgment against Paul Ogorzow, July 24, 1941. As mentioned in the author's note at the start of this book, the original documents from the criminal investigation into the S-Bahn murders are at the Landesarchiv Berlin, A.Pr. Br. Rep. 030-03 Tit. 198B Nr. 1782–1789.

## CHAPTER SIX

1 As the motive for these crimes had a strong sexual component, the German police wanted to know about the couple's sex life and interviewed them separately about this detail. Wilhelm Lüdtke and Georg Heuser, "Die Berliner S-Bahn-Morde," *Kriminalistik* 16, Issue 5 (May 1942), 68.

2 Phil Chalmers, *Inside the Mind of a Teen Killer* (Nashville, TN: Thomas Nelson, 2009), 132–133.

**CHAPTER SEVEN**

1 William L. Shirer, The *Rise and Fall of the Third Reich: A History of Nazi Germany* (New York: Simon & Schuster, 1st Touchstone edition, 1990), 778.

2 Andrew Roberts, *The Storm of War: A New History of the Second World War* (New York: HarperCollins, 2011), lv.

3 See, e.g., Stephen Frater, *Hell Above Earth: The Incredible True Story of an American WWII Bomber Commander and the Copilot Ordered to Kill Him* (New York: Macmillan, 2012), 179.

4 Shirer, *Rise and Fall,* 778.

5 "Appeal of President Franklin D. Roosevelt on Aerial Bombardment of Civilian Populations," addressed to the Governments of France, Germany, Italy, Poland, and His Britannic Majesty, September 1, 1939, quoted in Frits Kalshoven, *Reflections on the Law of War: Collected Essays* (Leiden, Netherlands: Martinus Nijhoff Publishers, 2007), 439, footnote 20.

6 United Press, "Hitler Agrees to FDR's Plan," *Telegraph-Herald* (Dubuque, Iowa), September 3, 1939.

7 Jack Fleischer, United Press, "Vicious Attacks on Channel Ports Aftermath of Berlin Bombing," *Leader-Post* (Regina, Saskatchewan, Canada), August 26, 1940, 1.

8 "Die Achte Durchführungsverordnung zum Luftschutzgesetz (Verdunklungsverordnung)," *Reichsgesetzblatt* I (May 23, 1939), 965.

9 Ibid., Section Sixteen, Clause 1.

10 Associated Press, "German Air Raid Maneuvers Staged for Berlin Residents," *Reading Eagle* (Reading, PA), July 27, 1939, 24.

11 Lothrop Stoddard, "People of Berlin Show Little Interest in War, Says Observer," *Calgary Herald*, December 16, 1939, 28.

12 In German, this poster said: *"Der Feind sieht Dein Licht! Verdunkeln!"* Author's collection.

13 In German, this poster said: *"Licht. Dein Tod!"* Author's collection.

14 Herbert R. Vogt, *My Memories of Berlin: A Young Boy's Amazing Survival Story* (Bloomington, IN: Xlibris Corporation, 2008), 74.

15 In German: *"Dieses Haus ist schlecht verdunkelt!"* Author's collection.

16 United States Holocaust Memorial Museum, "Background: Decree Against Public Enemies," *Holocaust Encyclopedia,* http://www.ushmm.org/wlc/en/article.php?ModuleId=10007906, accessed on February 1, 2013.

17 William D. Bayles, "Wartime Germany," *Life*, January 8, 1940, 55. The article is broken up into different letters. This quote is from the letter dated October 24.

18 Marianne Zappe, S-Bahn Berlin GmbH, *Kundenbetreuung*, e-mail to author, February 1, 2013.

**CHAPTER EIGHT**

1 Thomas Krickstadt, e-mail to author, March 3, 2013.

2 Marianne Zappe, S-Bahn Berlin GmbH, *Kundenbetreuung*, e-mail to author, February 1, 2013.

3 Dorothy Elkins, T. H. Elkins, and B. Hofmeister, *Berlin: The Spatial Structure of a Divided City* (New York: Methuen, 1988), 105–106.

# NOTES

4 Thomas Krickstadt and Mike Straschewski, joint e-mail to author, February 20, 2013.
5 The information on the rates for the S-Bahn is from Thomas Krickstadt and Mike Straschewski, joint e-mail to author, February 20, 2013. Note that later on, as the war progressed, this changed to a war ticket tariff system.
6 The information on how tickets were checked is from Thomas Krickstadt and Mike Straschewski, joint e-mail to author, February 25, 2013.
7 Robin Gottschlag, e-mail to author, December 28, 2012.
8 New York Prosecutors Training Institute, Inc., The Continuing Legal Education and Mutual Assistance Division of the New York State District Attorneys Association, "Strangulation in Domestic Violence and Sexual Assault," from the September 28–30, 1999, conference on Detection and Prosecution of Strangulation in Domestic Violence and Sexual Assault Cases.
9 Waldemar Weimann and Gerhard Jaeckel, *Diagnose Mord: Die Memoiren eines Gerichtsmediziners* (Bayreuth, Germany: Hestia, 1964), 274.

CHAPTER NINE
1 UPI, "Berlin Resident Given Death Penalty for Theft," *Reading Eagle* (Reading, PA), January 17, 1941.
2 Thomas Krickstadt and Mike Straschewski, joint e-mail to author, March 15, 2013.
3 William D. Bayles, "Wartime Germany," *Life*, January 8, 1940, 54–55.

CHAPTER TEN
1 Alan Gunn, *Essential Forensic Biology* (Hoboken, NJ: John Wiley & Sons, 2008), 181.
2 Don Bible, *Third Reich Warrant Discs, 1934–1945* (Atglen, PA: Schiffer Military History, 2001), 4.
3 Berlin *Kripo*, Murder Division Ditter document, October 5, 1940.
4 Forensic Institute of the Security Police at the Office of the Reich Criminal Investigations Department, "Examination of a kitchen knife for human blood," statement sent to the Criminal Investigations Department Headquarters, October 8, 1940.
5 Statement of Gertrud Ditter (born Kerwat), Murder Division Ditter document, October 4, 1940. Note that this is Arthur Ditter's mother, who spells her first name without an "e" at the end of it, not his murdered wife.
6 Statement of Arthur Ditter, Murder Division Ditter document, October 4, 1940.
7 Ibid.
8 Ibid.
9 This quote is from the second time the police interviewed Auguste Bohm. The wording is different, but the facts are the same as in her first statement. Statement of Mrs. Auguste Bohm (born Zimmermann), Murder Division Ditter document, October 16, 1940.
10 Statement of Arthur Ditter, Murder Division Ditter document, October 4, 1940.
11 Ibid.
12 Ibid. Note that some documents have Mrs. Ditter's maiden name misspelled as "Bath"— it is correctly spelled in this document as "Barth."
13 Laurenz Demps, quoted in Gabi Schlag and Benno Wenz, *Tatort Berlin—Der S-Bahn-Mörder von Rummelsburg*, TV documentary program, original airdate November 26, 2012, broadcast in Germany by Berlin-Brandenburg Broadcasting (rbb).
14 Berlin *Kripo*, Ditter Reward Poster, October 7, 1940.

15 Berlin *Kripo*, Announcement of Ditter Crime, *Deutsches Kriminalpolizeiblatt*, Berlin, October 7, 1940, volume 13, number 3793, 235.

16 Berlin *Kripo*, Status Report on Ditter Case, October 10, 1940.

17 Berlin *Kripo*, Ditter Reward Announcement, October 15, 1940.

18 Berlin *Kripo*, Notes on Information Provided by Mrs. Helene Schollain, October 11, 1940.

19 Statement of Mrs. Auguste Bohm, October 16, 1940.

20 Steve Hewitt, *Snitch!: A History of the Modern Intelligence Informer* (New York: Continuum, 2010), 105–106.


CHAPTER ELEVEN

1 Alan Gunn, *Essential Forensic Biology* (Hoboken, NJ: John Wiley & Sons, 2008), 184.

2 Lee B. Kennett, *For the Duration . . . : The United States Goes to War, Pearl Harbor–1942* (New York: Scribner, 1985), 162, note 23.

3 In German: "*Hilf auch Du mit!*" Author's collection.


CHAPTER THIRTEEN

1 Waldemar Weimann and Gerhard Jaeckel, *Diagnose Mord: Die Memoiren eines Gerichtsmediziners* (Bayreuth, Germany: Hestia, 1964), 261.

2 Ibid.

3 Ibid., 262.

4 Ibid. "Who, When, Where, How and Why" all start with "W" in German—"*Wer, Wann, Wo, Wie und Warum.*"

5 Ibid.

6 Ibid., 260.

7 Ibid., 262.


CHAPTER FOURTEEN

1 Supreme Headquarters Allied Expeditionary Force (SHAEF) Evaluation and Dissemination Section, G-2 (Counter Intelligence Sub-Division), complied by MIRS (London Branch), *The German Police*, April 1945, E.D.S./G/10, 3.

2 Michael Burleigh, *The Third Reich: A New History* (New York: Hill and Wang, 2001), 181.

3 SHAEF, *The German Police*, 47.

4 Ibid.

5 Ibid.

6 Burleigh, *The Third Reich*, 181.

7 SHAEF, *The German Police*, 47.

8 Ibid.

9 Dr. Jens Dobler, quoted in Gabi Schlag and Benno Wenz, *Tatort Berlin—Der S-Bahn-Mörder von Rummelsburg*, TV documentary program, original airdate November 26, 2012, broadcast in Germany by Berlin-Brandenburg Broadcasting (rbb).

10 Burleigh, *The Third Reich*, 681.

11 Shareen Blair Brysac, *Resisting Hitler: Mildred Harnack and the Red Orchestra* (Oxford, UK: Oxford University Press, 2000), 330.

12 For more on this issue, see the affidavit by Dr. Walter Zirpins, June 24, 1946, Nuremberg, Germany, contained in Wilhelm Lüdtke's denazification file.

13 The CIA thoroughly investigated Lüdtke after the war, and the only vices they could find were his moderate drinking and smoking. National Archives, Washington, D.C.,

RC Box #082, Location (RC) 230/86/23/05, "Ludtke Wilhelm." Note that the file name is missing the umlaut.

14 The CIA confirmed this information that Wilhelm Lüdtke gave them by looking him up in the 1941 and 1943 Berlin white pages. Ibid.

15 Ibid.

16 Ibid.

17 Ingeborg Heidenreich, quoted in Schlag and Wenz, *Tatort*.

18 Ibid.

19 Gerda Busch, quoted in Schlag and Wenz, *Tatort*.

20 This is from a once-secret record of the round table meeting Hitler held on August 20, 1942, to appoint a new Reich justice minister and a president of the People's Court. Lothar Gruchmann, "*Hitler über die Justiz. Das Tischgespräch vom 20. August 1942*," *Vierteljahrshefte für Zeitgeschichte* 12, Jahrg. 1. H. (January 1964), 86–101, 95. Footnote 23 on this page explains that Hitler was referring to Paul Ogorzow.

21 Ibid.

22 Dr. Jens Dobler, quoted in Schlag and Wenz, *Tatort*.

23 Michael Wildt, *An Uncompromising Generation: The Nazi Leadership of the Reich Security Main Office*, trans. Tom Lampert (Madison, WI: University of Wisconsin Press, 2009), 181 and endnote 48.

24 Dr. Christian Pfeiffer, quoted in Schlag and Wenz, *Tatort*.

## CHAPTER SIXTEEN

1 Waldemar Weimann and Gerhard Jaeckel, *Diagnose Mord: Die Memoiren eines Gerichtsmediziners* (Bayreuth, Germany: Hestia, 1964), 263.

2 Ibid., 263–264.

3 Professor Hans-Ludwig Kröber, quoted in Gabi Schlag and Benno Wenz, *Tatort Berlin—Der S-Bahn-Mörder von Rummelsburg*, TV documentary program, original airdate November 26, 2012, broadcast in Germany by Berlin-Brandenburg Broadcasting (rbb).

4 Wilhelm Lüdtke and Georg Heuser, "*Die Berliner S-Bahn-Morde*," *Kriminalistik* 16, Issue 5, May 1942, 50.

5 Weimann and Jaeckel, *Diagnose Mord*, 264.

6 Ibid.

7 Ibid., 265.

8 Ibid.

9 Thomas Krickstadt and Mike Straschewski, joint e-mail to author, March 15, 2013.

## CHAPTER SEVENTEEN

1 Diana Schulle, "Forced Labor," in *Jews in Nazi Berlin: From Kristallnacht to Liberation*, ed. Beate Meyer, Hermann Simon, and Chana Schütz (Chicago: University of Chicago Press, 2009), 148.

## CHAPTER EIGHTEEN

1 Thomas Krickstadt and Mike Straschewski, joint e-mail to author, March 15, 2013.

2 Stephan Harbort, quoted in Gabi Schlag and Benno Wenz, *Tatort Berlin—Der S-Bahn-Mörder von Rummelsburg*, TV documentary program, original airdate November 26, 2012, broadcast in Germany by Berlin-Brandenburg Broadcasting (rbb).

# NOTES

3 Thomas Krickstadt and Mike Straschewski, joint e-mail to author, February 20, 2013.
4 Frank Pfeiffer, e-mail to author, March 17, 2013.
5 Frank Pfeiffer, e-mail to author, March 16, 2013.

**CHAPTER NINETEEN**
1 Sunrise time from http://www.world-timedate.com, accessed on March 29, 2013.

**CHAPTER TWENTY**
1 "Ueberfälle in S-Bahnzügen," *Das 12 Uhr Blatt* (Berlin), January 7, 1941.

**CHAPTER TWENTY-ONE**
1 Manfred Woge, quoted in Gabi Schlag and Benno Wenz, *Tatort Berlin—Der S-Bahn-Mörder von Rummelsburg*, TV documentary program, original airdate November 26, 2012, broadcast in Germany by Berlin-Brandenburg Broadcasting (rbb).
2 Wilhelm Lüdtke and Georg Heuser, "*Die Berliner S-Bahn-Morde*," *Kriminalistik* 16, Issue 5 (May 1942), 52.
3 Ibid., 50.

**CHAPTER TWENTY-TWO**
1 "*Frauen wurden aus der S-Bahn-Zügen geworfen*," *Der Westen* (Berlin), February 14, 1941. The original misspelled the victim Voigt's last name. I corrected it in this translation.
2 Professor Laurenz Demps, quoted in Gabi Schlag and Benno Wenz, *Tatort Berlin—Der S-Bahn-Mörder von Rummelsburg*, TV documentary program, original airdate November 26, 2012, broadcast in Germany by Berlin-Brandenburg Broadcasting (rbb).
3 Manfred Woge, quoted in Schlag and Wenz, *Tatort*.
4 "Das Spiel ist aus—Arthur Nebe: Glanz und Elend der deutschen Kriminalpolizei," *Der Spiegel*, January 26, 1950, 24.

**CHAPTER TWENTY-THREE**
1 "Das Spiel ist aus—Arthur Nebe: Glanz und Elend der deutschen Kriminalpolizei," *Der Spiegel*, January 26, 1950, 24.
2 Wilhelm Lüdtke and Georg Heuser, "*Die Berliner S-Bahn-Morde*," *Kriminalistik* 16, Issue 5 (May 1942), 52.
3 Ibid.
4 Ibid.
5 Ibid.
6 Ibid.

**CHAPTER TWENTY-FOUR**
1 Wilhelm Lüdtke wrote that the prints were men's size 39.5. Some other reports have them at size 40.
2 "Impression and Pattern Evidence," National Institute of Justice, http://www.nij.gov/topics/forensics/evidence/impression/impression.htm, January 2, 2013, accessed on January 25, 2013.

# NOTES

## CHAPTER TWENTY-FIVE

1 This list was put together after Ogorzow was arrested as a suspect and consists of items that were taken from him and his home while he was under interrogation. Berlin Kripo Homicide Division Koziol, July 22, 1941. This list was received and certified on July 25, 1941.

## CHAPTER TWENTY-SEVEN

1 Wilhelm Lüdtke and Georg Heuser, "*Die Berliner S-Bahn-Morde,*" *Kriminalistik* 16, Issue 5 (May 1942), 68.

2 Ibid., 70.

3 Ibid., 68.

4 Ibid.

5 "Der Berliner S-Bahn-Mörder gefaßt!," *Berliner Morgenpost*, July 18, 1941.

6 Ibid., quoted and translated into English in Todd Herzog, *Crime Stories: Criminalistic Fantasy and the Culture of Crisis in Weimar Germany* (New York: Berghahn Books, 2009), 145.

## CHAPTER TWENTY-EIGHT

1 Robert Gellately, *Backing Hitler: Consent and Coercion in Nazi Germany* (Oxford, UK: Oxford University Press, 2002), 79 and endnote 56.

2 United States Holocaust Memorial Museum, "Translation: First Letter to All Judges," *Holocaust Encyclopedia,* http://www.ushmm.org/wlc/en/article.php?ModuleId=10007911, accessed on January 30, 2013, letter dated October 1, 1942. USHMM translated "Letter to All Judges—Announcement of the Reich Minister of Justice—Nr. 1," in Heinz Boberach, ed., *Richterbriefe: Dokumente zur Beeinflussung der deutschen rechtsprechung 1942–44* (Boppard am Rhein, Germany: Harold Boldt Verlag, 1975), 9–10.

3 Confession of Paul Ogorzow, July 1941. Kriminalpolizei file on the criminal investigation into the S-Bahn murders. Landesarchiv Berlin, A.Pr. Br. Rep. 030-03 Tit. 198B Nr. 1782–1789.

4 Some documents have this doctor's last name spelled "Schwarenbach."

5 Confession of Paul Ogorzow, July 1941.

6 Ibid.

7 Addendum to the Confession of Paul Ogorzow, July 1941.

## CHAPTER TWENTY-NINE

1 For more on the legal structure of the special courts, see, e.g., Andrew Szanajda, *The Restoration of Justice in Postwar Hesse, 1945–1949* (Lanham, MD: Lexington Books, 2007), 24–27.

2 Ibid., 26.

3 Indictment of Paul Ogorzow on July 23, 1941. Kriminalpolizei file on the criminal investigation into the S-Bahn murders. Landesarchiv Berlin, A.Pr. Br. Rep. 030-03 Tit. 198B Nr. 1782–1789.

4 Ibid.

5 Chief of Police in Berlin, press release, "Accusation of the Karlshorst Murderer," newspaper/print, Berlin Local Announcements, July 23, 1941, number 174.

6 "*Im Namen des Deutschen Volkes!*": Special Court of Berlin, judgment against Paul Ogorzow, July 24, 1941, 1.

7 US Army, "The Statutory Criminal Law of Germany: With Comments," *Department of the Army Pamphlet*, 31-122 (Washington, DC: War Department, 1946), 44.

8 Ibid.

9 Ibid.

10 Ibid., 45.

11 Special Court of Berlin, judgment against Paul Ogorzow, July 24, 1941. Kriminalpolizei file on the criminal investigation into the S-Bahn murders. Landesarchiv Berlin, A.Pr. Br. Rep. 030-03 Tit. 198B Nr. 1782–1789.

12 Ibid.

13 Ibid.

14 Ibid.

15 Ibid.

16 Ibid.

17 Ibid.

18 Wilhelm Lüdtke and Georg Heuser, "*Die Berliner S-Bahn-Morde,*" *Kriminalistik* 16, Issue 5 (May 1942), 70.

19 Chief of Police in Berlin, press release, "Ogorzow Found Fully Accountable," newspaper/print, Berlin Local Announcements, July 24, 1941, number 175.

**CHAPTER THIRTY**

1 Alex Small, "3 Nazi Traitors and 2 Slayers Die on Guillotine: Spy and Mass Murderer Among Five Executed," *Chicago Daily Tribune*, July 26, 1941.

2 Ibid.

3 Ibid.

4 Ibid.

5 Geoffrey Abbott, *What a Way to Go: The Guillotine, the Pendulum, the Thousand Cuts, the Spanish Donkey, and 66 Other Ways of Putting Someone to Death* (New York: St. Martin's Griffin, 2007), 139.

6 Kee D. Kim, M.D., associate professor, chief, spinal neurosurgery, Department of Neurological Surgery, UC Davis School of Medicine, e-mail to author, September 14, 2012.

7 Ibid.

8 Anne Nelson, *Red Orchestra: The Story of the Berlin Underground and the Circle of Friends Who Resisted Hitler* (New York: Random House Digital, Inc., 2009), 177.

**EPILOGUE**

1 Chief of Police in Berlin, press release, "Karlshorst S-Bahn Murderer Executed," newspaper/print, Berlin Local Announcements, July 26, 1941, number 178.

2 Todd Herzog, *Crime Stories: Criminalistic Fantasy and the Culture of Crisis in Weimar Germany* (New York: Berghahn Books, 2009), 145. In making this assessment, Professor Herzog refers to Joachim Linder and "his excellent study of Nazi crime fiction and the figure of the serial killer."

3 The information in this chapter on Wilhelm Lüdtke's life after the S-Bahn Murderer case comes primarily from the CIA files on him and his denazification file. His CIA file includes copies of his denazification paperwork, such as his *Fragebogen*. National Archives, Washington, D.C., RC Box #082, Location (RC) 230/86/23/05, "Ludtke Wilhelm." Note that the file name is missing the umlaut.

# NOTES

4 Ibid. *Fragebogen* Number N. 5042.

5 Ibid. Letter to Chief of Foreign Division "M," dated March 2, 1951.

6 Ibid.

7 Ibid. Letter to Chief of Foreign Division "M" from Chief of Station Karlsruhe, dated July 17, 1951.

8 Ibid.

9 CIA, "Research Aid: Cryptonyms and Terms in Declassified CIA Files—Nazi War Crimes and Japanese Imperial Government Records Disclosure Acts," June 2007, 12.

10 Ibid.

11 Wilhelm Lüdtke's CIA file.

12 Ibid.

13 Katharsis, Gemeinschaft für Philosophie und Geschichte e.V., Autorengruppe, *Geheimnisse deutscher und allgemeiner Geschichte*, Volume 1 (Frankfurt, Germany: Verlag West-Ost Renaissance, 2000), 27.

14 For details on Georg Heuser's crimes and trial, see Jürgen Matthäus, "No Ordinary Criminal: Georg Heuser, Other Mass Murderers, and West German Justice," in Patricia Heberer and Jürgen Matthäus, eds., *Atrocities on Trial: Historical Perspectives on the Politics of Prosecuting War Crimes* (Lincoln, NE: University of Nebraska Press, 2008), 187–209.

15 Dietrich Strothmann, "*Die gehorsamen Mörder*," *Die Zeit* (Hamburg, Germany), June 7, 1963.

16 Götz Aly, Peter Chroust, and Christian Pross, *Cleansing the Fatherland: Nazi Medicine and Racial Hygiene* (Baltimore: The Johns Hopkins University Press, 1994), 222.

17 *Entlang der Gleise*, "*Berliner Stellwerke* 2," http://www.entlang-der-gleise.de/stellwerke-berlin2.html, accessed on March 3, 2013.

# INDEX

Page numbers in *italic* indicate maps.

# INDEX

Berlin Special Court *(Sondergericht)*, 229, 236–238, 239, 241–244, 250
Berlin Wall, 262
BESMIRCH-2 (cryptonym for Lüdtke), 255
Betriebsbahnhof Rummelsburg S-Bahn station, *xiii, xv*, xvii, 141, 151
bicycle with dynamo light, Ogorzow, 217
bill for execution sent to Ogorzow's wife, 248
"blackout killer," 122–123
Blackout Regulation, 35–47
  accidents due to blackouts, 62
  conditions during blackouts, 2, 11, 18, 35–47, 50, 93, 106, 162, 164, 165, 177, 178, 209
  crimes committed during blackouts, 45–46, 61, 188, 193, 205, 223, 229–231, 237
  "Decree Against Public Enemies" *(Volksschädlingsverordnung)*, 45–46
  Eighth Regulation Implementing the Air Protection Act, 40–42
  propaganda posters, 43–44
blackouts used by Ogorzow, 7–8, 9, 13, 20, 22, 34, 69, 70, 81, 122–123, 126, 141, 149, 150, 154, 163, 166, 174, 187, 229, 235
Blitz, xx, 36
blood found on Ogorzow's uniform, 213–215
blows to the head of victims, Ogorzow, 4, 11–12, 24, 25–27
blunt object (iron rod, rebar) used by Ogorzow, 102, 103–104, 107, 110, 111, 130, 166, 170, 171, 179, 180, 197
blunt object (lead cable) used by Ogorzow, 26, 89, 90, 94, 95, 96, 98–99, 108, 110, 138, 225–226
bodies of victims (never concealing), Ogorzow, 197
Bohemia, 258
Bohm, Auguste (Herlitz's girlfriend), 78, 87
Bormann, Martin, 259
Braun, Konrad, 70–71, 74
break-in committed by Ogorzow, 210
British. *See* Great Britain
Brownshirts (SA), 31–33, 34, 102, 103, 154, 165, 178, 208, 209, 220, 222, 224, 228, 234, 244

Budzinski, Lina (attempted murder victim), *xiii*, xxi, 11–13, 17–18, 34, 49, 95, 156–157
Bulgaria, xx
Büngener, Elisabeth (murder victim), *xiii*, xxi, 165–167, 168–169
Busch, Gerda, 122
BVG (Berliner Verkehrsbetriebe), 52

carotid artery, 57, 69, 73
CAUTERY-4 (cryptonym for Lüdtke), 255
Central Intelligence Agency (CIA), 254–256
*Chicago Daily Tribune*, 246
childhood of Ogorzow, 2, 29–31
child welfare, Nazi Germany, 69–70, 71
Christmas celebration, Nazi Germany, 165
chronology of background events (August 1939–July 1941), xix–xx
Churchill, Winston (Prime Minister of United Kingdom), 36
CIA (Central Intelligence Agency), 254–256
Ciano, Galeazzo, 76
"city fast train" *(Stadtschnell-bahn)*, 50–51. *See also* S-Bahn
"city train" *(Stadtbahn)*, 51
"clap, the" (gonorrhea), 232–233
cleaning skulls of victims by Weimann, 221
climbing a fence to ditch work, Ogorzow, 207–208, 209, 211, 213
Cold War, 254
"collapse, the" *(Zusammenbruch)*, 253
colloidal silver, 233
"colonies," garden area, 5–6
color scheme used by S-Bahn, 47, 50
"Commencement and Duration of the Blackout," Blackout Regulation, 41
commuter train line in Berlin, 19. *See also* S-Bahn
"compromise," intelligence community, 256
conditions during blackouts, 2, 11, 18, 35–47, 50, 93, 106, 162, 164, 165, 177, 178, 209
confessions
  Heimann, 204–205
  Ogorzow, 220, 221–227, 256
connecting the garden and train attacks, 132–142, 148–150, 213, 226
consciousness (loss of) and guillotines, 247–248
control cars, S-Bahn, 153

280

# INDEX

# INDEX

# INDEX

# INDEX

# INDEX

# INDEX

pyromania (setting fires), serial killers, 30

"quarter trains," S-Bahn, 56
questioning of Ogorzow by Kripo, 209–220
quitting (rare), serial killers, 206

racial theory of crime, 124–125,
    143–147, 211
radio navigation used by Nazi Germany, 37
Rahnsdorf S-Bahn station, *xv*, xvii, 53,
    151, 166
railroad. *See* S-Bahn
rationalization of Koziol's murder by Lüdtke,
    198–199
rationing in Nazi Germany, 52, 201–202
rebar used by Ogorzow, 102, 103–104,
    107, 110, 111, 130, 166, 170, 171, 179,
    180, 197
REDCAP program (CIA), 255
red herring (shoes), 200–206, 222–223
"Regulation Against Folk Pests"
    *(Volksschädlingsverordnung)*, 45–46
Reich Chancellery bunker, 259–260
Reich Criminal Investigation Department
    newspaper *(Deutches
    Kriminalpolizeiblatt)*, 83–84
Reich Main Security Office
    *(Reichssicherheitshauptam*, RHSA),
    113–114, 115–119, 152, 190. *See also*
    Heydrich, Reinhard; Himmler,
    Heinrich; Kripo; Nebe, Arthur
*Reichsbahn* (German National Railroad
    Company), 49–50, 54, 55, 56, 78, 150,
    163, 262. *See also* S-Bahn
*Reichskriminalpolizeiamt* (RKPA), 116
*Reichssicherheitshauptam. See* Reich Main
    Security Office
Reinhardtstraße, 63
rent in Nazi Germany, 75, 76
returning to scene of crimes, serial killers,
    168, 226
revoking of Ogorzow's Nazi Party
    membership, 236
rewards offered by Kripo, 81–83, 87, 88,
    127, 140, 174, 185, 187
Rheydt, Germany, 123
Rhineland-Palatinate, 260
RHSA. *See* Reich Main Security Office
rights (none) of public, Nazi Germany, 216
"*Ringbahn*," 51–52, 54

Ritschel, Magda (Goebbels's wife), 123, 259
RKPA *(Reichskriminalpolizeiamt)*, 116
Roosevelt, Franklin (U.S. President), 38
Rosie the Riveter, 91
roundups of train riders at key times, 184
Royal Air Force (British), 43
Ruhr region, Germany, 36
Rummelsburg S-Bahn station, *xiii, xv,* xvii,
    25, 52–53, 67, 78, 99, 106, 129, 141,
    150, 151, 155, 158, 159, 172, 175, 180,
    183, 185, 196, 208

SA *(Sturmabteilung)*, 31–33, 34, 102, 103,
    154, 165, 178, 208, 209, 220, 222, 224,
    228, 234, 244
Saga, Marie (Ogorzow's mother), 30
Saga, Paul, 30. *See also* Ogorzow, Paul
Salamander, 201
S-Bahn, 19. *See also* S-Bahn Murderer
    air raid warning system, 63–64
    chronology of background events (August
        1939–July 1941), xix–xx
    "city fast train" *(Stadtschnell-bahn)*,
        50–51
    color scheme used by, 47, 50
    connecting the garden and train attacks,
        132–142, 148–150, 213, 226
    control cars, 153
    doors on, 57, 58, 93–94
    East German control of, 262
    electric traction motor sounds, 129–130
    employee, Ogorzow, *xiii,* xxii, 2, 7, 31,
        49–50, 52–53, 54, 55, 79, 157–160, 193,
        195, 209
    engine cars, 153
    first-class transport, 56
    garden area murders vs., 34, 111, 156, 195
    German National Railroad Company
        *(Reichsbahn)*, 49–50, 54, 55, 56, 78,
        150, 163, 262
    history of, 50–52
    logo, 50
    maps (1939), *xiii, xiv–xv*
    Olympics (Berlin, 1936) and, 51
    personnel interviewed by Kripo, 189,
        207–208, 209
    "quarter trains," 56
    *Ringbahn* (inner area of Berlin), 54
    second-class compartments, 54, 55, 56,
        92, 122, 126, 153, 175, 185, 186, 187

# INDEX

# INDEX

Soviet Union, xix, xx, 18, 48, 194, 209, 253, 254, 259, 260
special courts, Nazi Germany, 229, 236–238, 239, 241–244, 250
spy as attacker theory, 145
SS *(Schutzstaffel)*. *See also* Himmler, Heinrich
  Kripo and membership in, 120
  Lüdtke's membership, 252, 253
  member as suspect, 162–164
*"Staatliche Kriminalpolizei"* (State Criminal Police), 72
*Stadtbahn* ("city train"), 51
*Stadtschnell-bahn* ("city fast train"), 50–51. *See also* S-Bahn
*Stalag Luft* III POW camp, 257
State Criminal Police *("Staatliche Kriminalpolizei")*, 72
stations on key route, S-Bahn, *xiii*, xvii, 34, 35
stealing from victims (never), Ogorzow, 58, 167–168
stereotype, serial killers, 28, 210–211
stomach condition (excuse for murders), 234
Storm Troopers (SA), 31–33, 34, 102, 103, 154, 165, 178, 208, 209, 220, 222, 224, 228, 234, 244
strangulation by Ogorzow, 4, 17, 57, 68–69, 71, 74, 101, 107, 141, 172
Straschewski, Mike, 158
*Sturmabteilung* (SA), 31–33, 34, 102, 103, 154, 165, 178, 208, 209, 220, 222, 224, 228, 234, 244
suicide possibilities, 71, 167, 168
"summer-houses," garden area, 6
suspects, wrong kind, 143–147
swastikas, 31, 50, 72, 163
switch from normal to killer behavior, Ogorzow, 68
syphilis, 233

telephony cable laid alongside parts of S-Bahn, 99
Telschow, Otto, 16
Thierack, Otto (Minister of Justice), 229–231
third-class compartments, S-Bahn, 54, 55, 91–92, 152, 153
third rail and electroshock hazard, S-Bahn, 166–167
Third Reich. *See* Nazi Germany

"Threat to Kill, The" (MacDonald), 30
throwing victims from a moving train, Ogorzow, 59–60, 95–96, 102, 103, 104, 105, 108, 110, 111, 128, 156, 161, 166, 167, 171, 173, 181, 197
ticket inspector as attacker theory, 181–182
tickets and fines, S-Bahn, 53–55
time cards of S-Bahn workers reviewed by Kripo, 189–190
time period between attacks, Ogorzow, 128, 133, 138, 139, 142, 172
timetable, S-Bahn, 59–60, 101–102, 104
tracks (expansion joints) sound, S-Bahn, 129
trailer cars, S-Bahn, 153
train. *See* S-Bahn
train switching technology, S-Bahn, 159
trap set by Lüdtke, 192–199
trial of Ogorzow, 235, 236–244
Tripartite Pact, xx
trophies of kills (keeping), serial killers, 168
*12 O'Clock Journal (Das 12 Uhr Blatt)*, 174–175

U-Bahn *(Untergrundbahn)*, 51, 52, 150
uniform of attacker focus, Lüdtke, 161–164
uniform worn by
  Lüdtke, 252, 253, 260
  Ogorzow, 2, 49, 55, 57, 92, 93, 102, 141, 145, 149–150, 156, 157, 161, 170, 175, 186, 188–189, 197
United Kingdom, xix, xx, 18, 36, 48, 62–63, 209. *See also* Great Britain (British)
United States, xix
  Fifth Amendment right to silence, 216
  Rosie the Riveter, 91
  Sixth Amendment right to a lawyer, 216
  World War II and, xix, 38, 49
United States Holocaust Memorial Museum, 45
*Untergrundbahn* (U-Bahn), 51, 52, 150
U.S. Central Intelligence Agency (CIA), 254–256
utopian ideology, Nazi Germany, 124

*"Verbindung nach Küstrin"* ("Vnk"), 158, 159–160, 208, 262
*Vertrauensleute* (V-persons), 88
Vichy Regime, 49
"Vnk" *("Junction to Küstrin")*, 158, 159–160, 208, 262

# INDEX

## ABOUT THE AUTHOR

Scott Andrew Selby is a graduate of UC Berkeley and Harvard Law School. He also has a master's degree in Human Rights and Intellectual Property Law from Sweden's Lund University. He is the author of *The Axmann Conspiracy: The Nazi Plan for a Fourth Reich and How the U.S. Army Defeated It* and a coauthor of *Flawless: Inside the Largest Diamond Heist in History*. He is licensed to practice law in California and New York.

The website for this book is www.aSerialKiller.com.